S0-BWR-767

Also by Michael De Forrest

HOW TO BUY AT AUCTION

ANTIQUING FROM A TO Z

BUYING AND SELLING ANTIQUES, COLLECTIBLES AND OTHER OLD THINGS

Michael De Forrest

SIMON AND SCHUSTER · NEW YORK

PUBLISHED BY SIMON AND SCHUSTER
ROCKEFELLER CENTER, 630 FIFTH AVENUE
NEW YORK, NEW YORK 10020

In substantially different form, information included in the entries on dolls, flea markets, and wicker originally appeared in Newsday's LI *Magazine.*

DESIGNED BY EVE METZ
MANUFACTURED IN THE UNITED STATES OF AMERICA

1 2 3 4 5 6 7 8 9 10

LIBRARY OF CONGRESS CATALOGING IN PUBLICATION DATA

De Forrest, Michael Jean.
Antiquing from A to Z.

Includes index.
1. Art objects—Collectors and collecting. I. Title.
NK2115.D44 745.1 75-12860
ISBN 0-671-22075-6

With love and gratitude to Mary and Clara Berg,
who first took me antiquing,
and to my dear wife, Betty,
who, happily, still does

INTRODUCTION

The Antiques Trade

I cannot remember the first antique I bought—which makes me feel that it was something inexpensive, insignificant, and probably useless. It might have been a teakwood vase that was carved to look like bamboo and fiercely decorated with dragons that had fishy eyes made from beads of ivory. If not the first, that vase certainly was an early acquisition. It had been fitted with a metal liner, and when I took it out to clean it, I found that a large and lively family of insects inhabited the space between the liner and the wooden interior of the vase. Today I would spray everything with insecticide and scrub it up and polish it and have myself a treasure. But thirty years ago, having found the piece in a junk shop, I just said, "Well, what can you expect," and threw the whole business down the incinerator. One lives and, hopefully, one learns.

I do remember the first antique I sold. Vividly. Probably because it brought me a 700 percent profit. Since that return was based upon a five-dollar investment, it didn't exactly put me in the chips, but it did convince me that there was a whole world of wonderful antiques just waiting for me to come and conquer it. I don't know what I expected to do with the length of antique French brocade that I had impulsively bid in at $5 at a household auction. It was beautiful, old, and cheap—and at that time those seemed like three sensational recommendations for purchase. I thought that Betty, my wife, might like to use the brocade as a runner down the length of our dining table. "It's lovely," she said, "and about as tender as a dried leaf. At least you didn't pay much for it." Obviously the brocade was not for use, and not for us, which meant that it was suitable only for resale. "Very well," I said, anxious to be vindicated, "I'll sell it! After all, you don't pick up eighteenth-century fabrics on every remnant table."

I sandwiched the cloth between layers of tissue and gently rolled it and sailed defiantly into the marketplace. A couple of quick refusals took the wind out of my sails before I realized that the most likely customer for the brocade would be a specialist in French antiques. The telephone directory listings yielded several and I headed straight for the one nearest. There my reception was quite different. Yes, they would be interested in buying the fabric. "How much do you want for it?" the proprietor asked. "Oh," I said, "I don't know. How much would you be willing to pay?" He insisted that I name a price and I kept asking him to make an offer. We circled around like that for a few minutes before he finally relented and said that he would give $25 for the material. I thought that was splendid, but I also thought that he might be willing to pay a bit more. Alas, no. Business was slow. It was tax time. A broken glass in a display cabinet had to be replaced. And his only use for the brocade would be to line trinket boxes and showcases. Then he absolutely knocked me out by suggesting that I take the fabric to a competitor who probably would go as high as $50 for it. As it turned out, the competitor did not pay $50 for the cloth, but offered the same $25 that I previously had refused. We finally compromised on $40, and I stopped trying to play it cool and asked if I could be paid by check, because I knew that Betty would never believe I had sold the brocade for that much unless I showed up with such evidence.

In retrospect it is clear that I handled that sale like the amateur that I was. In the first place, I should never have wasted time and courted disappointment by soliciting general antiques dealers with an item only a specialist would appreciate—or use. In the second place, I should have decided on what would be a satisfactory price before I approached a buyer. If I had no way to estimate the possible worth of the article, I could at least have based a resale price on my cost and been content to let it go at that. Instead, I had tried to fish around, testing the market, hoping to find out what the traffic would bear. If that first dealer had not been such a prince, he would have told me to get out and not bother coming back. There is nothing more unprofessional than that dumb, evasive dance of the seller who refuses to quote a price. "How much do you want for it?" deserves a reply in terms of a specific amount instead of some shuffling, feinting answer like "What would you offer?" Many dealers are adamant about not negotiating with a seller who refuses to quote prices. Others will make an initial offer

and let the seller walk away if he rejects it. There are too m people who seek free appraisals for antiques that they have no tention of selling, or who run a progressive auction by using dealer's offer to boost the price asked of another. Most professio dealers are wary of such tactics and not only resist but quite righ resent them. Betty and I have sold a lot of antiques since my fort dollar triumph. On some pieces we have made a satisfactory profi On others we have taken a not-so-satisfactory loss. But not onc have we refused to quote a price to anyone who asked, "Ho much?"

I clearly recall the first antique that I wanted and did not buy. It was a Tiffany wisteria lamp that I saw illuminated in the window of an antiques shop. I had never seen one. Knew nothing about Tiffany. And less about antiques. I just knew that the colors and the design and the total effect were sensational and that it was something I could look at every day and enjoy and appreciate. The lamp was priced at $500. Today it would easily bring seventy or eighty times $500, and tomorrow it might be selling at one hundred or two hundred times $500. If it could be found. But $500 was out of sight to me then. As out of sight as Tiffany wisteria lamps have since become. Many years after I stumbled across and did not pick up that wisteria lamp, a major antiques dealer offered me a twelve-light Tiffany pond-lily lamp with a complete set of additional shades for $1,200. If I had bought it, I could today sell the extra shades alone for several times the cost of the lamp.

Such neglected opportunities would hardly seem to recommend me as one to give advice on buying and selling antiques. But those were far from being my only mistakes. At the first show in which Betty and I sold antiques I took $10 for a $600 Steuben glass bowl. At an auction, much more recently than I can comfortably admit, I paid a ridiculously high price for a figural urn that, on delivery, I discovered to be marked "Deenie's Ceramics Studio." I once lost a $10,000 painting to a competitor who took it with a winning bid of $60. At a flea market I wasted half a day waiting for a dealer to show me a promised "art glass vase" that turned out to be worthless, while my neighbor casually strolled to the next table and picked up a fine Mettlach stein for $25.

Betty and I have had our share of successes too. A $1,500 Fauré

enamel vase bought at auction for $90. A Rookwood ewer found for $4 at a flea market. A $200 historical blue Staffordshire plate purchased for $5 from an antiques shop. A delightful little Kewpie tea service picked up from a house sale. An unusual bentwood settee bought from a secondhand furniture dealer. And paintings. And lamps. And a period Queen Anne love seat found in a thrift shop. And a Georgian silver coffeepot had for a song at a charity bazaar. And a fantastic painting on ivory that sat unnoticed through three days at an antiques show. And . . .

Probably the most important lesson I have learned in the years that we have been buying and selling antiques is that if you buy generally—which we do—you can buy right almost everywhere and from just about everyone. This is something that many experienced dealers and advanced collectors would not agree with. They ignore the thrift shops, dismissing them as unproductive. They skip the auctions, considering them to be rigged. They bypass the antiques shows, figuring that the exhibitors are too much aware of the value of their merchandise to offer any reasonably good buys. For the same reason they almost never visit an antiques shop, except on a purely social basis. The flea markets are dirty. The antiques wholesalers are unfriendly. And prices everywhere are outrageous. There is Europe, of course. And there are house calls. And strangers who bring things to their shops or answer their advertisements. Well, I have news for whoever believes all that: you are missing half the fun and more than half the treasures by going down the antiques trail with blinders on. Certainly there are dealers, auctions, homes from which you cannot often buy successfully, but there are none that you can afford to ignore. Some of our best buys were made in some of the world's foremost auction rooms. A few of our biggest bargains were purchased from justly celebrated dealers—among the biggest in the business. We almost never leave a flea market, thrift shop, or antiques show without making a few purchases.

And you can do the same. You can make all the mistakes and repeat all the successes that have carried us through the years in the antiques trade. You can, no doubt, do much better than we have done. My principal hope is that you will have as much fun, as many good times, and as few regrets as we have.

Michael De Forrest

A

Abolitionists

Leaders of the antislavery movement appreciated the value of effective propaganda. Not only did they help make *Uncle Tom's Cabin* a monumental best seller but the publicity that they generated for John Rogers' early sculpture, "The Slave Auction," helped popularize Rogers' statuary, and eventually led to having a Rogers Group—as the plaster reproductions of Rogers' works were known—prominently featured in thousands upon thousands of Victorian parlors. It is said that more than 100,000 reproductions were sold of Rogers' eighty-odd groups.

The Emancipation Proclamation more or less did the job for the abolitionists, but *Uncle Tom's Cabin* remains a humdinger of a novel, and John Rogers Groups are now more widely collected than ever. A few years ago "The Slave Auction" was valued at less than $100. Today a good example would probably cost thousands.

Adolf Hitler wrote: "All propaganda has to be popular and has to adapt its spiritual level to the perception of the least intelligent of those towards whom it intends to direct itself." Much more appropriate to Mrs. Stowe's novel and Mr. Rogers' statues, I think, is what British essayist and poet Austin Dobson said in imitation of Théophile Gautier:

All passes. Art alone
Enduring stays to us;
The Bust outlasts the throne,—
The Coin, Tiberius.

Agata Glass

The famous rose-to-white New England Glass Company peachblow glass decorated with mineral stains to give it a deliberately blotchy complexion. In the 1880s, when the peachblow craze was at its crest, glassmakers tried various techniques to enhance the appeal of their products and to set them apart from peachblow glasses being merchandised by other companies. This rather odd, bubbly decoration was Joseph Locke's patented attempt to secure such extra sales for New England peachblow. Agata glass was in production for only a short time, in consequence of which it is extremely valuable today. Satin- (dull-) finished pieces of Agata are extremely hard to find, and so command still higher prices than those examples having glossy finishes.

Amazingly—especially in view of the extensive reproduction of peachblow glasses—Agata glass has not been reproduced. Not, at least, yet!

See Peachblow

Age (as in ". . . Before Beauty")

A famous auctioneer told me, "Age, condition, and use, all affect the value of an antique," and that certainly is true. But place not age before beauty, or even before trendy popularity. At an auction in New York the oldest object in the sale was an early seventeenth-century chair. It brought a forgettable $15. In the same sale a small twentieth-century occasional table of bamboo and rattan brought $60. Remember this the next time you are tempted to acquire something simply because it is old.

Age Lines in Porcelain

To paraphrase Shakespeare: "That which we call a crack, by any other name would still be a crack."

See Hairline

Ajax Liquid Cleanser

That famous "white tornado" is my secret weapon for cleaning bronze articles on which I do not wish to preserve a patina. For brightening gold-leaf finishes. For refreshing brass picture frames. For cleaning almost all enamels—especially for cutting through the grime on old cloisonné. For getting bisque, parian, unglazed earthenware, and other hard-to-clean ceramics to look as they should. Once they've come clean, ceramic pieces can be rinsed in clear water. Enamels and metals can just be wiped dry and polished, or not, as you prefer.

See Marble Polish

Amberina

Since this popular two-color glass continues to be made, the antiquer interested in acquiring original examples rather than recent reproductions must learn to distinguish between old and new. The colors in antique amberina pieces generally range from a rich deep fuchsia to a clear and brilliant amber—as if a fine Burgundy wine were being floated upon pure golden honey. Colors in the more recent amberina glasses may be anything from a watery pink that shades into pale straw, to wildly abandoned vermilion giving way to citric yellow. Examples of the latter are so brash that they would seem unlikely to fool anyone, but many of us are so anxious to unearth a treasure being sold for a trifle that we encourage ourselves to endow even such vulgarities with the rich and subtle characteristics of the originals.

Most blown pieces of antique amberina glass are quite thin. The more recent reproductions tend to be significantly thicker. Pressed antique amberina pieces, on the other hand, often are extremely thick, but can be distinguished from reproductions by careful consideration of the quality of the glass. Wear and grime notwithstanding, the old pieces have a polished brilliance that the newer examples do not equal. They also ring with a pure flintlike tone, which most copies do not.

There is another kind of amberina glass on the market, which isn't amberina at all, although it shades from red to gold and has other characteristics of the genuine article. This glass actually is painted with a transparent stain to give the typical amberina coloring. If you look carefully at an example of painted amberina, you will probably see that the red portion has the somewhat slick, shiny iridescence characteristic of mineral-stained glass. Although some stains are more permanent than others, this coloring usually will wear away with use, abrasive cleaning, or, perhaps, a few rounds in the automatic dishwasher.

One hears rather more than one sees of the famous and famously expensive plated amberina, which is rib-patterned amberina glass cased over a layer of milky-white opalescent glass. If you happen across a true example, you'll recognize it rightly enough. Only remember to look for the characteristic vertical ribs, which are typical of plated amberina. Otherwise you might confuse it with a piece of Wheeling peachblow. Not only will the vertical ribs help you distinguish between the two similar types of glass, but the peachblow colors are much darker, while the white lining is a thick, rather chalky white, in contrast to the thin layer of opalescent bluish-white glass that is used to line plated amberina. Since a good piece of plated amberina brings several thousand dollars more than a comparable example of Wheeling peachblow, these differences are worth bearing in mind.

Ammonia, Household

If there is anything better for making glass sparkle, I don't know what it is.

A mixture of ammonia (two parts), liquid detergent (one part), and chlorine laundry bleach (one-half part) added to a large volume of water makes a wonderful washup for deeply soiled, grime-encrusted glass. If you don't want to have to do a lot of brushwork, you can loosen most of the grime by letting a piece soak in this solution. Keep a nearby window open—and be sure that you add the ingredients *to* the water so that they are immediately diluted instead of risking asphyxiation by doing things the other way around. I almost did myself in once by stirring up a vast amount of this solution in the bathtub in preparation for cleaning a pair of lavishly beprismed candelabra. I coughed and cried for an hour and lost my voice for a day. I've since restricted this mixture to a portable plastic basin and large, airy chambers. You do the same, please.

Antique

In the United States the official minimum age for an antique is one hundred years. This is the standard applied by the U.S. Customs to determine which objects can be classified as antique and imported without payment of duty. By this definition Tiffany lamps,

Rookwood pottery, Crown Milano glass, R.S. Prussia porcelain, Royal Doulton ceramics, and about 99 percent of the items currently being sold as antiques aren't antique at all. Some will be eligible for the official designation within the next decade, but a lot of choice items, including many of those most avidly sought by collectors, are not going to become real antiques for another twenty-five or fifty years. This should be comforting to those who happily embrace the quasi antiques that some put down as mere "collectibles." It is time for the high and mighty to realize that the majority of their treasures also come under the "collectible" heading.

Age has little to do with the market value of most antiques or collectibles. In a friend's antiques shop I found a fine eighteenth-century delft charger and a Shirley Temple doll bearing identical price tags, even though the charger had a good hundred and fifty years' seniority over the doll. When I said that this seemed pretty ironic, the proprietor laughed and said, "Yes, and you know what? —the Shirley Temple doll will sell first, and next year it will be worth double the money, while I'm still trying to get my price out of the delft."

Probably we ought to leave the official definitions to the Customs Service, which is basically in the tax-collection and -protection business, and adopted the hundred-year criterion for antiques only in 1967, when the ridiculousness of limiting "antiques" to articles of pre-1830 origin could no longer be ignored. Still, if not all of our antiques can qualify as antiques, then what are we to call them?

To me "collectible" seems an especially pointless term. Rocks are collectible. So are burnt matches. Bottle caps. Paper clips. Shoelaces. You name it. All "collectible" really means is that it is possible to accumulate, gather, assemble a number of examples of whatever it is. In itself "collectible" carries no implication of age, as witness its application to the constantly proliferating commemorative plates, which are enormously "collectible."

I'd divide the field into two categories: old things and new things. Genuine antiques are older old things. The items that some antiques dealers refer to when they sneer "Collectibles!" are more recent old things. New things are decorators' items, reproductions, and new collectibles, such as those popular limited-edition plates.

The genuine antique is a thing of the past in more ways than one. There simply are not enough true antiques available to satisfy the demands of a large, enthusiastic, and growing public, most of whom have been eliminated from the antiques market by present prices. Like fine art, fine antiques are no longer for collection but for investment. Most of the shoppers currently in the antiques market are interested in acquiring useful articles of character and style rather than in collecting precious items that can only clutter up a display cabinet. At the same time most of them are buying with some anticipation that their purchases will appreciate in value. Although they might say that they are collecting antiques, what they are buying is collectibles. Since these customers are the lifeblood of the current collecting boom, let's hope that nothing happens to discourage them. Such as buying new things for old, or old things for older. Or damaged articles at mint prices. Or misrepresented reproductions. Or genuine pieces with spurious signatures.

And let's be realistic rather than rigid in considering "antiques." The most recent issues of several established guides to antiques prices devote more space to collectible depression glass of the 1930s than they do to Sandwich glass of the 1830s. As if that weren't enough, one of them carries more entries for Coca Cola items than for Canton porcelain. The future of the antiques trade is written there for anyone with sense enough to face it. If "antique" becomes increasingly inappropriate, then perhaps the meaning of the term will have to be modified to accommodate a changing market. The word has been misused for years anyway. We might as well go the distance and let it truly embrace all kinds of old things.

Antiques

I wish dealers and antiques show managers and other interested parties would be consistent about using the plural form when it applies. As in "antiques shop," "antiques exhibition," "antiques expert." Otherwise they are only saying "old." An "antique shop" is an old store. An "antiques shop" is a store where old things are sold. It makes a difference.

Antiques Shows, Shopping

The best time for shopping an antiques show is before it opens. The best way to guarantee yourself admission to the show in advance of its official opening is to be a participating exhibitor. If that is out of the question, some strategy is in order.

1. Ask an exhibitor who is participating in the show if you can come early and help him set up. This might or might not commit you to some genuine assistance. If it does, consider that one good turn does deserve another, and pitch in. You still will enjoy a good chance for an early look.

2. Ask the show manager if you can preview the show, because you plan to write a feature story about it for your hometown paper. Carry a notebook and a camera. You won't have to do any actual writing or photography—just look prepared. And don't worry about the fact that the coordinator has never heard of your publication; spend three minutes getting biographical data from him and you'll be home free. The manager will probably be much too busy taking care of 10,000 details to concern himself about you, so apologize profusely for disturbing him, wish him luck, and say that you'd like to get the feel of the show by just browsing around on your own. Promise not to get in anyone's way, and see that you don't. If you actually *do* write a story, send clippings.

3. If you can't imagine yourself in the role of journalist, try approaching the manager as a prospective exhibitor at a future show. Tell him that you would like to see what the setup looks like but can't possibly come during the regular exhibition hours. Should he

ask for it, graciously slip him the admission price. It's an early look you're after, you know, not a free one.

4. Sneak in. Get a couple of those covered banana boxes from the supermarket. Stuff them with crumpled newspaper. Carry them in through the exhibitors' entrance. Look distressed. Preoccupied. Confused. If anyone approaches you, pretend to be out of breath, anxious. Complain that the boxes are heavy. Carry them as if they were. I know a very important antiques dealer who brings this off to perfection.

5. Brazen it through. You still have to enter through the back door, but act as if you were approaching the throne room at Buckingham Palace. If you act boldly, with sufficient authority, no one will dream of interfering with you. If anyone should, tell him you are the husband/wife of the chairperson of the sponsoring committee. Never mind if the show turns out not to have a sponsor. Chances are only the manager will know that. If he appears and tries to turn you out, disarmingly offer him the price of admission and see if he doesn't change his tune.

6. Play dumb. Say that you thought the show opened the day before. Or hours earlier. Throw your poor incompetent self upon the manager's mercy. Say that you traveled for two hours just to attend his antiques show. Couldn't you just stay and look around for a few minutes since you're already there? Tactfully hand him the price of admission. Protest that you cannot possibly return later because you are scheduled for dental surgery—or something equally serious and unpopular—that afternoon. (If it happens to be a Sunday, better skip the medical plans and volunteer a church-related excuse. Show managers who operate on Sundays are extremely sensitive to church-related activities. Just saying that you are singing in the choir at vesper services usually bowls them over.)

7. Be candid. Tell the manager that you want to be admitted before the show opens because you want first crack at the antiques. Matter-of-factly proffer the admission price. Unless the manager or his mate also happens to be in the antiques trade—in which case he will want the field clear for his own first picking—he probably will let you pass.

Some exhibitors invariably will object to your appearance on the floor before the show officially opens. The reason for this is that they also want first crack at the best buys. Never mind their protests about possible theft, breakage, personal safety, and the like. It is the bargains that they are worried about. Since that is your primary interest too, just don't let them bug you.

Appraisal, Free

Many newcomers to the antiques field—and even occasional old hands—think that a clever way to find out the value of an antique without having to pay an appraisal fee is to show it to an established dealer under pretext of wanting to sell it. They assume, often incorrectly, that whatever the dealer offers will be a fraction—half, at best—of the item's actual worth. Since they have no intention of selling, but only want to pick the dealer's brains, they frequently wear out their welcomes after a couple of visits, and have to seek other fountainheads of information. In the process they learn which antiques dealers are willing to be prevailed upon (some patient souls go along with this gambit on the off chance that this nuisance eventually will turn up with a treasure he can be persuaded to part with) and which are not. But they seldom learn very much about the values of antiques.

In the first place, not all dealers know as much as they should, and very few know as much as they would like to know about everything. In the second place, the assumption that any antique for which a dealer willingly would pay $500 must be worth at least $1,000 is nonsense. Many dealers will pay $500 for an item that they feel they can immediately turn over at a markup as low as 20 percent, or even 10 percent, especially if they have a good customer whose patronage they can sustain and encourage with an occasional handpicked plum.

There also are dealers who deliberately reduce their offers for anything important, not because they are anxious to cheat anyone but because they fear that an intimation of the true worth of the piece would scare away the prospective seller. I know one dealer who offered a woman $40 for a pair of blue Aurene vases. She was about to sell them, too, until a customer who had overheard the discussion interrupted by saying, "Don't you dare do that! That's ridiculous! I'll give you $200 for each of those vases." This so alarmed the prospective seller that she decided not to part with the vases at any price. In this instance the woman actually had intended to sell the items, but if she had only been seeking this sort of free appraisal, and if the customer had not spoken up, she might have left the shop thinking that her vases might be worth $40 or $50 each, never dreaming of their true value.

An additional hazard of this kind of free appraisal is that not every dealer is at all times in the market for all kinds of antiques. If, instead of an offer, the answer to "Would you be interested in buying this?" turns out to be "No," the new antiquer is apt to get discouraged. Since he was not too certain of the value of the item, a couple of flat turndowns can get translated into "worthless," which might not be the case at all.

A more reliable free appraisal can sometimes be obtained by showing the item to an auctioneer and asking what price it might bring in one of his sales. Of course, you should imply that you intend having the auctioneer sell the article for you provided you find the estimate satisfactory and can agree on the terms of the sale. Almost any auctioneer will go along with this approach two or three times, and some will hold still for it indefinitely, again figuring that sooner or later something good actually will come through. It isn't exactly fair, and it certainly isn't something to do with every little nickle-and-dime collectible that happens your way, but if you have something unusual and possibly important and you would like to know more about it without having to spring for a stiff appraisal fee, you could give it a try.

Appraiser, Art

Before they look at a painting some appraisers first look in the reference books. I don't know if it pleases me or displeases me to find that certain appraisers are just as insecure as I am, but I do resent being asked to pay a fee to receive the same information I have already acquired in a few minutes at the library.

See Benezit

Appraiser, Museum

Every museum has a staff of resident or affiliated experts, but most museums have firm rules about not giving appraisals of art or antiques that are not destined for inclusion in the museum's collections. Exceptions have been made, but usually only in very special instances. If you have something so choice or unusual that a curator would give his eyeteeth to get a look at it, you may be sure that he will set aside some time for you. Just remember that he sees many more fine things than you probably do, so don't expect him to fall over at a chance to examine your Aunt Harriet's attic treasures. Even if the museum will not appraise your antiques, it probably will be glad to recommend an appraiser for you. It might even turn out to be one of the staff experts—by moonlight, of course.

Appraiser, Professional

I once showed two new satin glass bowls to a licensed appraiser who specializes in estate and insurance work. She told me that one was new and worth about $20, which was entirely correct. The other, she said, was old and worth about $200, which was entirely wrong. Which proves that in the antiques trade mistakes are made every day—including, sometimes, the selection of a professional appraiser.

If you are going to pay an appraiser's fee, you might as well go all the way and hire yourself a real expert. This can cost money.

There is an old story about a plumber who answered an emergency call to clear a blocked drain. The plumber arrived, took a look at the pipes, gave one bang with his hammer, dislodged the blockage, and was on his way in less than a minute. Later he sent a bill for $100 to his client. "What's the meaning of this?" the customer protested. "All you did was give the pipe one knock! You have some nerve charging $100 for that!" The plumber agreed that $100 was high for just hitting a pipe once and said that he would submit a new bill. Would the client agree that $1 would be a fair fee for hitting the pipe? The customer said that would be fine, and was surprised to receive a revised invoice that read: "For hitting the pipe: $1. For knowing where to hit it: $99." It is for what he knows that you pay an appraiser, not for the brief time he might take to evaluate your antiques.

At some of the larger antiques shows a special feature is an appraiser's booth where appraisals are given for a nominal charge or for a contribution to some charity. In such situations it is possible to save as much as 90 percent of an appraiser's usual fee. Unfortunately, however, some appraisers, anxious to send their customers away with a smile, will assign unrealistically high values to articles considered in such an informal situation.

Arcanist

Literally, one initiated into certain mysteries; the holder of an important, widely sought secret. In antiques the term designates someone familiar with the processes of porcelain making.

In Europe throughout the first decades of the eighteenth century, the techniques necessary for turning clay into true porcelain—as distinguished from earthenware—were indeed well kept and widely sought secrets. Those few who held them were called arcanists. The arcanist probably did whatever he could to sustain the image. There are records of arcanists who moved from factory to factory, from town to town, and from nation to nation selling their secrets or services, and sometimes even taking along a bit of earth or a few finished samples just to get things started. Is it any wonder, then, that much early-eighteenth-century European porcelain is difficult for most of us to attribute absolutely to this factory or that, or even to a particular town or country?

Art Deco

Currently used—and often misused—to designate a wide range of styles in design and decoration that were popular in the 1920s and 1930s. Some have trouble distinguishing between those objects that should be described as being in the Art Nouveau style and those that might be more correctly—and occasionally more profitably—termed Art Deco. The differences are significant and fundamental. In the Art Deco style the dynamic replaces the lyric. The familiar Art Nouveau maiden has been disencumbered. Her flowing hair is cropped or sleekly tucked beneath a well wrapped turban or modish cloche. No longer drifting in an iris-laden swamp, she now dances on the moon. Psyche has become Diana. Not for her the floating serpentine veils of Loïe Fuller. She struts, instead, in Josephine Baker's banana G-string. Proud. Powerful. The nymph made Amazon.

There was a certain chronological inevitability in the Art Deco revival. We had devoted several years of adoration to the Art Nouveau style. And there were the old movies. And the new respectability of camp. But I think it is interesting that this style, of which an important and recurring motif is the dynamic female celebrating not only her emancipation but her triumph, has found new public favor in tandem with the popularization of the women's liberation movement.

Art Nouveau

A style expressed in both the fine and applied arts, from the final years of the nineteenth century through World War I, in a radical but elegant departure from the corruption of eighteenth-century French styles, which had become a nightmare of Victorian tastelessness. Adherents to the Art Nouveau movement drew their inspirations from ancient forms, from nature—more particularly and most important, from plants.

When you have seen the towering cypripedia that the architect Guimard erected at entrances to the Paris subway, you know what Art Nouveau is all about. At night the giant flower buds glow with golden light that spills down the sweeping bronze stalks supporting them. The essence of the plants has been captured so powerfully that their reality prevails. Those flowers are not fantasy—the city is! You think that the roots of such plants must surely drink from a vast subterranean lake upon which Paris lightly floats. You descend the stairs, expecting enchanted caverns, and instead you are only in the métro. But above, there had been wonder rising tall as the trees along the Champs Élysées, or so they seemed—twin flowers from some secret forest, glorified into sentinels, at once delicate and strong, ephemeral and permanent. You return the next morning, half believing that you will find the buds have burst into full blossom. But they have not. The golden lights are darkened, and beneath the gracefully arched stems the neighborhood rushes on its way to work.

See Gallé, Émile; Phytomorphic

As Is

Dealers whose stock includes a lot of antiques marked "as is" really turn me off. Dealers who have a lot of "as is" antiques that they don't bother to inform you are "as is" turn me off even more.

Most of us readily compromise on condition when we first begin buying antiques. We agree when someone says, "If you were as old as this is, you'd be chipped [broken, cracked, missing a few parts] too!" It does seem logical, and the price seems right. And inexperience leads us to believe that a tiny "no harm" flake or an improperly fitted cover really isn't going to make all that much difference. China that has been mended with metal rivets seems especially appealing, since the rivets are considered to be confirmation of some age. And in the beginning, age is the principal quality that we seek in an antique. Quality and condition be damned. Because we are so new to the field, we are primarily concerned that the things we acquire be old.

I usually can tell how long a dealer has been in the antiques trade by the amount of "as is" merchandise on display. Only the very newest and a tiny, characterful band of the oldest ever stock much of it. The newcomers get away with it through a kind of positive thinking that is part ignorance, part enthusiasm. The old-timers are either sweet and folksy or arrogant and intimidating. In either role they have, over the years, mastered the art of selling "as is" antiques to those of us who really ought to know better than to buy them.

See Mint

Auctions, Antiques

Anticipation. Excitement. Competition. Triumph. Disappointment. Who has pointed a gun at you, forcing you to continue bidding? You have, that's who.

Auctions, Household

Good news—when they're genuine.

Aurenes

The iridescent art glass produced by the Steuben Glass Works at Corning, New York. Steuben produced iridescent glass in many colors, gold being the most generally available.

Blue Aurene is better than gold, green and brown are better than blue, and red—as in most kinds of art glass—is best of all.

Decorated Aurene is better than plain, richly decorated is better still, and acid cutback (acid-etched or cameo) is better yet.

Some pieces of Aurene show mirror-bright spots instead of the uniformly silken finish that is typical of this glass. These result from an uneven application of the chemical sprays used to develop the satiny iridescent surface. Although these bright areas are not considered flaws, many collectors prefer the pieces that do not have them.

Signed pieces are marked "Aurene" and/or "Steuben" in rather shaky script. This is quite easy to read on the blue glass, where it shows in blue-black lines. Signatures on gold Aurene are sometimes almost invisible unless the glass is held to the light.

Austria

The popular decorated porcelains manufactured in Carlsbad (or Karlsbad), Austria, were made before 1918. Otherwise they would have been made in Carlsbad (or Karlsbad, or Karlovy Vary), Czechoslovakia.

B

Baby Oil

If your ivory carvings need to be cleaned, you usually can do a fine and gentle job by applying a tiny bit of baby oil with a soft cloth and rubbing dry with another soft cloth. You can use mineral oil too. If you are dealing with pieces that have been decorated with colored pigments, be sure that the oil treatment will not smear or erase them before you and they get carried away. Either avoid the colored areas or make a careful test at some reasonably obscure spot.

Baccarat Glass

In operation for over a century and a half, this famous French glass works has produced commercial, practical, and art pieces in styles ranging from elaborately Victorian to Art Nouveau and Art Deco. Most articles are pressed, or molded, and many of the more complex items are composed of easily interchangeable elements: the base of a candelabrum, for example, could also be used as the foot of an epergne. Recognition of some of the more popular of these elements is enormously helpful in identification of Baccarat productions.

The easiest way to find the embossed Baccarat signature is to feel it. This is particularly helpful in discovering signatures on the fluted bobeches of Baccarat candlesticks. You can't always see those little raised letters, but you can feel them, even if the bobeches are dusty. Many elaborate Baccarat pieces are also marked under the base. Sometimes you can see the signature by looking down through the glass. A knack for reading upside down and backward is helpful. If you can't see anything resembling a signature, and the piece is too large or too complicated to recommend inverting it, lift it a bit and feel underneath along the inner edge. Work your way toward the center, and remember, if you find "*Déposé*" somewhere, you'll probably find the name of the firm that *déposé*'d it too. Using this tactile authentication has led me to acquire half a dozen Baccarat candelabra that were had for a fraction of what they would have cost if anyone else had discovered they were marked. Incidentally, some of the early Fostoria candelabra look an awful lot like Baccarat pieces, even as some of Baccarat's lacy pressed glass closely resembles lacy Sandwich glass items.

Baccarat still has some of its nineteenth-century patterns in production, but the new pieces carry the company's contemporary mark—a frosted circle containing a decanter and two glasses and "Baccarat/France." You have to look for this one.

Some dealers make a lot of fuss about Baccarat perfume bottles because they happen to be marked "Baccarat," but many of these bottles are commercial items that could be obtained filled with fine perfume for not much more than the prices asked for the empties. Those of us whose temperatures rise at the mention of the names of some of the world's great glassmakers have to keep reminding ourselves that it was not unusual for firms such as Baccarat and Lalique to fill orders for commercial containers, which orders kept the furnaces fired while the art-glass pieces sat around waiting to be sold.

The most famous Baccarat productions are the celebrated paperweights, which continue to be made. Even quite recent paperweights command high prices and are of interest to paperweight collectors, but I don't really think that they should be presented as antiques.

Bacon, Francis

"Knowledge," he said, "is power." He was not commenting on the antiques trade, but he could have been. Those of us who would like to "bring home the bacon" in that complicated and alluring business would do well to take Sir Francis Bacon's words to heart.

See Ignorance

Bargain

You bet it's what everyone dreams of.

See Inexpensive

Bateman, Hester

Eighteenth-century British silversmith, manager of her family's business, mother of six children, including Peter and Jonathan, and grandmother of William Bateman, all of whom, together with Anne Bateman—Hester's daughter-in-law, Jonathan's wife, William's mother, and Peter's partner—pursued the family trade.

Although as a female silversmith Ms. Hester Bateman was not the novelty one might expect her to have been, there is no doubt that her gender has contributed to the appeal that her silver holds for collectors, particularly in the United States, where she is one of the few British silversmiths whose names are sufficiently interesting to enhance the value of their works.

It is said that Hester Bateman did a good deal of free-lance work for other silversmiths, who sometimes would overstamp her maker's mark with marks of their own. Since the value of Hester Bateman silver has appreciated significantly, that unfortunate practice has undergone a complete reversal. It is now much more profitable to overstamp a piece made by someone else with the mark of Hester Bateman. This belated tribute might be very flattering to Hester Bateman, but it certainly complicates matters for an unsuspecting new collector.

Battersea Enamel Boxes

These little snuffboxes—seldom more than two or three inches in length—were introduced in the eighteenth century at Battersea, England, and have been popular items for collection just about ever since. Recently a whole series of new Battersea enamel boxes has been introduced into the antiques market. Since the new ones cost about 5 percent of the value of the antiques, be careful when selecting a Battersea snuffbox; try to obtain some sort of guarantee of authenticity before paying a premium price for it. You stand a better chance of acquiring a genuine old Battersea enamel box for $5 or $10 from someone who does not appreciate its value than you do of finding an old one presented as such for only $50 or $75.

Beatles, The

The four-boy revolution changed a lot of things besides music and haircuts. If one of the Beatles acquired a Tiffany lamp, a great many of his fans decided that a Tiffany lamp would, indeed, be a cool thing to have, especially since its flowing lines and glowing colors became even more flowing and glowing with a little help from the psychedelics.

See Nouveau Riche

Belleek Porcelain, American

Belleek porcelain wares produced in New Jersey and in Ohio during the last decades of the nineteenth century and the first decades of the twentieth are increasingly desired by collectors. If Belleek brings to mind only the paper-thin Irish porcelain—also extremely popular with collectors if the familiar Irish Belleek mark is printed in black—then not much of the American product will be recognized as Belleek. Most of the American factories produced a Belleek ware that was thicker and heavier and of quite different style and decoration than the Irish porcelains for which it was named.

Probably the finest of the American Belleeks is Lotus Ware, produced by Knowles, Taylor & Knowles of East Liverpool, Ohio. This company manufactured much other china and stoneware, so don't let that "thicker and heavier" qualification lead you to identify some of the lesser K. T. & K. products as Lotus Ware. The real article is finely made, quite light in weight, and a pearly white, often having floral or other hand-painted decoration. Some of this ware, like other American Belleek pieces, was sold as blanks for china painting by home decorators, which helps to explain why some of the hand-painted flowers are less well executed than you would expect on such excellent porcelain.

Ott & Brewer, the Willets Manufacturing Company, and the Ceramic Art Company, all of Trenton, New Jersey, produced Belleek wares, some of which more closely resemble the china of Limoges, France, than the porcelains of Ireland's Castle Caldwell. In 1906 Walter Scott Lenox, who had worked for Ott & Brewer and for Willets, and who was a partner in the Ceramic Art Company, established the china company that still bears his name. Lenox set out to duplicate Irish Belleek. Although the results were somewhat different, there are many who consider Lenox Belleek finer than the ware it was intended to copy.

Prices for choice examples of the antique American Belleeks are rising, with Lotus Ware at the top of the list. In the all-American aftermath of the Bicentennial celebration, further appreciation can be anticipated for these fine American porcelains.

Benezit

E. Benezit, *Dictionnaire des Peintres, Sculpteurs, Dessinateurs et Graveurs,* or just plain Benezit. The Bible of the art market. Six fat volumes and all in French. Even if your French barely makes it to *la plume de ma tante,* you can quickly learn to understand the simple and direct entries. Don't be intimidated. An hour of practice and a basic phrase book can do the trick. If you don't want to be bothered with that easy fundamental, then remember that, as a general rule, the longer the entry in Benezit, the more important the artist. The masters get pages and pages, the minors get a line or two. It is all relative, and you don't have to understand a word of French to use this instant evaluation. Representative prices are given for works by many artists, but most are listed in francs. Given the current art market and the international monetary situation, there is little to be gained from struggling with currency conversions in order to find out what something sold for in 1924. But you can use the prices as a guide to those artists whose works have shown steady or spectacular appreciation, and it is very comforting to know that someone somewhere shelled out a significant piece of change to acquire a painting by the artist who did the picture you discovered in a thrift shop. If your interest in painting and sculpture is not sufficient to justify owning your own Benezit, join a library that does own one. If your library doesn't have a set in the reference section, get to the board and tell them to skip a few of the pretty coffee-table art books and concentrate on an important reference work.

Bentwood Furniture

Bending wooden rods into curved elements for furniture construction was practiced long before the Thonet brothers of Vienna came along in the middle of the nineteenth century and turned the process into an international business. By applying mass-production techniques to the manufacture of bentwood furniture, the Thonets boosted their bentwood chair into, perhaps, the most famous piece of furniture ever made. If that seems to be an irresponsible observation, remember that the Thonets produced millions upon millions of these chairs before the close of the nineteenth century, and that other manufacturers copied the Thonet chairs with various modifications and adaptations, and still do. And remember all the cafés and coffeehouses and cabarets and cardrooms and . . . and . . . and . . . that bentwood chairs have furnished. Quite apart from which, of course, is the fact that the bentwood chair also inspired the tubular metal furniture that has immortalized its happy combination of lightness, strength, and economical yet fluid line.

When considering old bentwood furniture, look for breaks and splits along the crests of the curves. And at any tiny curling terminals.

The Thonet name adds considerable cachet for certain customers. Often it will be found on a printed label or burned into the undersides of seat hoops. You might have to search for it on pieces that have survived many coats of paint or varnish.

Most bentwood pieces are a joy to refinish, largely because they usually offer only small, smoothly rounded areas that are a cinch to rub down. But don't lightly assume that you can bleach one of those mahogany-finished bentwood pieces to match the rest of your honey-gold furniture. That dark-red stain soaked right into the pores of the wood. Maybe—just maybe—a professional stripper could successfully dispose of it, but trying to do it yourself probably won't yield anything better than a kind of purply wine-lees look. Never mind what it says on the can of paint remover! If you don't want to keep it in the mahogany family, and you don't want to visit a commercial stripper, why not just give your bentwood a nice coat of paint? Nothing wrong with a neat black-enamel finish as long as it isn't one of those high-gloss jobs. Don't get carried away, though, and paint over a Thonet signature, should your bentwood furniture happen to boast it.

See Thonet Brothers

Bisque

Unglazed porcelain. Like a lot of other terms describing or defining porcelain, this comes from the French. The French didn't discover porcelain in China, but French missionaries were the first to write home about the techniques and to describe glazes, colors, and decorative styles in terms that they either originated or translated into French, and that continue in use today. Which is why a French dictionary is a more practical guide to the field of Oriental ceramics than a short course in "Elementary Chinese" would be. The French missionaries went around naming and explaining methods and results that the Chinese had perfected and more or less taken for granted for centuries. So we still speak of the colors of the *grand feu* and the *petit feu*, and of *famille verte* and those other *familles—rose, jaune*, and *noire*—and whether it now comes from England or Germany or Japan or China, we call unglazed porcelain "bisque." Possibly because the porcelain, as it emerged from the kilns, before glaze or other decoration had been applied, had a dried, slightly toasted look that reminded the French missionaries of the brittle, twice-baked cookies that they called *bisquits*. If the reference to cakes seems a bit farfetched, it might help to remember that some of the other fanciful terms introduced by the French, and in continuing use, include such poetic or prosaic descriptives as *clair de lune* and *sang de boeuf*.

Strictly speaking, any unglazed porcelain can be called bisque, which means that all parian porcelain is bisque, although not all bisque is correctly described as parian.

Parian porcelain is fine-textured, unglazed, and technically speaking, supposed to be bone-white. Originally called parian (from the island of Paros, known in ancient times for its fine marble) because it was said to resemble marble, it becomes as self-contradictory as "chocolate blancmange" in colored decoration. Widely copied examples of the famous Bennington (Vermont) parian porcelain pieces are found with touches of blue decoration, but that is about as colorful as true parian is supposed to become, and many purists insist that only the dead-white bisque of finest quality is worthy of the designation.

The distinctions between bisque, parian, and china become terribly blurred in considering porcelain heads for dolls, since some authorities consider all unglazed porcelain heads as bisque, while others subdivide bisque into categories called bisque if it is colored and parian if the bisque has been left pure white, with, perhaps, tinted features. Glazed porcelain heads, on the other hand, are called china by some, although others call all porcelain dolls' heads china, and subcategorize into glazed and unglazed—or bisque. 'Tis a veritable merry-go-round.

Dealers and collectors insist that you can tell the difference between new bisque and old by the feel of the paste. Old bisque usually is smooth. Newer bisque tends to feel slightly sandy or sticky. Old bisque can also feel slightly sticky if it is not too clean, but it is quickly restored to silken smoothness by a good washing. (*See* Ajax, Liquid.) Old bisque sometimes shows tiny black flecks of dirt in the paste as a result of having been formed in improperly cleaned molds. You cannot assume, however, that a piece lacking these telltale imperfections is necessarily new. Finally, the colored decoration of most old bisque is usually soft, mellow—almost appearing to sink into the paste rather than to be imposed upon it—and finely executed. The decoration of most new bisques often is crude, leaving a thick painted surface that nearly masks the character of the porcelain. The colors used frequently are rather fundamental paint-box primaries.

Boasting

What a wise antiquer never does. It must take enormous self-control to stay mum about your latest coup, but it's better sense and better manners than lording it over the poor cluck from whom you copped a treasure for a fraction of its worth. Such remarks as "Now that I've bought it, I'll tell you—it *is* jade!" should subject the braggart to heavy financial penalties. Those who gloat have only themselves to blame for having to pay through the nose the next time around.

See Maven

Bottles

Collecting antique bottles is an important hobby, but I think some of the excitement that powered its enormous surge of popularity has subsided since so many dumps have been dug out. Ten years ago all anyone needed to become a bottle collector was a shovel and the curiosity and common sense to figure out a good place to dig. This made it easy for a lot of new collectors to come into the field. Such phenomenal growth eventually becomes self-limiting. A decade of digging has left precious little ground for new prospectors to explore. The thrill of discovering a rare or unusual bottle is much more likely to be experienced at a bottle-club meeting or show than at the heart of a unmined dump.

Bottle collectors are almost the only antiquers who will not reject an example because the glass is "sick." This cloudy decomposition definitely delights some of them, and the more speckled and spattered and flaked and frosted a specimen is, the more fascinating they seem to find it. The rainbow iridescence that makes some old bottles look as if they had been dug from the ruins of Byzantium is another result of surface decomposition. Be suspicious of this attractive effect if the colors are particularly bright and the entire bottle evenly bathed in them. It might be new. In minutes, chemical sprays can accomplish things that wouldn't occur naturally for years and years and years. "Purpling," the development of a delicate lilac tint as a result of long exposure, contributes to the appeal of some old bottles, but the introduction of do-it-yourself kits for quickly purpling glass has placed some well-purpled specimens slightly beyond the pale.

Bradley and Hubbard

The passion for things signed with recognizable names has brought about an unbelievable rise in prices for Bradley and Hubbard pieces, especially for Bradley and Hubbard lamps. Some of the lamps are attractively designed, but the quality of the materials and workmanship that went into them varies enormously. The best of the lot might be considered "lesser Handel-types." The poorest of the lamps rank much lower and do not merit higher prices than any of the inexpensive lamps with glass-panel shades, simply because the often badly constructed shades are stamped "Bradley and Hubbard." And yet the customers' hunger for names, names, names often bestows upon an ordinary Bradley and Hubbard lamp a value equal to that of a much superior Handel. Since the signature apparently is paramount in establishing the value of these lamps, it is necessary to know what the marks are and where to look for them.

When the glass-panel shades are marked, they usually are stamped "Bradley and Hubbard" on one or more of the metal strips at the inner circumference.

Some of the lamp bases carry the name or the "B&H" monogram under the foot. Bradley and Hubbard oil lamps sometimes have the monogram embossed on the font cap. Two unexpected places in which later Bradley and Hubbard lamps are frequently signed are on the pipe extending from the base to the sockets, and on the cup housing the wire connections to the sockets.

See Jefferson Lamps

Brass, Lacquered

Over the years a lot of useful brass articles have been coated with lacquer in order to eliminate the need for polishing. Unfortunately this protective coating often got scratched or worn away in spots, permitting the metal beneath it to tarnish. On lamps the lacquer sometimes became discolored or scorched. Such pieces can wind up looking pretty sick.

Generally there is a cure. What you have to do is get rid of the lacquer so that you can properly polish the brass. In many cases this is the major effort of a commercial refinisher in the costly polishing of an old brass bed. You can tackle the job with a regular liquid brass polish, such as Noxon, applied with a steel-wool pad. You can remove the lacquer with paint solvent too, but then you still have to go back with the brass polish and do a thorough polishing job. By using brass polish for step one, you combine stripping and shining, which cuts your work in half. Or nearly.

After you have removed the lacquer and the metal is uniformly shining, you can decide whether or not you want to have the newly gleaming surface given a fresh coat of protective lacquer. I never do—but, then, I don't mind polishing brass.

That's why I never pass up a terrific buy on an antique brass student's lamp simply because the finish looks shot.

Bride's Basket

A popular Victorian decorative accessory consisting of a metal stand, usually with an elaborate ornamental handle, in which is set an open glass bowl. Presumably these were called Bride's baskets because of their popularity as wedding gifts, but the name is still appropriate, since many of those on the market today are marriages of bowls and stands that were never intended for each other. Don't for a moment think that the original bowl did not perfectly fit its holder. It always did. And check along the often ruffled edge of the bowl to be sure it isn't chipped or cracked.

If the metal stand is marked "Pairpoint Mfg. Co." and the glass bowl is original, the bride's basket probably was made at the Mt. Washington Glass Company.

Brimfield (Massachusetts)

For buying antiques, for selling antiques, this is the Mecca to which the faithful must return three times each year. The largest outdoor antiques market in the eastern United States. A small city of tents and trailers mushrooming at dawn in what minutes earlier had been a great muddy field. Either it is your scene or it isn't. If it is, you can continue shopping throughout the night. If it isn't, you can see many of the same dealers at shows in Boston and in New York. But only at Brimfield will you find them all together in the same place at the same time. The promoters call it a flea market, but it isn't. Not really. Prices may not be low, but the variety of merchandise displayed is tremendous. The whole town gets into the spirit of the event. The church runs a parking field and sells food. The service station sprouts a lemonade stand. If I had to choose between going to Paris and going to Brimfield, I would choose Paris, but I would regret it, because I love Brimfield.

Britannia

What a confusing term. When someone describes a metal item as Britannia, he almost always means that it is made of the white metal alloy in general use for plated pieces. The same term, however, also applies to a standard for silver having a higher proportion of pure silver than does sterling, which is 925/1000. Britannia silver is 958/1000 pure silver, which was the standard required for English silver from 1697 in London (provincial silversmiths were covered in 1700) until 1720. This higher standard was made mandatory in order to stop the sterling coins of the realm from being converted into trays, tankards, spoons and what have you—a practice that was threatening to result in a national shortage of silver coins. After 1720 the Britannia standard was no longer required, although silversmiths sometimes did, and occasionally do, employ it. Such English pieces carry a mark showing the seated figure of Britannia, in addition to the appropriate hallmarks indicating maker, date, and place of manufacture. Articles made of Britannia metal, on the other hand, sometimes are marked "Britannia." Because this alloy has been used since late in the eighteenth century, some Britannia metal items can be desirable antiques, but please don't confuse them with pieces crafted from Britannia standard silver. Most of the "Britannia" marked pieces are of late-nineteenth –early-twentieth-century manufacture and certainly ought to be instantly recognizable to any reasonably informed dealer or collector.

Bru, Casimir, Jne.

French doll maker of the second half of the nineteenth century. His dolls are the Tiffany of the doll collector's world.

Watch out for reproductions and improper marriages of heads and bodies for Bru dolls. An average Bru commands such a significant price that a little flimflammery in the authenticity department can pay huge dividends. Which means that unless you are an expert in such matters, you had better be darned certain that you are purchasing your Bru doll from a reliable person before you part with all that long green. If you are lucky enough to run into one of those trustworthy venders who immediately tells you, "This is a reproduction Bru head on a genuine Bru body," then you certainly ought to be able to buy with confidence. But why not wait until you can buy something that is totally original from that reputable individual? And don't try to pick up a Bru doll as a bargain by bidding one in at an auction where there is no possibility of return or refund if you find that you have made a mistake. In spite of all the encouraging stories about Bru dolls' turning up at flea markets and garage sales and in uncataloged auction lots, chances are that you will overpay rather than underpay in order to obtain this currently most desired of French dolls. Take comfort from the fact that whatever you pay for such a doll today will probably look like a steal tomorrow!

See Marseille, Armand

Burmese Glass

A friend once showed me a painted glass lampshade that obviously had been manufactured for use on an electric fixture. "Is this Burmese?" she asked hopefully. "Not at all," I said, much to her dissatisfaction. "But it shades from pink to yellow," she argued, "just like the book says."

Which is one of the problems with many books about antiques—this book not excluded. No matter how we try not to spread misinformation, some readers will latch on to a properly expressed fact and try to apply it to situations that it simply doesn't fit.

"To begin with," I told my friend, "what you have is a shade of frosted colorless glass that has been sprayed with pink and yellow paint."

She was unimpressed. In rebuttal she showed me a passage in an antiques book that said that Burmese glass items often had painted decorations. "True," I said, "but the kind of painted decorations the writer has in mind is not the sort of painted decoration that you have here." We circled around like that for a while, and, frankly, I don't think she was ever entirely convinced that her shade was not a treasure direct from the Mt. Washington Glass Company. I wouldn't even be surprised if, with an untroubled conscience, she sold the darned thing for a ridiculous price to someone who agreed with her definition of "Burmese."

Genuine Burmese glass is expensive. And well it might be, because it is really beautiful. It was made by only two firms—the Mt. Washington Glass Company of New Bedford, Massachusetts, for which the patent for Burmese glass was secured in 1885, and by Thomas Webb and Sons of Stourbridge, England, which produced Burmese under a licensing arrangement with the Mt. Washington management. Other factories attempted to produce and market similar types of glass, but such production was quite limited, either because of problems of production or through patent-infringement actions on the part of the proprietor. Queen Victoria gave Burmese glass a huge boost in popularity by ordering a tea service in the decorated ware from the Mt. Washington Glass Company, which may explain the successful licensing arrangement subsequently completed with the Webb firm, which called their glass Queen's Burmese Ware.

Genuine Burmese is an opaque glass of a soft yellow color. Contrary to my friend's misinterpretation, the yellow is not a surface decoration but the basic color of the glass. Certain areas of the pieces were reheated, which caused the glass in those places to develop a pink color. This pink is variously described as salmon pink, blush pink, coral, and other fairly imprecise shades. Let's face it, one man's blush pink could be another's dusty rose, while salmon and coral always make me think of the color of Tropicana roses, which actually is much closer to the shading on reproduction Burmese. The pink of genuine Burmese is a soft, melting color that blends gradually into the yellow portions of the piece. It is not at all the rusty red or dead orange that turns up sometimes on new "Burmese-type" pieces. Even with an acid finish, genuine Burmese has a lovely creamy look and a fine silken surface. The reproductions have either a chalky mat surface or a dewy, wet look. The yellow portions of the new pieces tend toward green. I think I've already been thoroughly confusing on the subject of the proper shadings of pink. Suffice it to say that dark shadings leaning to orange and red are not characteristic of any old Burmese glass that I have seen. Reproduction pieces also tend to be much heavier and thicker than the finely made genuine Burmese articles. You really need to handle examples of true and false Burmese in order to know the difference.

C

Cameo Glass

An ancient technique for decorating glass articles by cutting through an outer casing of one or more layers of contrasting colored glass to create a design in relief. Revived with much success in the second half of the nineteenth century by English and French glassmakers. English cameo glass articles are generally quite Victorian in style and feature much intricate carving. The great flowering of French cameo glass took place as part of the Art Nouveau movement, with Émile Gallé its most famous practitioner.

Except for the most unusual pieces, French cameo glass probably will not continue to be a spectacular category for the investment-minded collector. Likely to enjoy some appreciation, but—with the reservation that must always be made for exceptional pieces—hardly spectacular. Prices for average pieces were and are high, and while they may rise, the rate of increase seems to be lagging well behind the astonishing gains being made in such currently dynamic collecting categories as dolls, American art pottery, and Tiffany, Handel, and puffy Pairpoint lamps.

English cameo glass, on the other hand, appears to be enjoying an enormous rise. And although American cameo glass was hardly distinguished, except for a few rare Tiffany cameo pieces, production was never large, so that even quite average examples command exceptional prices, which can be expected to continue to climb.

Collectors irrevocably committed to French art glass, but who buy with an eye to the financial future, might consider acquiring prime examples of French *pâte de verre* instead. Already costly, these pieces have been gaining the sort of status-symbol acceptance that usually goes hand in hand with a healthy increase in value.

Cameo Jewelry

The best cameo is made from a single stone slab, the relief design being developed by carving away portions of one vein to expose a contrastingly colored vein, which serves as a background. Customarily, a light-color vein is chosen for the relief design, leaving a darker vein to be polished into a softly gleaming base, but occasional and sometimes quite attractive cameos are found with a darker relief design carved upon a lighter background. Naturally, the richer and finer the detail of the carving, the better the cameo. Less substantial cameos are carved from shells, the technique being much the same, but the material is thinner and significantly easier to work—which means that all other things being equal, a shell cameo is generally worth considerably less than one carved from stone. False cameos have been created from various materials, including thin layers of stone laminated together, and going all the way down the line to pressed wax and molded plastic.

Stones and shells have been used for cameos for thousands of years. The ancient Greeks not only used cameos for personal adornment but also as ornamental settings on caskets, cups, and other furnishings and decorative articles. When the ancient Romans began adopting and adapting all things Grecian, they also took to making cameos, the production of which continues to flourish in and near present-day Rome.

On the return trip to Rome some of the bus tours to the ruins of the villa of Emperor Hadrian include a little side excursion through a cameo factory. I never quite figured out whether the guide or the driver or the sight-seeing bureau had made the arrangements, but some buses made the detour to the cameo works and others did not. And although Betty and I often took the tour—it being an agreeable way to spend a summer afternoon—there never seemed to be any pattern to the inclusion or omission of this extra feature. At the factory, visitors could watch cameos being made, and could purchase their favorites set into inexpensive pins and pendants and rings and earrings and bracelets and buckles and just about any other mounting into which a cameo might be set. Too bad that those buying this new cameo jewelry in American antiques shops don't at least get a chance to see what is left of Hadrian's villa or to appreciate the incredible gray-green beauty of the hillside olive groves along the road.

Most of the ladies on the new cameos are carved in thin right-face profile and have slightly retroussé noses. Their hair is not well detailed and their chins either jut forward angularly or are unfortunately receding. A scenic cameo of a maiden in a romantic landscape might look properly antique but will reveal its newness to anyone who carefully compares it to a fine old one. Never mind about the mounting—a lot of antique cameos have been reset over the years. By the same token, only discretion would prevent someone from putting a new cameo into an antique setting.

Canton Wares, Blue-and-White

The most generally available eighteenth- and nineteenth-century Chinese tablewares are the blue-and-white underglaze-decorated pieces showing simple Oriental landscapes within blue borders. The design—a bridge in the foreground, a willow tree, a simply suggested house or pagoda, a boat in the water, perhaps a bird or two in the air—eventually evolved into the perennially popular Willow pattern, which has been transfer-printed on tons of English, American, and Japanese ceramics. Remember that the old Canton ware is hand-painted rather than transfer-decorated and that the decorations are rather school-book simple instead of involved. Sometimes stylized stick figures appear in the house or in one of the boats, but there are no people on the bridge in the old Canton ware. The bridge personnel made their debuts later—in England, Japan, and other places. Since eighteenth-century delft sometimes copied the Canton decorations, there aren't any people on the bridges on it either.

See Rose Medallion

Capo di Monte

It means "mountaintop," which is where this important eighteenth-century Italian porcelain factory was located—on a hilltop near Naples. Although a variety of works were produced there, most familiar are the distinctively decorated pieces having mythological figures in molded relief and lively colors. Similarly decorated pieces are now rather generously called Capo di Monte, whether they originated in Naples, at the Ginori porcelain factory near Florence, or in Germany or France. There are, in fact, so many Capo di Monte–type porcelains on the market, and there is, in truth, so little real antique Capo di Monte porcelain for sale that most of us can comfortably assume that whatever pieces we may encounter are anything but genuine. The famous blue "crowned N" mark has been used on so much porcelain that it might as well stand for "Nippon" as for "Napoli."

Most of the Capo di Monte–style little boxes and cups in the antiques shops today are late-nineteenth- and twentieth-century products. Some of them have some age and considerable decorative appeal. Inexpensively acquired, they make exciting finds until someone points out that no matter how much they resemble the pictures in the antiques books, they are neither as old nor as rare as they seemed.

Carder, Frederick

The Steuben glass that antiques dealers and collectors rave about is not the costly contemporary crystal but the astonishing variety of wares produced at the Steuben Glass Works between 1903 and 1932 while the company was under the direction of Frederick Carder.

Carder was a genius, the experimental genius of American glass. He did everything. And he did most of it himself. The results were never as sensuous or seductive as those achieved by Tiffany's glassmakers, but they combine technical perfection with an often rather "moderne" styling that can be considered quite characteristically "Steuben."

I could write a book about Steuben glass of the Carder period, but fortunately I do not have to, because Paul V. Gardner has done that in *The Glass of Frederick Carder*. For the new antiquer—and for plenty of us older antiquers as well—the most useful section of the book consists of more than a hundred pages of line drawings from the Steuben catalogs of the Carder years. Study them. You will soon find that you can recognize many unmarked Steuben pieces at a glance. You will also find that many presumably unmarked pieces are actually signed, but that it takes a bit of looking to spot some signatures.

Almost the only thing that Mr. Gardner's book doesn't tell you is that it is sometimes very easy to acquire the beautiful Steuben colored crystals for a fraction of their worth, since many dealers do not associate these pieces with the Steuben factory. The drawings in Gardner's book will help you recognize them. And then won't you feel superior!

Besides the colored crystals, look for sneakily good buys in Steuben's ivory, alabaster, jades, Ivrene and *verre de soie*. The ivory glass is a soft custard, alabaster looks very much like unflavored gelatine, the jades resemble most opaline glasses (except that they are thinner and gum-drop pretty), Ivrene is a satiny iridescent gleaming white, and *verre de soie* has a soft, shadowy iridescence over a faintly gray body. (P.S. Those grayish light shades with a splotchy mineral-stain iridescence are not *verre de soie,* although there *are verre de soie* light shades. Confusing? Not after you've seen the real thing.)

Carnival Glass

A novelty pressed glassware with an iridescent finish that was introduced about 1900 as an inexpensive version of the costly art glass then being produced by Tiffany, Steuben, Quezal, and others. That carnival glass was sometimes called "poor man's Tiffany" not only tells us a great deal about the intended market for carnival glass but also about the sort of customers for whom Mr. Tiffany's wares were intended. Much carnival glass was manufactured for use as merchandising premiums or prizes to be given at fairs and carnivals, from which purpose comes its generic name. To have their wares as captivating as possible, the makers of carnival glass came up with an astonishing variety of patterns and combinations of patterns, even employing different designs on the inner and outer faces of many pieces. When the public's fancy for the costly iridescent artwares faded in the final years of the 1920s, so did the popularity of the heavily decorated iridized carnival glass, which had been accepted as caviar by the general. Oddly enough, carnival glass collecting became a respectable and important part of the antiques business at about the same time that the public began to rediscover its enthusiasm for Tiffany and other iridescent art glass. In consequence of this renewed interest, manufacturers dusted off their old molds and resumed the production of carnival glass to satisfy a suddenly revitalized market.

How to tell old from new? It isn't easy. Some carnival glass experts forthrightly say that to them the old pieces look old and the new pieces look new, and let it go at that. You can't even be guided by signs of wear, because anyone can age the base of a piece of glass by turning it a few times in a bit of gravel or running it around in a tray of sand, or scratching it with a file or a bit of emery board or a piece of sandpaper. Plus which, some genuine old pieces stored away in cabinets, unused when they were new because they were too splendid and left unused through the years when carnival glass was unfashionable, show no signs of wear whatever. Pieces marked "Fenton" or with the overlapping "I" and "G" monogram of the Imperial Glass Company are new, or comparatively new, dating from the big carnival glass revival that got under way in the 1960s. There's that, at least, to go on. Unless someone has gotten industrious and had the marks polished off.

According to one collector, most of the new carnival glass pieces have a somewhat shiny finish, in contrast to the richer, more fully developed iridescence that is characteristic of the well-made, well-finished pieces produced between 1905 and 1925. Another equally experienced carnival glass collector discomfortingly points out that in some of the new marigold pieces the color is remarkably good.

More than 600 carnival glass patterns have been identified, and occasional finds continue to surface to swell the total. Plates, oddly enough, are among the more uncommon carnival glass items. Evidently not too many plates were made in a ware intended to be as lavishly decorated and as showy as possible. One carnival glass collector maintains that there were no complete dinner services made in true old carnival glass. Not, at least, until near the end of the era, perhaps as late as 1925.

Pattern popularity and rarity have much to do with the value of old carnival glass. Animal patterns are particularly desired by many collectors.

In addition to the ubiquitous marigold, carnival glass was produced in blue, green, purple, white, and red, and also in pastel shades of pink, blue, and green. Because the iridized surface often makes it difficult to determine the true color of the glass, it is best to hold the piece to light to see the basic color. No doubt about this: the real old red carnival glass is the most valuable.

Chalkware

Doesn't "chalkware" sound more valuable than "plaster"?
See Composition

Chapman, Robert William

In an essay, "Silver Spoons," he wrote:

> *A collector should not be too careful to be sure of what he buys, or the sporting spirit will atrophy; and he who collects that he may have the best collection, or a better than his friend's is little more than a miser.*

I agree. I really do. And if Mr. Chapman would change that "should" to "could," I would agree even more heartily.

Chewing Gum

At an auction preview, two days prior to the sale, I found a pair of Handel boudoir lamps not identified in the catalog and lotted together with a pair of worthless "decorator" table lamps. Both the shades and bases of the Handel lamps were signed, the bases being marked with embossed metal strips. From the incomplete catalog description and the inclusion in a lot with two zero lamps, I concluded that the Handel lamps had been unrecognized by the auctioneer and might be sold for much less than they would bring if properly identified. Nevertheless Betty and I estimated a maximum bid based on the full value of the Handel lamps. We figured that we could always get $5 or $10 for the other pair of lamps if we sold them at a flea market, which would cover our gas and toll expenses in returning to the auction. After a prolonged contest with a single rival we finally won the lot for a little more than we had wanted to pay but also a bit less than we thought we could realize on the Handels. Plus which, since the sale included no other items of interest to us, our only hope of getting any return from our investment in time and travel was to buy the lamps. When they were delivered to us I immediately checked the shades to be certain they had not been damaged during the course of the exhibition. The shades were fine, and I started examining the bases to make sure that the shade fitters and finials and other elements had not been misplaced. When I turned the bases over, I found that each Handel signature had carefully been concealed by a large smear of chewing gum. I showed the apparently unmarked bases to Betty. "Don't tell me," she said, "that those embossed labels fell off!" I carefully peeled away one glob of gum and uncovered the Handel tag, which was just as I had seen it during the exhibition. When the chewing gum was removed from the other lamp, that signature also proved to be intact. "The underbidder!" Betty said. I nodded. "He favors Spearmint," I said. Betty said that she was really glad that we had outbid our tricky competitor. "If we hadn't seen the lamps before he stuck those gum wads over the signatures, we might not have known . . ." I said that we would have known, since the shades were signed and the lamps unmistakable, but that we might not have been as eager to pay top dollar for a pair of incompletely marked lamps. Things being as they are in the antiques market today, those little signatures greatly increased the salability of the lamps. I probably would have bid much less if I had not seen them, which meant that for the cost of a couple of sticks of chewing gum our competitor might have saved a few hundred dollars. Who knows how many potential rivals he did discourage with those strategically placed seals? For that matter, who can guess how many times the chewing-gum trick actually has worked to his advantage!

Chlorine Laundry Bleach

Ordinary undiluted chlorine laundry bleach usually will remove the network of fine brown veins that discolors many old ceramics. Don't be afraid that it will also remove a painted or transfer-printed decoration. It won't. Just fill up a plastic basin, slip in the item, and let time and chlorine do the rest. It often bleaches the discolored hair-fine cracks in porcelain, which many dealers euphemistically call "age lines," to near invisibility. Of course the piece or the glaze might still be cracked, but if the lines come clean, its appearance will be markedly improved. Occasional pieces emerge from this bleach bath with a faintly powdered surface. A thorough rinsing in clear water usually will correct this, although it might not restore the original texture and gloss of the glaze. If you have several pieces from a dinner service or tea set that you would like to bleach, experiment with a damaged or unimportant piece and see how well you like the result before you try the treatment on a tureen or a teapot. You probably will be delighted. It would be a pity to risk one of your treasures, though, wouldn't it? If treasures are all you own, go out and buy a cracked cup or a chipped saucer of the same vintage from the same maker and experiment with that. Then you can proceed with confidence or accept the fact that your unbleached pieces are going to go on hiding a measure of their original beauty behind a tea-brown veil.

If you happen to be one of those who think that these discolorations add a touch of the antique, remember that they were not there way back when the piece was made. By removing them you actually are bringing the article nearer to its original condition.

Cinnabar

Red lacquered ware. Some of the choice older pieces contain thousands of layers of lacquer carved into intricate designs of great variety and depth. Good cinnabar lacquer has a rich surface with a gleaming waxy luster.

There are a lot of junky new cinnabar-type pieces on the market. These are molded rather than carved and have none of the depth or richness that mark fine cinnabar items. The finish is either dry and powdery-looking—which shouldn't fool anyone but frequently does—or the thin, brittle, painted surface is often chipped. It stands to reason, doesn't it, that if beneath one layer of lacquer there is another layer of lacquer and another and another and another, and on and on and on, a tiny flake wouldn't immediately expose white plaster? These new cinnabar-style pieces are usually priced low and are worth less. Or worthless, if you prefer.

Clocks

Among the most popular of antiques. With surprising frequency, an old clock is the first acquisition of a new enthusiast. Probably because a clock can be both decorative and practical. Those who would like their new old clocks to remain practical as well as decorative must either know how to do repairs or have access to a reliable—and not just a widely recommended—clock fixer. Some dealers and auctioneers will guarantee the clocks purchased from them, in which case disappointment and inconvenience might be offset by a refund or free repairs.

A friend who knows much of such matters insists that most old clockworks require nothing more than a good cleaning and oiling to put them right. I'm sure he knows, because he buys and sells a great many clocks. I think he also oversimplifies, because he enjoys tinkering with clocks, which turns what might be tedious or forbidding to most of us into child's play for him. There are some clockworks for which broken or missing parts are unobtainable and must be adapted from other works or especially crafted. Such things are decidedly not child's play and probably are not worth undertaking unless you happen to be dealing with a very important clock.

Oddly enough, the more important a clock is, the less likely it will be to need repair. Not only was it probably well made in the first place but the chances are good that it received proper care over the years. It isn't unusual to find a fine eighteenth-century clock running perfectly. The tricky part is to find a fine eighteenth-century clock offered for sale. On the other hand, not many of those fanciful Art Deco clocks produced in the years between World Wars I and II seem to have survived in working order. So much for the wizardry of mass production.

Cloisonné

A method of decorating in which various colored enamels are separated by thin metal strips that are set on edge into a supporting form, which is usually, although not necessarily, of metal. Contrary to a widely held misconception, some of the finest cloisonné work is not at all heavy, having been executed on extremely thin sheets of copper, while some of the crudest pieces are made on weighty shapes of stamped brass. Some of the cheapest work is done on base metal that has been thinly plated with bronze.

The best way to check for damages or repairs on cloisonné pieces is with your fingers. Even an expert restoration will reveal a slightly different texture. You won't need the sensitive fingertips of a

Jimmy Valentine to detect it. Defects are sometimes difficult to see, especially in a piece with an involved design. You will do much better to take off your gloves, close your eyes, and explore the surface with your fingers.

Recently much new cloisonné has come onto the antiques market, where it does not belong. The colors in the new pieces look harder and brighter than those found in the richer-looking, older cloisonné. Most of the new items are also considerably heavier than their antique counterparts. Such comparisons are absolutely meaningless, of course, until you have examined some old and new pieces. When you have, it will be much harder for an unscrupulous dealer or auctioneer to stick you with some of the new items at antiques prices.

A good deal of not new but not very fine early-twentieth-century Japanese and Chinese cloisonné is available, and probably because choice pieces are increasingly hard to obtain, these production items often carry pretty substantial prices. Many of the Japanese pieces have large areas of undecorated metal accented by bands or panels of rather muddy multicolor enamel, and if they still boast their original bases, they will be impressed with the word "Japan." The Chinese examples generally have over-all enamel in simple floral and/or geometric designs. These are more finely finished than the Japanese pieces. Some have "China" impressed in the metal, others are so marked, often with red paint or a paper label. Any such designation of country of origin immediately suggests post-1890 manufacture, which is not usually the cloisonné that collectors will pawn the family jewels to acquire.

Coffee and Tea

If the English had not become so inordinately fond of these once exotic beverages, the ceramics industry that developed at Staffordshire might never have flourished. Before this taste was acquired, the wealthy were accustomed to drink from vessels of silver or glass. The less fortunates drank from pewter, horn, shell, wood, gourds, cupped palms—just about anything that didn't leak—and too bad if along with their beer or cider they also got lead poisoning, cankers, and assorted social diseases. Until the popularity of drinking hot tea and coffee quite democratically ruled out everything from the silver chalice to the tin cup, for the excellent reason that when filled with boiling liquid those containers became hot enough to burn the fingers. Thus there was a practical reason for turning to ceramics. There was an esthetic one too, since Oriental tradition decreed pottery and porcelains for tea service. The British upper class bought its chinawares from the Far East and from continental factories. Such imports were far beyond the means of the masses, which, however, did not rule out the need for an occasional "dish" of tea or coffee. As the custom of drinking tea and coffee spread, so did the demand for inexpensive ceramic cups. To supply this demand, English potters began to adopt various techniques, including the use of molds, in order to speed production. This marked the beginnings of industry (as distinguished from crafts and from art) at the Staffordshire potteries.

See Wine

Composition

Cardboard, pressed wood dust, pressed marble dust, pressed ivory dust, celluloid, plaster, *papier-mâché*, you name it—whenever the composition of something seems doubtful, or perhaps inferior, someone is certain to describe it as being "composition." This catch-all term has become a fairly specific one in reference to the composition of some antique and collectible dolls, but it is otherwise fairly meaningless. How seriously would we take a weather forecaster who told us that the weather was going to be weather?

Consignment Piece

When an antiques dealer tells you that an item in which you are interested is on consignment, he might or might not be telling the truth. Either way, what he means to tell you is that the price is not terribly negotiable. The only graceful way to press for further concession is to go along with the gambit and suggest that the dealer get in touch with the consignor and ask if a lower price would be acceptable. This gives the dealer a chance to come back to you later if he wants to offer you a more favorable deal.

Consignment Shops

Many consignment shops charge their consignors a commission of one-third of the gross proceeds of a sale. Which means that if you find something that you would like to buy priced at $300, the owner-consignor is going to be satisfied to receive $200 for it, while the proprietor of the shop retains $100 to cover his expenses and whatever profit he can take from the transaction. Sometimes—especially if an item remains unsold for a month or more—the proprietor will agree to reduce his customary share of the proceeds, or will prevail upon the consignor to accept a lower price, often at a substantial saving to you. So don't be afraid to ask. And don't be shy about checking a day or two later if the owner suggests that he will have to consult the consignor.

Although consignment shops seldom yield the undervalued treasure that antiquers dream of stumbling over—most items having been quite carefully appraised by both the consignor and the proprietor before being offered for sale—they do sometimes include fine items from private collections that would not otherwise reach the market. And one of the principal services that the proprietor of a consignment shop can provide is to know who has what to sell and which customers would be interested in it. Never hesitate to list your special wants with the manager of a consignment shop. But if he succeeds in coming up with an item that you've been pining for, don't expect him to take a beating on the price. Not if you want him to bother digging up item number two. Or number seventy.

The best consignment shops for antiques are those serving neighborhoods of old homes and quiet wealth. New housing developments and middle-class suburbs are the provinces of the garage and tag sales.

Coordinator

The organizer or promoter of an antiques show. I wish some of them were better organized and interested in better promotion for their shows. The coordinator is sometimes the only one to derive any profit from a show. The exhibitors' fees are calculated to cover all of his expenses, with an allowance for profit included. This usually puts the coordinator in the black before the show opens. This is not true of the exhibitors, whose booth expenses—often including non-interest-bearing deposits paid as much as a year in advance—must be recovered through sales made at the show. If the coordinator also receives all or a percentage of the gate, he can carry home a tidy bit of money after the show. The exhibitors can carry home their unsold merchandise and whatever profit remains after their expenses have been covered.

The antiques show is one of the few promotional efforts in which the financial risk is most often sustained by those with no claim to a share in the principal financial returns. Too many exhibitors think of an entry fee in a show as comparable to the rent paid for a retail shop. That is not quite correct. They should ask themselves if they would pay the same rent if their landlord also charged a dollar, or two, or three to every retail customer who crossed their thresholds. Of course allowance must be made for the cost of advertising and promotion incurred by the coordinator—if, that is, there is any. If antiques dealers weren't so polite, timid, grateful for small favors, and otherwise eager to kiss the hand that milks them, they would band together and insist that interest be paid on deposits held longer than six months, and that their contributions to the show be recognized by a prorated sharing of a percentage of the profits. This might be no more than a few dollars refunded on each entry fee, or it could be substantial. Before coordinators and exhibitors press the panic button at such suggestions they ought to ask themselves how many tickets would be sold for admission to an empty arena.

Copper Luster

Although metallic lusters have been used to decorate ceramics since the Middle Ages, it was not until early in the nineteenth century that luster-decorated pottery reached widespread commercial production in England, where copper, silver, ruby, and purple metallic finishes were applied to inexpensive ceramics designed to appeal to a large and not generally selective market. Perhaps the shiny metallic finishes were intended to serve as a kind of poorman's plated ware, much as carnival glass, at the close of the nineteenth century, was intended to provide the American general public with a cheap but flashy substitute for the costly iridescent art glass that Tiffany supplied to the upper crust. In some lusterwares the metallic finish is applied to glazed pottery, in others it is imposed directly upon the clay. When used over a glaze the luster sometimes appears quite thin, and might be completely worn away in spots.

An antiques expert once told me that the way to judge the age of a piece of copper lusterware was by the depth of the luster finish on the interior of the piece. In the oldest pieces, he said, the metallic finish went all the way to the bottom. On later pieces it stopped about three-fourths of the way, and retreated farther with the march of time until fairly recent items would have only a thin margin of luster on the inner rim. I thought that this was true until I ran into some brand-new little creamers that had been entirely covered—inside and out.

Close examination of old copper luster will usually reveal a certain amount of crazing; look especially around and under the foot. And check all nonlustered areas. You won't find crazing on the recent reproductions.

Copper Polish, Paste

You are not going to believe this—I didn't either until I tried it—but the same paste that you shine your copper pots with can be used to restore the brilliance to iridescent art glass.

Caution: Do not use this or any other strong or abrasive cleaner on pieces that rely on painted mineral stains for their color or decoration. Almost any stained finish eventually will wear away; no sense hastening the process through your cleaning efforts. The difference between painted or "flashed" iridizing, such as you find on carnival glass, and the iridescent effects achieved by Tiffany, Steuben, Quezal, and their peers is that in the finer art-glass items the iridizing is *in* the surface of the glass, while the flashed effects are *on* the surface of the glass. There's a world of difference between those two prepositions, including the difference between a luster that is permanent, needing only to be thoroughly clean to reveal its brilliance, and one that use and repeated cleaning ultimately will erase. Copper polish is especially useful for cleaning large or metal-mounted or repaired pieces that might not be convenient, easy, or safe to bathe in ammonia and detergent solution.

Cranberry Glass

True cranberry glass takes its color from gold, which makes it a rich and pretty transparent pink. A cheaper glass, colored by copper instead of gold, is more red than pink and should not be called cranberry. If the color strays, it is toward a delicate blue-rose that has nothing to do with yellow. Sometimes the pink glass is only a thin casing for a layer of colorless crystal. You can see this by looking across the rim or through the base. Although the pink glass usually is the outer surface, I have an elaborately enameled Victorian cranberry-glass water service that has the colored layer on the interior. Painted cranberry glass gets its color not from gold but from a transparent mineral stain. Most painted pieces look thick, as opposed to crisp and brilliant, and have an even color, without the variations that genuine cranberry shows where there are bubbles, molded patterns, or expanded areas.

Crooks

It is easier to be deceived in the antiques trade than in most other commerce. How desperately we want to believe the wonderful things we are told! How eager we are to think that we have outsmarted someone else!

Crown Milano Glass

Speaking strictly, this is not a kind of glass, but rather the name for a line of decorated glasswares produced by the Mt. Washington Glass Company, which in 1893 registered the crowned "CM" monogram as its trademark for Crown Milano wares. The glass itself is not remarkably different from the white opal glass produced at other American and European factories, but it usually has been blown or pressed into one of the wonderfully characteristic forms associated with the Mt. Washington Glass Company. Except that they tend to be more elaborate, the painted and enameled decorations quite closely resemble those found on articles decorated by Smith Brothers. This is not surprising in view of the fact that the Smith brothers had been in charge of the Mt. Washington Glass Company's decorating department before going into business for themselves. The satin-smooth mat surface given to most Crown Milano pieces, and the customary—although not exclusive—color schemes of a soft ivory or beige background highlighted by thin pastels and rich gold, and even the majestic name and trademark suggest that Crown Milano glass was intended to resemble and perhaps directly compete with such popular Victorian decorative porcelains as those produced by England's Royal Worcester Porcelain Company Ltd.

This apparent similarity to porcelain made possible the acquisition of our first Crown Milano piece.

The auction gallery, a famous one, had it cataloged as "Porcelain Ewer now mounted as a table lamp," but there was no mistaking the bulbous shape, the twisted rope handle that collared the slender neck, the vaguely Near Eastern curve of the uptipped lip, or the fact that beneath its painted decoration the ewer was not porcelain but the milky-white opal glass that the Mt. Washington Glass Company used for its Crown Milano ware.

"There's no way to be certain it is signed until the whole business is dismounted, and when it is, who knows what you are going to find?" I said. "Maybe the entire bottom will be shattered or cut away or cracked, because there are only two things I can swear to—it's a Crown Milano glass ewer, and it has been drilled through the base." Betty said, "If it doesn't go too high, maybe we should buy it and take our chances that it will be all right when the lamp mountings are removed." I asked if she would be very unhappy if the ewer happened to break while I tried to detach the fittings that converted it into a lamp. "I can't guarantee that if it isn't broken already, it will come through unscathed," I said. "Let's risk it," Betty said.

If the piece hadn't been drilled, it would have been worth about $2,000, because not only was it an important shape but the decoration was outstanding. Most Crown Milano pieces are painted with flowers. A few are scenic. On one side this ewer had a medallion showing a shepherdess with sheep framed in a gold-enameled laurel wreath. On the other was a nest of birds and roses within a similar wreath. The delicate ivory background was completely patterned with miniature laurel wreaths in soft gray-blue. "Let's bid up to three hundred and fifty," I said, "and hope for the best. After all, it's drilled—which pretty well wipes out its resale value." Betty agreed, and we marked our catalog accordingly.

A dozen well known dealers showed up at that sale. "Are you sure you don't want to increase our limit?" Betty asked as she surveyed the crowd. "Let it go if it goes higher," I said. "We can't afford to risk even three fifty on a drilled piece that might not be signed and could be broken. At the same time, it's such a great piece, I really would like to have it." As the sale progressed, so did the number of potential competitors we recognized in the audience. "Maybe another fifty," I reluctantly conceded when the lamp finally reached the auction block.

"Now we have the decorated porcelain ewer mounted as a table lamp," the auctioneer announced. I was relieved that no one had bothered to correct the description during the days of exhibition. The lot was opened at $50 and generated only casual interest. A dealer who supplies accessories for a prominent interior decorator dropped out at $100, and the lamp was ours at $120. I took an easy breath—my first that day and my last until, surrounded by pillows, prayers, and incantations, the glass emerged, neatly drilled but otherwise unharmed, plainly marked with the painted five-point crown and "CM" that authenticated my attribution.

"Just tell me one thing," Betty said. "How come you were so certain it had to be Crown Milano? It doesn't appear that anyone else at the sale recognized it."

"Because," I said, beaming in immodest triumph, "the shape is exactly like a Crown Milano ewer pictured in one of the art-glass books."

"But you always insist that pictures in books aren't too helpful," Betty reminded me.

"This," I confessed, "was one time they paid off!"

The other moral of this story is that there is absolutely no auction house from which an occasional unrecognized treasure cannot occasionally be acquired for a fraction of its worth.

Crown Tuscan Glass

It is sometimes possible to acquire pieces of this lovely semiopaque, or translucent, pink glass produced by the Cambridge Glass Company of Cambridge, Ohio, for a fraction of its worth. It also is possible to confuse it with an inexpensive opaque pinkish "milk" glass of negligible value. If you are not familiar with the Cambridge shapes and decorative motifs, you might want to remember that the true Crown Tuscan glass will show a beautiful golden-peach opalescence when thinner portions of an article are held to the light. You won't find that effect in your inexpensive pink "milk" glass. No, sir!

Custard Glass

A translucent, opalescent glass of soft ivory color that was widely distributed and well received near the close of the nineteenth century. Most often found in pressed pieces for useful tablewares—water services, berry sets, matching butter dish–cream pitcher–sugar bowl combinations, which might or might not include a similarly patterned and decorated spoon vase—this creamy, rather waxy-looking glass often has raised decorations accented with colored enamels and touches of gold metallic stain. For maximum value, acquire full sets in matched mint condition. Don't, however, neglect an excellent buy of a perfect individual piece just because you think you will not be able to collect a complete set. Keep your eyes open. Butter-dish covers, berry bowls, tumblers, creamers—you name it—turn up from time to time. Only don't mistake a brand-new piece of custard glass for an older example.

The colors of old custard glasses vary, but most are pale, more ivory than yellow. Reproduction pieces overdo the yellow coloring and occasionally show a slight greenish tint. The glass in some of the new pieces makes me think of synthetic vanilla pudding. The old custard glass looks more like rich country cream.

Blue custard glass is another of those misnomers that turn up from time to time in the antiques business. Don't fight it. Just don't mistake blue milk glass—how's that for another misnomer?—for it. Blue custard glass was a Northwood product in the popular chrysanthemum sprig pattern. It is decorated with gold enamel. Choice examples in good condition bring premium prices. Blue milk glass was produced all over the place and still is. As far as I know, there aren't any pieces in the chrysanthemum sprig pattern, but I wouldn't want to take an oath on it. Since there is a significant distinction in values, it is worth remembering that blue custard glass, like its cream-colored relative, is translucent and opalescent, while blue milk glass is opaque; and that blue milk glass has a rather dull surface, while blue custard glass has a slightly glossy finish.

Examine all custard glass items with light passing through them, and tap them gently as a safeguard against acquiring cracked pieces. Use your fingers to check for rough edges; for some reason, aside from the obvious one that these pieces were useful rather than ornamental wares, this glass is often chipped, especially along the slight ridges that indicate mold seams. And remember that condition of the colored and gilt decorations affects worth. Some custard glass patterns are more readily available in green decoration than in blue, which means that blue enameling on those patterns can command a higher price. Some patterns—including some of the most generally available—were and remain more popular than others, and continue to be more widely collected. In the antiques trade this is one of the rare instances in which scarcity does not significantly enhance value.

Cut Glass

Decorating glass articles by cutting designs into the surface is a well documented ancient technique. While examples from many eras and many countries give evidence that the craft never entirely disappeared, cut-decorated glass reached its greatest technical and artistic achievement in the late 1800s and through the early years of the twentieth century in works produced at American factories. America's *nouveaux riches* and expanding upper middle class took to the busily carved objects of fine crystal like ducks to water. An astonishing variety of articles were executed in cut glass at the turn of the century—not only such expectables as bowls, pitchers, and ordinary tablewares but tables, floor lamps, umbrella stands, even the humble (in this instance not-so-humble) chamber pot.

I used to think that it was difficult to tell a fine piece of cut glass from one that was not too fine. But that was before I really started looking at cut glass. It was stupid of me not to realize that quality invariably speaks for itself. Sometimes loudly. Sometimes subtly. But given half a chance, it makes itself heard. The reason we do not hear from fine quality more often is simply that there just aren't that many items of real quality sitting around waiting to declare themselves—in cut glass or in almost any other category.

A few years ago, except for some passionate collectors and regional preferences, interest in cut glass seemed to be waning. It appears to be back now in full force. Signed pieces and important or unusual items (coffeepots, teapots, and don't forget those chamber pots!) are bringing premium prices, and the trend looks to be up, up, and away!

Czechoslovakia

It didn't exist as such before 1918—which means that glass and ceramics from Czechoslovakia didn't either.
See Austria

D

Delft

Strictly speaking, a tin-glazed earthenware, although the word is now generally—and incorrectly—used to describe a wide range of blue-and-white-decorated wares in porcelain, pottery, even opaque white glass.

Pieces marked "Delft" and "Holland" are not the old Dutch or English faience considered to be antique delft. But they are decorative, and blue-and-white wares are enormously popular, so customers and dealers just can't seem to get enough of them—no matter that they are more new than old and often even newer than new!

Delftwares were first made in Italy. They were introduced into Holland and England in the sixteenth century and enjoyed great popularity there for the next two hundred years. Early pieces are not exclusively decorated in blue and white; they sometimes include yellow, red, green, purple, and orange. The Dutch faience industry received an enormous boost early in the seventeenth century when many Dutch breweries went out of business. Buildings no longer used for making beer were soon converted into potteries, and unemployed workmen were soon back on the job—turning out delft. Quantities of delftwares were shipped all over the world, as they continue to be, whether they originate in Holland or England or Spain or Hong Kong or Germany or anywhere else that blue-and-white-decorated delft-type wares originate.

Most common of the new delft-type wares are chargers transfer-printed in grayish blue on bluish gray. They don't even look like old delft to anyone who knows what old delft looks like.

Denture Cleanser

It has been widely reported that the effervescent tablets sold for cleaning false teeth could also cure sick glass. Since sick glass is the result of surface decomposition, I thought this remedy belonged in the realm of wishful thinking. Years ago I tried all the recommended treatments on a terribly sick decanter that I had bought from an antiques peddler who assured me that the cloudy deposits to which I objected were only dirt and sediment and would vanish with a little soap and water. Well, they did not vanish after washing. They looked worse. When the rest of the decanter was sparkling clean the sick spots really showed for what they were. Neither did they vanish when treated with vinegar, as one friend recommended, or baking soda, as another suggested. They withstood the liquid drain cleaner that an auctioneer swore was infallible. The cosmetic application of a thin film of mineral oil caused the sick spots to hide temporarily, but the next washing removed the oil, which had only masked the spots, and they were back, like the bloodstains on Lady Macbeth's hands, only a lot less imaginary. Little wonder, then, that I thought the simple denture-cleaning tablet unlikely to succeed.

And it didn't. The glass looked improved for a day or two, but the cloudy sick spots soon reappeared—every bit as unfortunate as before. I think the only reliable cure for sick glass is to have the decomposed surface polished off. Since the shapes of decanters, bottles, vases, and the like usually will not permit this, you might as well try the denture-cleanser treatment. It probably won't do any harm—as long as you don't do anything that might break the glass, such as shock it with a rush of hot water. If it doesn't work, you can always clean jewelry with the rest of the tablets. They're very effective for that.

Depression Glass

Mass-produced American pressed glass tablewares of the 1930s, often having mold-etched patterns in imitation of more costly engraved glassware. Usually colored—pink, green, amber being the most common—with some variation in values for different colors in different patterns. Usually clear, although some opaques were produced. It used to be given away at the movies or as merchandising premiums. No one gives away depression glass now. Whether you love it or hate it, depression glass has become such an important collecting category that it should no longer be ignored. What once seemed a passing bit of regional madness now approaches the level of a national craze. And with occasional depression glass rarities reaching prices in the hundreds and even crossing the thousand-dollar line, the probability of a much predicted decline in values becomes increasingly unlikely. How significant depression glass has become in the antiques trade is confirmed by the reports that certain pieces, especially the much desired butter dishes, are being reproduced!

Except for the rarer items, depression glass continues to be inexpensive. Pieces so acquired should provide a quick profit for the new dealer, or a modest investment with some potential appreciation for the beginning collector. Either should keep on the lookout for serving dishes, covered pieces (complete with the proper cover, of course), salt-and-pepper shakers, butter dishes, pitcher-and-tumbler sets, and other, harder-to-find items. In good condition, which means not chipped, cracked, or badly scratched. Some depression glass patterns are more popular than others. Some are much more widely available. Some pieces command a better price in one color than they do in another. Indeed, the intricacies of depression glass collecting have reached near-Byzantine complexity. This probably is especially satisfying to depression glass enthusiasts, because it gives them something more to concern themselves with in buying and selling these mass-produced tablewares that until quite recently were objects for ridicule and rejection to most antiques dealers. Some of us who are inclined to go right on ridiculing and rejecting ought to remember the years when we felt the same way about carnival glass. At least one enterprising depression glass dealer-craftsman has climbed on the bandwagon with depression glass jewelry, making pendants and earrings out of etched-pattern motifs salvaged from damaged pieces. So collectors can wear examples of their favorite patterns as well as set their tables or fill their cabinets or picture windows with them. For several years some custom jewelers have been doing similar things with scarabs and stoppers and prisms and turtlebacks and tiles of iridescent Tiffany glass. We all know what has happened to that market. Suffice it to say that when collectors identify so deeply with a hobby that they wear tokens of it for all the world to see—a Mickey Mouse wristwatch, an Art Deco Clip, a tiny doll framed in a Victorian locket, or a medallion cut from a green "cameo" depression glass cake plate—that hobby is not going to evaporate into the thin air of sudden unpopularity. Not soon, certainly.

Diapers, Cloth

Excellent to use for polishing. And you won't have to worry about lint and frayed hems and trailing threads and other such nuisances that plague users of the discarded T-shirt or devotees of the frayed-towel or old-blanket schools. Moreover, you can wash and reuse cloth diapers, which makes them convenient, inexpensive, and a lot safer than oily or waxy rags that you might be tempted to keep around for a second application or pending proper disposal. Toss them into a pail of water, add some detergent, and let them soak until you're ready to give them a real laundering. Believe it or not, there still are some accommodating shops that will sell you a dozen old-fashioned cloth diapers, even in these highly "disposable" days.

Diapers, Disposable

A very good first wrapping for breakable antiques. Some dealers who exhibit priceless porcelains and glass at antiques shows all over the country absolutely swear by them. You can use them repeatedly too, which, over the long haul, makes them not only more reliable but more economical than tissue paper. If you frequently acquire antiques at flea markets, country auctions, and from other sources that offer haphazard wrapping, it is convenient to have a dozen disposable diapers on hand. At an important doll auction in New York, when all of the buyers lined up to claim their purchases at the end of the sale, it was amusing to see each produce a package of disposable diapers for wrapping the latest acquisitions.

See Plastic Foam

Disneyana

Mickey Mouse, Minnie, Pluto, Goofy, Donald Duck, Dumbo, and Snow White and the Seven Dwarfs are not too many decades removed from Rose O'Neill's Kewpies or Palmer Cox's Brownies. Their antics are responsible for the appeal of an enormous range of collectible articles from the 1930s, even as frolicking Kewpies or cavorting Brownies formerly helped sell humidors or jam jars or clocks or whatever. Whimsical characters from literary and popular works have decorated everything from ancient Egyptian faience obscenities to Mother Goose plates. That Disney's creations made their debuts on film rather than on paper—or papyrus—does not diminish their legitimacy. Film was the popular literature of the 1930s, even as television became the popular literature of the 1950s. Which means that Howdy Doody, too, will have his collectible day. Just wait!

See Shirley Temple

Dolls

Of all collectors, doll collectors are the most emotionally involved with their hobby. In connection with no other collecting category are words of love spoken so often or so appropriately. A dedicated doll collector who might display remarkable restraint in all other affairs can become instantly irresponsible, extravagant, aggressive, lyrical, grim, jolly, and unwaveringly determined when faced with a desired doll. For no other merchandise is the checkbook whipped out so quickly, the cash advanced—even forced on a seller—so eagerly. Politeness is not uncommon along the antiques trail, but usually it is a vender who says "Thank you" to his customer, unless the customer has purchased a doll, in which case the expression of gratitude is often reversed. Not only are doll collectors the most appreciative but they are also the most fiercely competitive. The most numerous too. Authorities hesitate to rank the world's Big Three of collecting, but there is general agreement that in indeterminate order they are: stamps, coins, and dolls. And of the three, doll collecting is currently ranked as the fastest growing.

As a hobby, collecting dolls is far from new. Marie Antoinette collected dolls before the French Revolution sent her to the guillotine and exiled her favorite doll maker to triumphant popularity in England. Queen Victoria assembled a famous collection of wooden dolls, for many of which she designed and sewed the costumes.

No one knows when or where dolls were first used as toys—as distinguished from the diverse religious roles that dolls have played in countless societies from the most primitive to the most cultivated. Early and folk dolls have been made from clay, corn, bone, leaves, straw, gourds, ivory, feathers, grasses, seashells, nuts, and fruits. At the time of the Roman Empire and for centuries thereafter, wax dolls were made in Italy. In the seventeenth and eighteenth centuries wax dolls were produced throughout Europe. Wax also was used as a surface coating and to improve the modeling of doll heads made from other materials, including wood, plaster, and paper. A true hard-paste porcelain comparable to that produced in the Orient was finally developed in Germany in the early 1700s, but it did not come into widespread use for dolls' heads until the middle of the nineteenth century, when doll makers in Germany and France began producing bisque and china-head dolls, which soon captured a worldwide market.

In porcelain, doll manufacturers found a perfect material for their product. The unglazed bisque had a fine texture that took painted decoration with appealingly realistic results. Porcelain was infinitely more durable than wax and it was suited to mass-production processes. Industrialization made new manufacturing techniques possible and also provided a prosperous new middle class anxious and finally able to enjoy some of the luxuries formerly reserved for the rich and royal. Without too much fear of disappointment, even the merchant's daughter could hope to own at least one beautiful bisque-head doll. Perhaps with big glass eyes that opened and closed and a lovely wig made from real human hair. By 1900, dolls had become a big business, especially in Germany, which, until World War I, made two-thirds of all dolls produced in Europe.

The greater number of German-made dolls helps in part to account for the generally higher prices now commanded by French dolls, but an even more significant factor is the superior workmanship that is characteristic of much of the better French product.

Rarity, age, and condition all affect the value of a doll. Serious collectors want their dolls to be as completely original as possible. A minor damage might not discourage them as much as would a poorly executed repair. Both experienced and beginning doll collectors place maximum importance upon the doll's head, often insisting that the head represents 90 percent of the value of a doll. For that reason the head is the first element to be examined—and thoroughly. If the doll has a wig, off it comes, so that the head can be inspected for damages and repairs.

Since most dolls are made in parts, a good deal of interchanging and replacement has been and continues to be possible. Some manufacturers marked various elements of their dolls, usually for convenience in assembly rather than out of consideration for future collectors. These marks help serve as a guide to originality, but even they are not always consistent, since it was not uncommon for one company to produce doll heads for use on bodies made by another manufacturer, the finished product being distributed (and often identified) by still another firm. All of which makes the matter of complete "originality" something even doll experts occasionally have problems with.

Some dealers make much of the fact that certain antique dolls still wear their original costumes. It is extremely difficult to be absolutely sure of this in most cases. A great many dolls cannot be said to have "original" clothes, since a majority of the German girl dolls originally were dressed only in little guaze slips. In such instances "old" clothes might be the more accurate designation—if, indeed, the clothes are old. Original costumes that can be documented through markings, advertisements, family records, and other means do add to the value of a doll that is otherwise in proper condition. And certainly a full outfit of well-made old clothes contributes much to a doll's appeal.

The doll collector's vocabulary abounds in language that seems contradictory or mysterious to the uninitiated, who are apt to be put off by such an apparently senseless term as "open-closed mouth." (An open-closed mouth is a mouth that appears to be open but is actually backed with porcelain or composition or whatever material the head is made of. This is distinguished from a closed mouth, which is just plain closed and painted that way, and from an open mouth, which is, indeed, open, meaning that there is space between the parted lips. Simple?) As one becomes more thoroughly immersed in the world of dolls these designations not only become meaningful but assume critical dimensions.

As the number of doll collectors has dramatically increased, the number of collectible dolls has radically decreased. This has spurred an incredible jump in doll prices, many of which have doubled and tripled in less than a year. It also has caused many newcomers to the field to include composition and vinyl dolls from the 1930s right up to the 1970s in their collections. This, in turn, has inspired dramatic price increases for such now widely sought dolls as the early Shirley Temple and Dionne Quintuplets dolls.

Dollhouses, doll furniture, carriages, dishes, and other accessories have enjoyed an enormous increase in popularity and are quickly assuming status as collectible categories in their own rights. Dollhouses loom particularly large as bright items for the future.

See Lillie, Beatrice; Marseille, Armand; Repairs: Dolls

Double or Nothing

It is widely believed that antiques dealers double their money on anything they buy. Not many do. In truth, the return usually is either far less or much greater.

See Profit

E

Elmer's Glue-All

My lifeblood. For paper. For wood. For fabric. For felting lamp bases. For leathering tabletops. For bonding anything porous . . .

See Epoxy

Emeralite Lamps

It is easy to tell if the green-and-white-cased glass shades for these now popular lamps are chipped, but you sometimes have to see light passing through the shade to know whether or not a shade is cracked. If there is no available electrical outlet, or the lamp needs rewiring before it can be used, shine the beam of a flashlight through the shade or hold it out to the sun. And examine the shade from all sides.

Some Emeralite models have a tricky arrangement of clamps that holds the shade in place. If you do not know how these work, you probably would be well advised to keep the shade installed. When you want to wash the shade, just leave it in place, disconnect the lamp, and wipe the shade with a sponge lightly moistened with a weak ammonia solution. Yes, it is possible to remove and replace the shades, but it takes a certain amount of know-how and a lot of courage. If you have never done it, think twice before you try, no matter how much you enjoy responding to a challenge. Or how do you think so many of those shades became chipped and cracked in the first place?

Encyclopedia

When the library is closed and you just can't wait to find out about a particular artist or artisan, give your old encyclopedia a break. It won't reward you every time, but it just might surprise you. I wish I owned all the reference books I need. Until such time, my old one-volume encyclopedia certainly comes in handy. Funny that so many of us think the information we seek would be far too specialized for inclusion in such a general reference work. Try to latch onto a good one published twenty-five or thirty years ago. The world's changed so much since then that the brand-new editions have chosen to eliminate entries for some of the lesser artists and illustrators that I find particularly helpful.

EPNS

EP(electroplated) N(ickel) S(ilver).

That's all it means, no matter how fancy it may look. And it's Victorian silverplate, which may be very decorative but probably isn't worth a great deal.

Epoxy

The fast-setting crystal-clear epoxies are very good for bonding glass and other nonporous materials. And if you are careful to avoid dribbles and drips, your repairs could be virtually undetectable. Which means that you probably will be able to use the piece. But, please, if you sell it, point out that it has been repaired.

Export Ware

These eighteenth- and early-nineteenth-century porcelains produced in China for export to those nations that either had not mastered the making of hard-paste porcelain, or could not supply it in quantities sufficient to satisfy the growing demand for "China-wares" for table service, used to be called Lowestoft porcelains. The name is still used, although the trend is definitely toward calling this china export ware or China Trade porcelain. The funny part is that for years this enormous quantity of Chinese porcelain was attributed to a small factory at Lowestoft, England, which is not now thought to have produced any hard-paste porcelain. It also has been suggested that the china was made in China but sent to Lowestoft for decoration—a theory that seemed supportable enough, since the decorations on export ware are painted over the glazed porcelain. The decorated-in-Lowestoft theory does not stand up too well, however, in view of the frequently Oriental aspect of many of the European-style decorations.

Much export ware was decorated to order with the crests or monograms of the purchaser or of the newly wedded couple to whom a dinner service would be given. Probably this originated as a carryover from the custom of identifying the family silver with the arms or initials of its owner. It helps to remember that much detail that we consider pure decoration was introduced for such practical purposes as discouraging theft or establishing ownership, even as we are currently urged to mark our treasures with our Social Security numbers or similar individual identification. Families that could not or would not employ armorial decorations were provided with monogrammed shields as central motifs for their dinner services. It is said that tablewares so decorated were in such demand that they eventually were produced on something like an assembly-line basis —completely finished except for the insertion of whatever monogram the customer might require. When an order came through, the appropriate initials were applied, and another export ware dinner service could be packed and ready for shipment in a trice. Needless to say, this quite expeditious process made no allowance for a little detour to Lowestoft, England.

Many books and plenty of antiques dealers still call export ware Lowestoft. So hard do some legends die—even among those of us who really know better.

See Samson of Paris

F

Fabergé, Carl

In precious metals, superb enamels, and in precious and semiprecious stones, he fiddled for the last of the czars. Some of his works—especially the small animals carved from agate, jade, rhodonite, and other stones, together with the naturalistic branches of mineral berries and stone flowers on gold stems—have recently been copied. Since the reproductions are carved from the same kinds of stones that Fabergé used, they are extremely difficult for the inexperienced to identify as reproductions. They also are not inexpensive, although they usually sell for a fraction of the price that an authentic Fabergé piece would command. The copies are easy enough to recognize as such if you happen upon a full display of them. The seller, in fact, often proudly points out that each piece is a replica of a fantastically costly original. You might find it harder going if an antiques dealer selectively blends two or three of the new items into his display. The thought of acquiring a $6,000 carving for a paltry investment of $250 can be pretty compelling. Awareness that these reproductions are being marketed should help reason to prevail. So should some familiarity with the proper dimensions and detailing of the originals. The Fabergé animals are little masterpieces of sculpture in miniature. They often measure only one or two inches. Most of the copies that I have seen are carved to a slightly larger scale, although I am told that some series exactly duplicate their costly counterparts. The Fabergé stone animals were not marked, so if you are offered one bearing a Fabergé signature, you can be sure that the marks are not genuine, even though the sculpture might be. I would like to think that I could distinguish between the quality of the stones Fabergé used and those in the reproductions, but I would only be deceiving myself if I did. And self-deception can be costly.

Some of the imperial Easter eggs, which were Fabergé's most celebrated creations, remain unaccounted for. In 1974, one reportedly was acquired for a fraction of its worth from an antiques shop in Texas. Such finds tend to support the theory that there are Fabergé eggs lying all over the place just waiting for someone to gather them up. Perish the thought! Your best chance for obtaining an example of Fabergé's work for less than its ever-ascending value is to pick up a cigarette box or a card case, a cane or an umbrella handle, any of which might easily go unrecognized as the work of the master goldsmith and jeweler to the imperial Russian court.

Find, Antique

A good one is better than a Martini for lifting my spirits.

Flea Markets

I love them. Especially the big outdoor markets with hundreds of dealers and miles of aisles lined with everything from fine antiques to outright junk. I like the no-nonsense attitude of most flea-market dealers. The general lack of affectation. Of course it would be pretty hard to be pretentious in the chill hour before sunrise, especially while standing ankle-deep in mud or snow or swirling red dirt. I like walking through the field on a clear night while around me the market blossoms like some magical village reappearing out of the past—a Brigadoon defined by the occasional brightness of gas lanterns showing where the first arrivals are setting up their displays. The early hours at any flea market always give me an enormous rush of optimism.

Antiques are not always inexpensive at the flea markets. Plenty of dealers at the major flea markets are knowledgeable professionals with years of experiencc in the trade. But if you find something good—if the piece is one you want and the price is fair—what difference does it make if you pick it up at a show or in a shop or at a flea market? I overheard a shopper complain to a flea-market dealer, "You ask antique prices," to which the dealer replied, "Lady, I sell antique things." Indignantly the woman said, "Well, then you should be in a shop. After all, this is a flea market!" It takes a while for many of us to rise above that kind of doublethink. Until we do we miss a lot of good buys.

The most important piece of equipment for successful flea-market shopping is a sturdy pair of comfortable shoes. Shoes (boots are even better, because they protect your ankles from brambles, wires, gravel, snakes, and the other 996 "natural shocks that flesh is heir to") that you can walk in all day, or all day and all night, or all day and all night and all day, without complaint. If you do not own such a pair, get some right away, or restrict your shopping to the indoor flea markets.

The second essential for shopping any of the early outdoor markets is a portable light. A powerful and dependable flashlight, if you can find one. Or one of those gas lanterns such as the dealers use to light their displays. The trouble with most gas lanterns is that their metal shades get hot, making the lantern awkward, if not perilous, to carry around. You'd think the manufacturers could devise a heat-resistant shade for their lanterns, or that they would at least come up with an insulated replacement for that searing metal surmount that has blistered the fingers of more than one predawn flea-market shopper. The trouble with flashlights is that those large enough to have significant power are usually also heavy. If you are going out to buy a flashlight especially for use at flea markets, choose one with a handle, which will make holding it much less tiring and will also enable you to strap the flashlight onto your belt, or tie it to your wrist, or improvise some other easy method of carrying it when you need to use both hands to transport a treasure.

Some devotees take metal folding shopping carts—the kind used for groceries and laundry—to the flea markets. These lightweight two-wheeled carts would seem perfect for carrying purchases, but actually they are difficult to maneuver over rough terrain or through crowded aisles. A four-wheeled cart, a toy wagon, or even an old baby carriage is easier to handle. A couple of sturdy shopping bags (double them up or use those woven from plastic cord) usually will be sufficient for all but the most bulky purchases, which you usually can arrange to pay for and collect by car.

There are a few potential risks involved in leaving an object to be picked up later from the vender who sold it to you. The first is that your purchase will get accidentally broken, damaged, or stolen. It's your property after you pay for it, and the dealer who sold it to you may or may not choose to act responsibly. Another risk is that some self-appointed "expert" will suggest to the dealer that he sold the article for a fraction of its worth, which can cause the seller to suffer severe second thoughts, frequently unfounded, and might even encourage an unethical dealer to refuse to deliver your purchase to you, insisting instead that he will give your money back. He might even suggest that breakage or theft obliges him to do so. An equally drastic possibility is that, having collected your money, a truly unscrupulous operator will pack his wares—and yours along with them—and vamoose. The best way to avoid such unpleasant situations is to pay for whatever you're buying and immediately take possession of it. If this involves hiking several miles to your car in order to cart away something huge or heavy, then ask your wife, husband, mistress, lover, friend, second cousin, or whomever you're shopping with to stay with your treasure until you can drive back. If you are alone at an open-air market and can't possibly claim your purchase until later, make a mental note of the number of the dealer's auto license plate and make a literal note of it as soon as you discreetly can. Situations of this sort do occur, sometimes for perfectly innocent reasons. With the immediacy of a lightning flash, a sudden storm can send dealers hurrying from the scene. And which would be the more honest action under such circumstances: to pack your purchase and take it along, intending to deliver it to you at a subsequent flea market, or to leave it unprotected and hope that only the rightful owner would remove it from the field? No, no matter how inconvenient it might be, you are much better off immediately taking whatever you buy. This applies to antiques bought at shows and shops and auctions too, where something tagged "Sold" but left on view can give rise to all manner of complications and misunderstandings.

Some antiquers worry about the possibility of acquiring stolen merchandise from a flea-market vender. This never has happened to me, nor have I heard anyone register a specific complaint, but there are some markets about which such rumors abound. A lot of flea-market venders get huffy if you ask them to give you a receipt for your purchase, but their principal resistance seems to stem from offense that their integrity has been questioned. If you suspect that a particular article has not been come by honestly, you probably will rest much easier if you just don't buy it. If you can't resist it but are plagued by doubt, then at least memorize and record the number on the seller's vehicle license plate. Probably you will never need to refer to it, but you can take some comfort from knowing that you have it to fall back on. I know one passionate flea-market shopper who snaps pictures of any dealer unfamiliar to him from whom he buys something costing more than $250. He handles the situation skillfully. Flatters the seller into posing for him. Suggests that it would be nice if he held, or stood beside, or otherwise related to the object in question. So far only one dealer, an out-of-work salesman afraid that a record of his flea-market activity would curtail his unemployment benefits, refused to have his picture taken.

At the larger flea markets, where a majority of the dealers are regulars, you can sometimes, especially if you are making a significant purchase, persuade a seller to accept a check. Sometimes. But just as the temporary aspect of the flea market makes some customers suspicious of venders, so does it encourage venders to be extremely cautious about trusting the public. After all, if you give a seller a check, you are going to drive off with his goods, and he is going to be left with what might turn out to be a worthless piece of paper. Since it can be risky to carry large amounts of cash, a book of traveler's checks can provide a reasonable solution. Many sellers who would reject a personal check will accept a traveler's check. Those who refuse the latter usually do so to avoid even that record of income—a matter perhaps best left to conscience and the stalwarts of the IRS. With various degrees of success, the managers of a few of the major flea markets have experimented with credit-card arrangements for sellers and shoppers, but for the most part, cash remains the primary medium of exchange. If you make many small purchases, it is convenient to have a batch of dollar bills available to pay for them. A hundred singles are usually a nuisance, but at a flea market they can be more convenient than a pair of fifties. No one ever refuses small bills, but some sellers either can't or won't change larger ones.

Take a bottle of drinking water and a package of Wash 'n Dri towelettes to any of the large outdoor flea markets at which you might spend several hours. In hot weather I like to freeze a gallon plastic jug of bottled water and store it in a plastic cooler. Along about midday, when only a Tiffany jeweled dragonfly lamp would be more welcome than a good cold drink of water, it is pretty well melted and deliciously chilled. (Just remember to open the bottle and pour out about three inches of water before you put it into the freezer or the ice will form right up into the bottle neck and will become a bottleneck.) If you pack your lunch in the cooler, the bottle of frozen water will keep it fresh and appetizing, and you won't have to worry about having food sloshing around in puddles of melted ice. A Wash 'n Dri not only is good for quick cleanups but is very soothing to insect bites and incipient sunburn.

Florentia Glass

A frosty gray glass spangled with mica flakes and having a design of large green leaves or pink flower petals. I dream of finding an example of this rare Steuben glass at a price that I can afford. Since I have seen exactly four pieces offered for sale in the last ten years, the dream begins to seem impossible indeed. Still, I keep hoping. There is, in fact, a particular Florentia compote about which I feel every bit as compulsive as Captain Ahab did about that big white whale.

Flour

A pinch of ordinary wheat flour can be enormously helpful when polishing metals. If a black residue results from application of your metal polish, sprinkle it with a tiny bit of flour and wipe the whole business clean with a soft cloth before continuing to polish with a clean cloth. This is a reliable technique that I learned while watching antiques-repairs expert David Rubin of Springfield, Massachusetts, demonstrate his Rubin-Brite Metal Polish. Don't coat the article with flour as if it were a piece of chicken you were about to fry—a light dusting does the trick. I keep an odd salt shaker filled with flour and have it at my elbow whenever I sit down with my jar of Rubin-Brite for a shine-up session. Since Mr. Rubin's clients include the National Museum of the Smithsonian Institution, using his polish and his flour-dusting technique makes me feel like a top professional. The results are pretty professional too.

Flow Blue Ceramics

Also known as "flo blue" and, especially in England, as "flown blue," this popular blue-printed ceramic ware has a purposely smeared decoration in which the blue pattern flows beyond its proper borders into a smudged background. Perhaps the manufacture of flow-blue wares began quite accidentally when a pattern "ran" just enough to provide a shadowy halo for itself, but if so, it was one of those happy accidents that paid off, because the results found immediate public favor. Wedgwood and other British potters developed various techniques for causing the blue designs to flow, and from 1820 until the end of the nineteenth century flowing-blue decorations continued to appear on tablewares and other practical pieces produced by many of the Staffordshire factories. As might be expected, the quality of the decoration varies greatly, as does the quality of the articles so decorated.

In another of those nominal contradictions that keep turning up along the antiques trail, flow-blue wares also come in yellow, brown, and green. Of course they then should be called "flow yellow," "flow brown," or "flow green," but they seldom are. Since these colors are quite uncommon, it probably is just as well that when they do turn up, they too usually are described as "flow blue," with or without explanation or qualification.

British ceramics made between 1843 and 1883—when flow-blue decoration reached its greatest popularity—can be accurately dated from the familiar Registry of Design marks. Pieces marked "England" date from the final decade of the nineteenth century, which was about the time that fondness for the old flow-blue wares began to fade. Flowing-blue-decorated ceramics marked "flow blue" or "flo blue" on the reverse aren't the old flow-blue pieces that collectors seek. A lot of the flow-blue wares on the American market today are so brand-new that they should make their sellers and/or purchasers blush blood-red with shame. European porcelains decorated with big smears of blue paint are sometimes presented as flow-blue china, but they shouldn't be. If you happen to like smeary blue-and-white china, these might make you happy, but if you are collecting flow-blue ceramics for their antique value, the new painted jobs will probably never produce a profit for you.

Frustration

Never go shopping for antiques when you are feeling dissatisfied with life in general or with anything in particular. The most unfavorable times are those when an especially desirable antique has eluded you. You will often feel inclined to buy something that you later will find to have been overpriced or otherwise unsatisfactory. Instead of an antidote to frustration, you will have acquired an additional source of frustration. It is unfortunate that the serendipitous treasure almost never presents itself when you are most in need of it.

See Find

Fulper Pottery

American commercial and art pottery established in 1805 in Flemington, New Jersey. The pieces in which most collectors are interested were produced during the final decades of the firm's operation under the Fulper name, before it was changed to Stangl.

I happen to like Fulper pottery. Not only for itself but also because it has always been easily acquired and easy to sell. It is becoming somewhat less easy to acquire as prices continue to rise and collectibility increases. I suppose if prices rise sufficiently it will eventually become difficult to sell Fulper pottery—unless, of course, one is offering something unusual, such as a mushroom lamp with glass inserts in the ceramic-formed shade, or a Fulper doll.

After handling a few pieces of Fulper pottery it is possible to identify other pieces without reference to the familiar Fulper signatures. All the same, it is comforting to know that most pieces are marked "Fulper." Incised signatures. Stamped signatures. Hand-executed paper labels.

Furniture

Many general books on antiques devote a good deal of space to descriptions of fine furniture. This permits a lot of interesting discussion concerning cabriole legs and mortise-and-tenon joints and drake feet and broken-bonnet tops, and sometimes it allows for the inclusion of handsome photographs of important pieces from museum collections or major galleries. None of which is particularly helpful to the average dealer or beginning collector. Neither is it needed by those who are more advanced. Fine furniture is the easiest of all categories of antiques to explore with confidence. Moreover, the seldom-told but inescapable truth is that there is not much fine American or French antique furniture to be found in the shops, at antiques shows, or at 90 percent of the auctions. This explains the increasing emphasis being given to bric-a-brac and so-called collectibles. When an important piece of furniture does come onto the market it seldom has any trouble reaching a price that would seem prohibitive to any but the most prestigious dealers or collectors.

There are still occasional buys to be made in antique English furniture, but reports of thrift-shop finds and auction steals in American and French furniture are becoming increasingly rare. The last that I heard about was a Federal piece that turned up in a Salvation Army store and needed $300 in restoration to put it right. I doubt very much that the buyer would have picked it up if it had been found in restored condition wearing a $300 price tag. The last antique chair that I observed sneaking by an auctioneer wound up bringing $100 more than it should have simply because two excited bidders had recognized it as a potential find. The fine-furniture shortage has inspired many dealers and decorators to greater enthusiasm for things they once ignored.

See Wicker

G

Gallé, Emile

French glassmaker, ceramicist, furniture designer. A major contributor to the Art Nouveau movement and a founder of the celebrated Nancy School, which served as a center for artists working in the Art Nouveau style.

"Our roots," he wrote, "are deep within the woods, at the edge of the springs, upon the mosses." His words unlock the magic in his work, releasing a near-mystical power from objects that formerly had seemed remarkable only on account of pleasing designs and careful execution.

Prices for good examples of Gallé cameo glass have risen steadily, but there are still bargains to be found in enamel-decorated Gallé pieces, which often go unrecognized as examples of his work. Although they seem less exciting than the familiar cameo pieces, Gallé enameled works actually can command higher prices from advanced collectors and dealers. Gallé pottery offers an even better opportunity for an alert antiquer to make a real steal. Often signed "Gallé/Nancy," or marked "E.G." with the cross of Lorraine, the pottery is not always identified with its maker and can sometimes be acquired quite inexpensively.

Those who cherish signatures on their art-glass articles will give Gallé a nod of gratitude. He was one of the first artists to consistently mark his work. Consequently, Tiffany and others decided that signing their creations in glass might have some advantages—including the implication that a signed vase was not just a utilitarian or decorative piece but deserved consideration as a work of art, the artist who created it having signed it proudly, even as he might have put his name on a painting or piece of sculpture.

Garage Sales

Some antiquers and collectors swear by them. Some antiques dealers deplore them. The thing about garage sales is that either you are addicted to them or you are not. If you are, nothing could possibly keep you away. If you are not, you probably are going to go on grumbling and wasting a lot of time looking for obscure addresses and not finding anything worthwhile until one day you make a truly sensational buy at a garage sale, and then you will become addicted to them, and you will still waste a lot of time looking for obscure addresses, but you will no longer grumble, because it will all be done in an attitude of high adventure.

I have never found any very wonderful antiques at garage sales. I know those who have. And news of a great buy usually makes me devote a few hopeful and concentrated weeks to covering every garage sale listed in the newspapers or announced in a hand-lettered placard tacked to a telephone pole. I suppose that if I went to five garage sales every week for a year, somewhere along the way I would acquire at least one terrific antique. This is rather like the story about the chimpanzees with typewriters eventually pecking out all the books ever written. What the garage-sale question boils down to is deciding whether or not the game is worth the candle. Include in your calculations gas, oil, wear and tear on the car, lunches, and if you wouldn't get better results shopping a flea market, visiting an antiques show, or making the rounds of the retailers in your area.

Garage-sale addicts—whose concept of paradise is finding two garage sales on the same block—submit the following suggestions:

1. Go early. Even the day before the sale begins, if you have advance notice and sufficient nerve. It won't always work. If there's a

telephone number to call instead of an advertised address, you can always call ahead and say that you plan to be out of town, or sick in bed, or whatever on the day of the sale, and try to wangle an advance look in that way. If you can't manage to get your nose in the door ahead of the rest of the world, arrive early enough to be sure you don't come dragging in on the heels of the pack.

2. Collect street maps and road maps of the area. Define your targets in advance. This is really much more efficient than getting directions from the man at the filling station or the postman or the girl at the luncheonette. If no commercially distributed street guide is available, go to the town hall or the county courthouse and ask for one—it might even be free.

3. Keep lists. Some garage sales are practically continuous operations that advertise occasionally. For the most part, these can be ignored. They seldom yield the kind of bargains garage-sale shoppers are looking for and they can waste much valuable time. Certain addresses or telephone numbers you will remember, but the true garage-sale addict maintains a file of sales not to attend, and checks it over before venturing forth. Best sales for antiques are those held by elderly couples on their way to sunny retirement.

4. Consider the condition of a roadside sign announcing an undated garage sale before detouring down a circuitous route to a sale that might have been held a week or two earlier. Does the sign look fresh and new? If it doesn't have sale dates and looks in any way weathered, ignore it, because it probably is a leftover.

5. Always ask if there is anything else for sale. In the house? Up in the attic? Down in the cellar? That's often where the unexpected treasures are waiting.

Gaudy Dutch

There is more than nominal similarity between Gaudy Dutch and Gaudy Welsh tablewares. The decorations and pattern names resemble each other, and if you know them only from illustrations in antiques books, you might find it hard not to confuse these two nineteenth-century English ceramics that were especially designed for export to the United States. If you have an opportunity to consider authentic examples of each, you will not have any trouble mistaking Gaudy Welsh for Gaudy Dutch. (For some reason—probably because its value is about ten times that of Gaudy Welsh—Gaudy Dutch is almost never mistaken for Gaudy Welsh!) The decoration of Gaudy Dutch is painted over the glaze. Gaudy Welsh decorations are painted under the glaze. This gives Gaudy Dutch a dry, mat surface in contrast to Gaudy Welsh ware, which has a glossy finish. Because the Gaudy Dutch decorations are painted over the glaze, they frequently are found to be scratched or flaking. Gaudy Welsh decorations sometimes show a flowing, running color, especially in the characteristic cobalt blue. Such streaking is not associated with Gaudy Dutch. Neither are the occasional touches of luster that are found on some Gaudy Welsh.

Strawberry and King's Rose pattern gaudywares closely resemble Gaudy Dutch, with which they are contemporary. Gaudy Ironstone is something else again. Thicker and heavier than any of the other gaudy ceramics, much of the ironstone is marked. Gaudy Ironstone is hand-decorated in patterns resembling those of Gaudy Dutch and Gaudy Welsh. It should not be confused with decorated ironstone that has been transfer-printed with some touches of hand-applied color. Some people call Imari-style decorated ironstone Gaudy Ironstone. The decorations are quite different, and so are the prices.

Glass

Of all categories of antiques, glass articles are the easiest to steal and the easiest to get stung with. Which is why this book includes a disproportionately large number of entries concerning various kinds of glass. It isn't at all hard to learn to recognize proper period furniture, and while even experts have been known to make mistakes in identifying antique porcelains, the odds, on the whole, favor correctness. But glass objects frequently are, in the memorable words of Anna's King of Siam, "a puzzlement." And if you are lucky enough to find an authentic item, it sometimes is extremely difficult for the uninitiated to judge whether or not it is in proper condition, or has been restored, or has been, perhaps, mutilated into some semblance of perfection.

New collectors of glass often are amazed at the repertoire of tricks available to correct, conceal, or disguise defects, damages, or indications of recent manufacture. To start at the top: a chipped rim can be polished smooth. A broken rim can be cut down—and polished to look as if it were fresh from the blowpipe. Broken pieces of opaque glass frequently can be repaired and painted over, even as broken porcelains often are. Interior cracks, which frequently are a problem in multilayered glass objects such as cameo-cut or cased pieces, sometimes are invisible except when viewed from the proper angle in just the right light. Ditto for pieces having a brilliantly iridized surface or an elaborate over-all design. And an item with a broken base can be redeemed in an incredible variety of ways, ranging from mounting what is left of the article in a stand of metal or wood to applying a new glass or plastic foot. Many of the signatures that would identify a piece as recent can be ground away in a trice, while more significant marks—if not more significant value—can be added with a rubber stamp and a bit of acid or by a fast workout with a dentist's drill or with some other engraving tool.

On the other hand, a great many sellers are blissfully unaware that there are glass articles worth hundreds of dollars—even thousands. And there are others who are familiar with the values of these rarities but are unable to identify them correctly when they practically leap into their hands. Fine glass objects are the most frequently underestimated of auction lots, and, as such, can be the genuine sleepers in many sales. Much more often, however, auctioneers are able to dispose of glass reproductions at prices not far below those at which the buyer could have acquired genuine examples.

Greed

One of the seven deadly sins. In the antiques trade it can be fatal indeed. Greed can motivate two quite different kinds of behavior: insane and insatiable acquisition, born of the fear that if someone else happens to buy something, he might be the one to make a profit from it; and total stagnation, resulting from the fear that if something is sold, it might, no matter what the price, have been possible to sell it for more.

Greedy antiques dealers are accumulators. They really do not want to part with anything. Either they resent your interest in buying one of their antiques or they are terrified of it.

H

Haggle

At the flea market in Rome you are expected to haggle. Most of the dealers will feel that their work is only half done if you do not try to bargain. They will laugh, shout, argue, weep, plead, cajole, curse, bless, and threaten—but don't for a minute fret that they will grow so angry that they will permit you to walk away until you have made a purchase. It's all part of the game, and you miss half the fun if you do not take time to play it.

At the flea market in Paris you can haggle with some of the dealers set up along the edges of the market, but for the most part you can forget about trying to bargain with merchants in the various antiques *marchés* unless you first win their goodwill by purchasing a number of items at full price. Once the ice is broken, however, Parisian dealers can be quite human, even those who work hard at being intimidating.

Most American dealers subscribe to either the Rome or Paris school of thought where haggling is concerned. Some expect it and will quote prices geared to accommodate a certain amount of concession. Others resent it and, on principle, will hold prices firm unless and until they can save face by collecting the full amount for several items—then they may yield on something else.

If you don't have the temperament for haggling, however, forget it, because you never will carry it off successfully. Any astute dealer will see through you and immediately recognize his superior position.

Whatever you do, don't open negotiations by saying "I'll give you . . ." or "Would you take . . . ?" Almost any self-respecting dealer will back away from such an approach, and rightly so. Asking someone if he could do a little better on the price is a less offensive opening. And don't knock an item in hope of bringing down the price. The seller probably knows that the piece is broken, repaired, or whatever, and he also knows that you're interested in it or you would not bother pointing this out.

Some dealers come on very strong when trying to bargain. They create an impression that they are about to buy everything in the place. They get prices on a number of pieces and then persuade the seller to give them a more favorable price based on the purchase of quite a lot of things. After the seller figures and refigures the best possible discount he can give, perhaps even sacrificing his profit on one or two items in anticipation of a large sale, the buyer eliminates many of the things, deducting their initially quoted prices from the total, thereby taking advantage of a favorable discount that he did not deserve, and further reducing his cost by the full prices of rejected pieces. It isn't very nice, but I have to admit that I have from time to time seen it work effectively, either because the seller is too confused to recalculate correctly or because he does not want to risk losing what is left of a potential sale.

Hair Dryer

When you're doing it yourself, and you are anxious for that glue to harden, that paint to dry, try hurrying the process with a few well-directed passes of a portable hair dryer.

Hairline in Porcelain

To paraphrase Gertrude Stein: "A crack is a crack is a crack . . ."
See Spider

Hallmarks on British Silver at a Glance

Since 1300—don't worry about identifying examples of silver from that time, for the excellent reason that you simply aren't going to encounter any—the leopard's-head mark has been used to confirm the sterling standard of British silver. Although primarily associated with London silver, this mark has been used by other assay offices and cannot be considered absolute proof of London origin without the confirmation of other marks. The leopard's-head mark appears in various designs upon variously shaped shields, which require close study to distinguish one from another. However, you can immediately tell the marks used before 1821 from those used thereafter simply by noting whether or not the leopard's head wears a crown. From the last quarter of the fifteenth century until 1821 the leopard's head is crowned; from 1821 to the present the leopard's head is bare. Now, what could be easier—especially when one considers that the greatest period in British silver ended just about the time that the leopard lost his crown? The single exception to this is the substitution of the Britannia mark—a seated figure of Britannia—from 1697 to 1719, when the Britannia standard for silver (*see* Britannia) replaced sterling and the Britannia mark replaced the leopard's head. Don't worry too much about the Britannia mark, because you are not going to see it often. Concentrate on the leopard's head, and remember to take your hat off to choice pieces upon which the leopard wears his crown.

The second most helpful mark is the lion passant, which made its debut in 1544, and which in 1720 became a required mark on all sterling silver wrought in England. Like the leopard's head, the lion passant is an extremely useful mark for those of us who would like to do some instant identifying before trying to pin down such fascinating particulars as years and makers and towns. I mean, if you find a piece of British silver in a box lot at a country auction or sitting around unappreciated at a flea market, you are not going to have a chance to whip out a table of marks for a good half hour of research. So in spite of the varying styles and shapes in which the lion passant has appeared, it is very helpful to remember that from 1544 to 1821 the lion passant is sort of looking over his shoulder, full face right into the camera, as it were; while after 1821 the lion prances along looking straight ahead of himself, so that we see his head in profile. Now, isn't that easy? If it doesn't seem so, I'll try to make it a bit easier. For the first 277 years the lion passant has two eyes showing. Tiny, perhaps, but nevertheless two eyes. After 1821 the lion is shown in profile, so naturally you see only one eye. Even when marks become worn or blurred, you can usually figure out whether or not the critter had one or two eyes. The earlier, full-face lion is called "lion passant gardant," and in his earliest presentation he wears a little crown. Don't worry about the crown on this one, though, because the lion passant gardant doffed its crown in 1550, only six years after he came prancing onto the British silver scene.

The third mark that can be helpful for bracketing a piece of British silver at a glance is the sovereign's-head mark, which first appears in 1784. This mark was introduced as a tax stamp and indicated that the appropriate newly enacted duty had been paid on the silver. The mark shows the monarch in profile. It is very difficult to distinguish details in these tiny marks, but it is fairly easy to see whether or not the royal profile faces left or right. So if the sovereign's-head mark appears, it indicates that the piece dates from 1784 to 1890, when the duty was discontinued. To narrow things down a bit further—that being a pretty uncomfortable range—the sovereign's head looks to the left for only two years, 1784 to 1786.

After that the head looks to the right until 1837, when it becomes the head of Queen Victoria—which mark, if not identifiably female, is at least looking to the left for the first time in fifty years. Now Victoria appears upon an oval shield, whereas George III appears for only two years looking left upon a rectangular shield with cut corners, after which he and his son shaped up and faced right upon oval shields. So a sovereign's head looking left upon an oval shield is indicative of nineteenth-century origin, and while certainly not without value, is decidedly not Georgian.

Two fairly recent sovereign's-head marks appear briefly on British silver and should not be confused with the earlier duty marks. One shows two crowned monarchs in left-face profile and was used from 1933 to 1936 to commemorate the silver jubilee of George V and Queen Mary. A single sovereign, this one facing right and prominently crowned, was used in 1952 to commemorate the coronation of Queen Elizabeth.

The other marks that you will find on British silver are the famous year marks and other town marks and the individual marks of the silversmith who made the piece. When you get to these, it is library time. But even without reference guides and registry tables, you can at a glance separate eighteenth-century and earlier British silver from that produced in the nineteenth and twentieth centuries.

Many new collectors worry about acquiring pieces with forged marks. Take comfort—improper marks are the exception rather than the rule. For many years, and well into the first decades of the nineteenth century, the counterfeiting of makers' marks was punishable by death, and British law still provides stiff penalties for such forgeries. There are relatively few British silversmiths whose marks sufficiently enhance the value of a piece beyond its intrinsic and customary antique worth to make them worth the quite considerable effort that it would take to duplicate them successfully.

See Bateman, Hester; Lamerie, Paul

Handel, Philip J.

In 1885, before he was twenty, Philip J. Handel organized his own glass-decorating business in Meriden, Connecticut, where the Handel Company remained in operation for over fifty years. With this in mind, the rumors that Handel was at one time or another employed by Tiffany are much more easily discounted. While certain Handel lamps might qualify for the "Tiffany-type" description, some study of Handel's work will make its differences from Tiffany lamps immediately apparent. Both Handel and Tiffany used a tree-trunk-form lamp base and a lily-pad-styled lamp base, but the differences in design, material, and workmanship are significant. On no count would a comparison favor the Handel products. Moreover, Tiffany produced nothing at all resembling the most numerous of Handel lampshades—a reverse-painted glass shade sometimes having a glue-chipped outer surface and sometimes decorated with enamels, coralene beading, and other treatments not associated with Tiffany's work. Styles of Handel humidors, vases, coffee services, and other accessories range from Victorian to Edwardian to modestly Art Deco without ever quite capturing the distinctive elegance or superb craftsmanship that is characteristic of Tiffany's works. Many Handel pieces described as being hand-painted actually rely on printed motifs that were subsequently hand-colored. Some of the truly hand-painted pieces, especially the floral-decorated Handel porcelains, are extremely well done and quite beautiful, particularly when the floral areas are contrasted with Handel's familiar mossy-green textured backgrounds.

As values of genuine Tiffany lamps have skyrocketed, prices for better Handel lamps have increased significantly. This, in turn, has influenced the prices of other Handel items.

Fortunately for today's dealers and collectors, the Handel Company was quite generous about marking its products. Except for some easily recognized leaded-glass shades, most of the lampshades are signed. On painted glass shades the word "Handel"—with or without an identifying number, artist's name or initials—usually will be found on the interior at the lower rim. Such signatures are easy to fake with a bit of brown or black tempera, which gives the dull, slightly blistered look of the real thing. The genuine Handel marks, however, were fired on, as was other painted decoration, and although the signatures might succumb to a good deal of hard, abrasive scrubbing or some diligently applied solvent, they are not going to wash off with ordinary soap and water such as you might use to clean a glass shade, and they won't soften and smear and threaten to vanish at the first touch of a damp cloth or a licked fingertip. A lot of inferior lamps have been sold at superior prices because no one bothered to check the authenticity of a recently applied "Handel" signature. Handel lamp bases are marked in several ways, including the famous woven silk label that often was stitched to the felt glued under the foot. If a lamp so marked has been rewired—and many of them have been, because another characteristic of some Handel lamps is that they originally boasted some of the shortest electric cords on record—there's every good chance that the original felt was ripped off and discarded and the Handel label along with it. Lamps having more or less open bases that would not have been felted often have the Handel name cast quite prominently into the metal. Some of the small boudoir bases have "Handel" impressed near the foot, frequently near the cord outlet. Others have a small metal strip embossed "Handel" soldered to the base. These strips can be easily lost, or easily duplicated, so invest not your faith in them unless everything else about the lamp confirms its authenticity. Many of the metal mounts that held molded glass or glass-panel shades also are impressed with the Handel mark and often carry identifying patent numbers.

Humidors, cigar and match holders, and other opal glass items usually are stamped "Handel ware," although the mark may be very faint or even have faded to invisibility.

Hand-Painted

It is so easy to distinguish hand-painted decorations from those that were mechanically applied that the frequency with which the latter are successfully represented as the former puzzles me no end.

Not only can you not rely on some professionals for the correct description, but many transfer-decorated porcelains do their own misleading by having "hand-painted" or "hand-decorated" (sometimes in French—very jazzy!) stamped on their reverses. These terms often refer to a few splashes of raised enamel or a bit of colored background or border enhancing a printed subject. Take all such claims with a grain of salt. In fact, the more elaborately a piece is marked, the more suspicious you should be.

You cannot even consider an artist's signature as confirmation that a particular decoration was done by hand. Some dealers will point out a printed signature—"Angelica Kaufmann," for example—as proof that a famous artist actually painted a decal scene. Like Mayflower ancestors and beds in which George Washington reputedly slept, "Angelica Kaufmann" decorations are too numerous to be genuine. Additionally, the real Angelica Kaufmann died in 1807—nearly a century before most of the pieces she supposedly executed saw the light of day. Plus which Ms. Kaufmann's reputation rests on her portraits, oils, drawings, etchings, and engravings. It appears that the real Angelica Kaufmann never did any china painting. So much for the "artist's signature" most often found on transfer-decorated porcelains.

Another kind of misleading signature is a genuinely hand-painted one—often a first or last name only, such as "Henri" or "Michel"—on an article that has primarily been transfer-decorated, but which a workman has garnished with some simple hand-applied details. Strands of seaweed, for instance, to enliven a printed fish, or some healthily brushed-in foliage or flowers around a pair of mechanically reproduced lovers. The factory-retained artist usually signs his work quite prominently. Not surprisingly, such pieces are frequently presented as "hand-painted and artist-signed."

A somewhat more legitimate kind of hand-painting involves the individual completion of transfer-applied outlines. In a sense, such pieces are hand-painted, although "hand-colored" would be a more precise description. Usually these have about as much individuality and interest as the pictures in a child's coloring book or one of those paint-by-numbers masterpieces that used to be the rage. This technique is especially common on sets of dishes, such as fish, game, fruit, and dessert services. A close look usually will reveal the printed outlines—often done in sepia—that the artist has followed.

With a bit of practice and a few minutes' study you can learn to distinguish between painted and transfer-printed decorations. And when you have learned, you probably will be able to identify items at a glance. You might find it helpful to use a magnifying glass at first, although you will be able to dispense with it early on.

The most obvious thing to look for is the tiny dots, or rosettes, that characterize most transfer decorations. The finer the work, the smaller the dots will be, which is when the magnifying glass comes in handy. A painted decoration will almost always reveal some brushwork. Again, the finer the work, the more closely you will have to look to see the tiny strokes with which colors were applied. Some artists achieved certain effects by using a dotting technique for shading or foliage. You can distinguish hand-applied dots from the dots characteristic of transfer printing by remembering that transfer dots are uniform, while even the most meticulously stippled painting will show variations.

Transfer decorations applied to bowls, bulbous vases, and other curved shapes frequently will show irregularities—gaps, stretched edges, streaks of color—not found in hand-painted pieces. If you notice such flaws, you do not have to bother looking for dots to know that the article has been mechanically decorated—signatures, marks, and seller's assurances notwithstanding.

Hard-Luck Hannah

There is an old song about a girl called "Hard-Hearted Hannah," and I suppose that description would also apply to many of these damsels in distress who pop up with amazing frequency along the antiques trail.

What Hannah is, basically, is a confidence woman. And until you have seen her in action, you haven't lived. She might be old or young or anything in between. She can look surprisingly chic and almost embarrassingly well heeled, or pathetically bedraggled. I met her once at the check-out counter in a supermarket. She was redeeming food stamps and blinking back tears at having to dispose of all her elderly aunt's lovely old things. I watched her operate at an auction, gradually involving the couple seated next to her in increasingly intimate conversation until they were moved to tears by her tale of woe. They finally left with her, arms linked in camaraderie, to see if they could not help her out by purchasing a few of the treasures she had been reduced to selling. I encountered her again over the telephone when I answered a "Selling my lifetime antique collection," newspaper ad.

Hannah really laid it on with a trowel that time. Her husband had just abandoned her, leaving her with unpaid bills, unfed children, and a house filled with antiques. I even had to listen to Hannah do a good five minutes on the shameless little tramp who had lured friend husband from his cozy home. In counterpoint to Hannah's breathless outpouring of intimate and impending tragedies, I could hear children squalling and a television set blasting out Saturday-morning cartoons. Yes, Hannah said, I could come to see the things she had for sale. And it would be best if I came before dark, because her husband had skipped off with the money she had given him to pay the electricity bill and her lights had been shut off, so if I wanted to see the things I had better arrive before sundown. I started to ask if the television was running on batteries, but decided not to. I realized that no matter how many unhappy details Hannah might choose to enhance her story, she probably was not forced to sell at quite the sacrifice she would have liked to picture to her prospective customers.

When I got there the cupboard was convincingly bare, all right, and the children were properly unkempt, and the big color television stared blindly into a darkened room. Hannah packed the kids upstairs and steered me into her shop, which she euphemistically termed "the parlor." Admittedly, she had a great many things, and some of them were first-rate, too. But her prices were far from sacrificial—unless, of course, the sacrifice was to be made by the buyer. I had not gone there expecting to steal anything from some destitute soul, but I had not expected to be asked several times the price at which I could have acquired similar items from almost any reputable antiques dealer. I suppose some of Hannah's other customers were more readily sold than I, because a few weeks later I saw Hannah at one of the big Manhattan auctions. She was buying like mad, and she was wearing a really sensational fur coat. She seemed not to remember me, so I pretended not to recognize her. I telephoned Hannah after her next newspaper ad ran, a month or so later. Again she was in tears. This time her husband had suffered a heart attack. He was hospitalized. Hannah was—understandably—frantic. The children were hysterical. There was no money for medical expenses. If I hurried right over I would be able to name my own price for almost anything I wanted, and I would be doing the family a great favor at the same time. I didn't bother to go or to respond to any of Hannah's subsequent ads. I suppose the logical finale to desertion and illness would be death, and I didn't think myself able to cope with Hannah's bereavement.

From time to time I run into Hannah, who obviously shares my passion for antiques shopping. Whenever I see her buttonholing a new mark I wonder what fresh catastrophe she has concocted to force her to reluctantly sell her treasures. Occasionally she ruins her entire pitch by offering her business card to prospective buyers, who, if they had any sense, would realize that no damsel in distress bothers stopping off at the printer to have a batch of cards run up.

That card would be a sure giveaway, except that most of Hannah's clients are so anxious to take advantage of a situation that seems ripe for it that reason flees in the wake of Hannah's hard-luck scenarios.

Most of the hard-luck sisterhood are seasoned professionals who hype their ongoing businesses with sporadic bids for sympathy. Too bad that their tactics have caused some of us to be skeptical of any situation in which the sale of antiques is tied in with an intense recital of personal problems. Those with genuine problems usually call in an auctioneer or a dealer instead of exposing themselves to a parade of private customers who might pick and choose only one or two items and take a great deal of time doing it.

House Calls

The most advantageous opportunity for buying antiques. Dealers dream of them. Some spend a small fortune soliciting them through advertisements in newspapers and neighborhood periodicals, and backing up their ads with multiple telephone lines and answering services and recording devices. They insist that only such total effort can produce worthwhile results.

Other dealers operate on the basis of personal referrals, primarily through real estate brokers or attorneys, although there are imaginative and aggressive souls who ferret out sources from the obituary columns, from morticians and hospital attendants. A friend of ours took a more wholesome approach and posted notices on local activities bulletin boards in shopping centers and supermarkets, but received not one response.

Another friend beats his way through back roads in rural areas that suggest potentially good pickings. With more aplomb than most of us could muster, he goes ringing doorbells. "Hello," he says, "would you be good enough to tell Mrs. Murphy that the man is here to buy the old things she wanted to get rid of?" When told, as he always is, that he has come to the wrong house, he launches into a terribly convincing line that runs something like: "But I don't understand. . . . I only just met her down in the town, and she was telling me about all the old furniture and pictures and lamps and rugs and things that she was going to sell, and . . . I'm sure I followed her directions. . . ." If the householder fails to rise to the bait, my friend apologizes for the intrusion and, almost as an afterthought as he is about to take off, pauses long enough to add, "I don't suppose you folks'd have any things you want to sell? I mean, after all, as long as I'm here . . ." This is not, I am assured, unfailingly productive, but possibly because my friend has the instincts of a truffle hound when it comes to sniffing out potential sources of antiques, and probably because he is an ingratiating type who could, as they used to say, "charm the paper off the walls," and has inherited the shrewdness of a long line of Yankee traders, it succeeds more often than skeptics like you and I would anticipate. Myself, I could never bring it off.

I get occasional house calls, however, by answering advertisements and through the recommendations of friends. Dealers who handle only paintings or rugs or jewelry, or other specialties, sometimes will share a house call on the promise that our interests will not conflict. And, of course, there is always the possibility that the person from whom one is buying antiques will know someone else who might have things to sell.

House calls almost never follow the straightforward path typical of most selling/buying situations. Prices are seldom firm and frequently depend upon an opening offer suggested by the buyer. Changes of mind, withdrawals of merchandise, even postsale recisions are frequent. I once bought a charming Victorian doll's house from a retail antiques shop. The following day the owner telephoned to say that he regretted having to ask that I return the doll's house. Since I was perfectly pleased with it, I asked why. For a moment I thought that the seller had received a better offer or had decided that he had not priced it high enough, although I felt that I had paid a fair, in fact a fairly healthy, retail price for it. "Look," the dealer said, "I'm in a bind. I bought the doll's house and a lot of other things on a house call, and now the people are demanding most of the stuff back, because the man I dealt with wasn't the sole owner and had no right to sell anything, and they're very unhappy—especially about the doll's house, because it's a family favorite. Maybe they wouldn't have a leg to stand on from a legal point of view, but this is more an emotional thing and they're terribly upset, and, frankly, at this point, I just want to get them off my back." I asked the dealer if he didn't think there was a certain breach of faith on his part, since we had made an agreement that I was perfectly willing to stand by. "Listen," he apologized, "I fell like a real ass, but if you'll help me out, I promise you special consideration on anything you want from my shop." I asked if such things happened very often. "All the time," he said, "but always before anything got sold. This is the first time I had to call a customer and ask to have something returned. Usually the people change their minds right away and the phone'll be ringing even before I get the stuff off the truck. Believe me, I don't like to lose sales any more than the next guy, but there isn't enough profit in the whole deal to make it worth listening to more of their complaints. Last month I went on a call from a couple who were going to sell their home and move to Florida. All over the house they had beautiful art-glass shades over the bulbs in the ceiling lights. We agreed on a price for the shades, and I got a ladder and spent three hours getting them down, because when the ceilings were painted, the painters had just gone over the shade holders and everything, so most of the shades were stuck tight. It took me another three hours that night to clean all the paint off the shades, but when I got through, I figured I could probably make $50, maybe $100 on the deal, which wouldn't be too bad. So the next morning the wife called and said that she wanted all the shades back, because she hadn't realized how awful the place would look without any shades on the light bulbs, and how would they sell the house and their other things when the lighting was so ugly? 'Just give me back the shades until we sell the house and then you can have them,' she offered. So I said, 'Okay, if it's going to make such a difference to you,' and I took the shades back and had her give me a receipt for them. Two days later in the mail I get a check refunding what I'd paid for the shades. I called her and said that I was not going to accept the check and that I expected her to return the shades as we had agreed. 'Oh,' she said, 'I'm sorry, but we've run into a little change of plan and we're not going to sell the house after all, so I'm afraid you'd have rather a long wait before we could give back the shades.' What could I do? Everyone knows you aren't going to court over some dumb deal that would bring you maybe $100 at the outside. And if you did it on a matter of principle, you'd wind up looking like the heavy, because you're the shrewd antiques dealer out to fleece these poor defenseless civilians. No one ever considers the house calls that are wasted because the people only want a free appraisal of their things. Or the time and travel I spend following up on fruitless leads. Believe me, I would rather buy from a professional dealer any day in the week!" I suggested that there might be one major exception. He agreed. "Sure," he said, "because when you do make a good buy on a house call, it can be truly spectacular!"

The first house call Betty and I answered had Gothic overtones that might have persuaded us to forswear such future adventures, except that we are much too committed to antiquing to be discouraged by a little thing like sheer terror. The house itself would have been better suited to location in some Transylvanian forest than to its lonely outlook above the gray waters of Long Island Sound. It was a huge multisteepled structure, with crazy balconies and widow's walks decorating the upper stories, and crumbling verandas and porches with tattered, out-of-season screens sloping away from the lower ones. There was a poorly penciled note stuck in a crack by the door. "Knock and enter. Bell not working." The floorboards obligingly creaked as we went in. Betty and I looked at each other. "I thought you said these people were named Rawlings?" I whispered. Betty nodded. "It has to be Karloff," I said. "Come on—we're at the wrong house." At that instant, from somewhere far up in the dim reaches of that house, came the most bloodcurdling wail that I have heard in a lifetime of Saturday-matinee horror films. "You're right," Betty said, "this definitely is the wrong place!" Before we could retreat, a small but undeniably stalwart creature emerged from behind the dusty portieres that curtained away the rest of the house. She looked as old and as indomitable as

Maria Ouspenskaya in *Son of the Wolf Man*, and she wore a lumberjack's black-and-red-plaid mackinaw and an apron that time and grime had turned a peculiar putty color. Her hair was white and shingled into a modified Dutch bob, which she topped with a Lindberg-type leather helmet, the flaps pulled up and snapped together. I thought that she was much too quaint to be truly sinister and took brief encouragement from that observation. "You the people about the antiques?" she asked briskly. We started to say that we were, but our answer was overtaken by another piercing shriek from the upper regions. Since our hostess seemed to take no notice, we felt that common courtesy decreed that we pretend to do likewise. "Through here," the woman said, and turned and disappeared between the thick drapes. "I think we should leave right now," I said emphatically. Betty said, "We can't. Think how it would look!" I said, "Think how we would look hanging by our thumbs up in that attic!"—and was only half kidding. "She would be offended if we left without even looking at her things," Betty insisted. "That," I said, "would be a real pity! Probably she has a big oven in there where she turns unsuspecting customers into gingerbread."

Undaunted by another ungodly outcry from upstairs, Betty hurried after the old woman. There was no oven in the other room, but there was a potbellied stove, big as a blast furnace and furiously red from the blaze it contained. The room was tropical. Also the air was thick with smoldering incense. Patchouli. Exotic and overwhelming. "Out on that side porch," the woman directed. I was relieved that she didn't follow us but remained unbelieveably close to the blistering stove. We could hear frantic scuffling and thrashing-about on the floor above us. The struggle was climaxed by a strangled outcry. "Cats," Betty said encouragingly. I nodded, although both of us knew that whatever was up there was not cats.

Three sides of the porch were stacked with old-fashioned life jackets. Hundreds, perhaps thousands of them. The kind that were used on liners before the Mae West was developed. I told myself that the old gal must be a smuggler. A white-slaver. A dope pusher. I was working up quite a fantasy when Betty broke into it with a delighted "Look!"

I followed her gaze to a beautiful old chandelier dangling from a hook in the roof. "Nice," I muttered. "It's perfect for our entry," Betty said. I had to admit that it would be. At which point the old lady just happened to call out, "Find anything you like?" She might as well have asked if we liked the chandelier, because it and a broken kitchen table were all there was—except, of course, for the life jackets. "What would anyone do with a thousand old life jackets?" I asked. Betty shrugged. "Maybe they have problems at high tide," she said brightly. "Now—about that chandelier?"

"How much do you want for the fixture?" I asked. The old woman laughed. "Like that, huh?" she asked. I said that I thought we might be able to use it. The worst of all screams cut through our negotiations, and the woman turned abruptly and, hurrying us off as if we had suddenly donned leper's bells, rushed us out the door with a brusque, "I can't get it down now. You'll have to come back Sunday at two if you want it."

I don't think either of us spoke until we were well away and down the road. Then we both started laughing, and when we were able to talk, we began cooking up suitable scenarios to explain the incredible screams and the life jackets and the incense and the unbearable heat. "I thought she was kind of cute," Betty said. "I wonder how much she's going to charge us for that chandelier." I couldn't believe that having escaped, we actually were going to return voluntarily to that house, but I could tell from her smile that Betty was conjuring up pictures of that antique chandelier hanging in our entryway—and I realized that we would return.

On Sunday at two we knocked, pushed open the creaking door, and walked into the furiously overheated, incense-laden room. A gaunt and shaggy young man greeted us, and I, putting two and two together and getting seven, decided that my previous theories about drugs had been confirmed. "You here for that hall light?" he asked. I swallowed hard and managed a hasty "Yes," lest he think we had other, less innocent motives. He lumbered off into the inferno behind the closed portieres. "Notice anything different?" Betty asked. "No screaming," I admitted, not entirely certain the silence was not ominous. The old woman appeared. She wore the same mackinaw and the same aviator's helmet, but there was something different about her. She seemed to have put on a great deal of weight since our meeting. As she approached, however, I saw that her bulky woolen jacket was partially open and that something large and dark was cradled within it. Eyes stared up at me from beneath the hooding folds. The old woman gave a fierce and delirious cackle and dramatically pulled open her mackinaw to reveal the largest, ugliest monkey I ever saw. "He's a howler!" the woman said, howling delightedly, and Betty said, "Oh, he's adorable," from which I knew that we were going to buy that chandelier whatever the cost, since she was trying to flatter the old lady into a friendly frame of mind. "He isn't housebroken," the woman announced cheerfully, at which moment I became enamored of the fragrance of patchouli. "Was that . . . ?" Betty began. The old lady grinned. "Taking on something fierce when you were here. He doesn't take to staying alone upstairs, but if my son isn't here to take after him, I don't trust him down here when I have callers."

The young man returned with the chandelier. "I hope you're buying this," he said, "now that I finally took it down." We paid a price that was a shade higher than we had hoped, but still less than we would have had to pay for a similar fixture at an antiques shop—if, for that matter, we could have found a similar fixture. "Do you have anything else that you want to sell?" Betty asked brightly as the young man and I took the fixture to the car. The woman shook her head. "Only those old life jackets," she said, "but I guess you wouldn't have too much use for them." Quickly I agreed that we wouldn't, and we left, greatly relieved that our sinister visions had resolved into such simple reality.

Another house call that we made early in our antiquing experience was equally weird, although on an entirely different level. A newspaper ad generated this one. "Disposing of my entire collection of fine art glass," the ad said, so we telephoned and made an appointment and received surprisingly precise directions for finding the place. "I think this is a pro," I told Betty, "running a shop from her apartment." Betty said that we would find out soon enough, and soon enough we did. The woman who received us was charming. Her home was beautifully furnished. The entrance foyer and one entire wall of the living room were lined with mirror-backed cabinets that held hundreds of pieces of glass. And every item was brand new! "This is a piece of Nicholas Lutz," we were told as the lady offered us a little Venetian vase. "It is priceless," she added with a sigh. "This is peachblow. This is old English hobnail. This is your satin glass. This is Burmese. All the pieces in this case are definitely Sandwich." I nodded, too appalled to speak. "What do you think of this?" she went on, singling out a reproduction of an amberina pitcher. "Or this?" she asked, forcing a crudely transfer-printed biscuit jar into my hands. "It is Mount Washington," she added almost reverently. "Very nice," I said, handing it back to her and wondering how long we would have to continue the charade before we could leave without hurting the woman's feelings. "I love beautiful glass," the woman went on, explaining that she had been collecting for just years and years. I was tempted to ask where her collection was, because I hadn't seen anything old enough to have been collected all that long ago, but Betty and I had from the first agreed that we never would willfully insult anyone, and even if we hadn't had that understanding, there was something touching about the woman's deep commitment to her worthless collection. "Now, tell me," the woman said, "are you dealers?" We said that we were. "On a rather limited basis," Betty pointed out. "Of course." The woman beamed. "I understand. Well, pick out whatever you like, because I am going to give you really wonderful prices. I love working with new dealers." Betty cleared her throat and took the plunge. "We really were looking for some of the older types of glass," she said pleasantly. "Older?" the woman cried, greatly offended. "What makes you suggest my glass isn't old?" Betty smiled and explained that she had meant that we were more interested in seventeenth-century and eighteenth-century pieces—which was not true, but then it was not exactly an occasion for honesty. "Why didn't you tell me?" the woman asked, delighted. She led us into what would have been her dining room if it had not been converted into a glass museum. "Not many people appreciate this fascinating early glass," she said, removing a couple of cheap Mexican goblets from a locked cabinet. "Aren't these exquisite?" she demanded. "And to think that they survive in such perfect condition! They are your genuine Stiegel glass, made in Manheim, Pennsylvania, in 1770." She turned them slowly to better appreciate the passage of light through the deeply molded swirl pattern. "Yes," I said. "Well, that's very interesting, and we thank you for showing us your things." She seemed bewildered. "Then there's nothing you want?" she asked uncomprehendingly. "I'm sorry," Betty said sincerely, "I'm afraid we're not quite ready for glass of this type." The woman smiled. "I understand completely," she said. "And now that you know where I am, feel free to come back at any time, even if you only want to look at these beautiful examples of the glassmaker's art." We said that we would, and went, in silence, to our car. "That poor woman," Betty said sadly. "I know what you mean," I said. "She really believes . . . When we went in, I figured she was just another con artist trying to palm off her new stuff on unsuspecting customers. I wonder where she acquired all that junk." "From a true con artist," Betty said, "who stuck her with a lot of misinformation and a bunch of good names and a fortune in worthless glass."

At a flea market we were approached by a cheerfully extroverted woman who said that she had "a few things to sell," and asked if we would like to stop by her house and see them. We said that we would, indeed, and were surprised to be handed a mimeographed flyer complete with a little map giving directions to her house from all principal parkways. "Obviously," Betty said, "just a spur-of-the-moment thing! Probably she'll have searchlights on the lawn, like at the opening of a Hollywood supermarket." There weren't any searchlights, but there were carefully executed price tickets on everything, including a lot of novelty giftwares that obviously had been assembled for the occasion.

The problem with such calls is that they take time. Time in traveling to and from the house and time to get clear. You can walk in and out of an antiques shop in five minutes, and probably the owner will be glad to be rid of you if you have found nothing of interest, but it is difficult to be in someone's home and try to be equally impersonal. Plus which, not everything is always out on display, which means that your good luck, or no luck at all, is not apparent until you have repeatedly asked, "Anything else?" Since the last item that the seller thinks of will sometimes turn out to be your buy of the day, it is a good idea to train yourself to suffer through those "What else have you?" questions with patience and grace. I remember one call that seemed particularly unrewarding because the house itself was so promising. We had spent the afternoon traipsing upstairs and down, exploring wings and servants' quarters and barns and bathhouses—yes, millionaires have house sales, too!—and finding absolutely nothing, until Betty finally asked, "Would you have any lamps?" And the recently widowed lady of the house rather vaguely said, "Oh, there are one or two old lamps down in the laundry." Visions of Tiffany instantly danced through my head, but, alas, the lamps were only a pair of jeweled peacocks with illuminated tails. Disappointing, perhaps, but still very nice. "I think we can use these," I said, relieved to have finally found something to buy and some way to squeeze a small profit out of what otherwise would have been a wasted afternoon.

If you go on a house call, expect to pay cash for whatever you buy. And plan to pay and take immediately. It is very discouraging to find something you want and then have to leave it because you do not have enough money to pay for it or cannot immediately remove it. Even if the seller doesn't change his mind about parting with his treasures, there always is a possibility that another buyer will come along and dazzle him with a better offer. It happens. Lots of luck if you go back prepared to pay or to cart away and are greeted with the news that your find is even then on its way to another, happier owner.

Howe, Edgar Watson (Editor, 1877–1911, Atchison, Kansas, "Daily Globe")

> *There is nothing so well known as that we should not expect something for nothing—but we all do and call it Hope.*

We all sure do, Mr. Howe—especially we antiquers. The great

thing about the antiques trade is that on rare occasions we find it! Too bad those occasional finds encourage so many of us to unreasonable hopes.

See Florentia

I

Icart, Louis

In the 1920s and 1930s, he was the most popular artist in Paris. And also one of the most prolific. Some of his etchings—"Blue Hydrangeas," for example—were published in enormous editions. Other editions were considerably more limited. Prints of Icart works were widely distributed and are being issued again. Not long ago a flea-market dealer offered us a folder of Icart prints at $2.50 each. "If you frame them," he suggested, "you can't tell them from the real thing. Especially if you cut a mat so it covers where it says 'Reproduction.' "

"Come to my shop," a retail dealer said, "I have plenty of Icarts that you can buy for $50, $75." When we went to the shop, the Icarts were not etchings but prints. "I was looking for original editions," I said. "That's what these are," I was told, "original-edition prints, published in the twenties."

" 'The Apple Girl and the Letter,' by Louis Icart. Two original prints circa 1930, mint, 18″ x 22″. Beautiful color, both for $20.00" (advertisement in the *Antique Trader Weekly*).

Not long ago we sold Icart etchings for $20. And sometimes for $30. And once I charged the daring sum of $47.50 for the one showing a tall blond girl with a magnificent black stallion. I think the current asking price for that one is $300 or $400. But not all Icart pictures bring such prices. The nudes are the most avidly sought. And etchings that had severely limited editions. What do not—or should not—command more than nominal prices are the ubiquitous prints, for which some dealers demand the price of an etching. If you can't tell the difference at a glance, whip out your magnifying glass. The prints will show the fine pattern of the printer's screen. Colored areas on the etchings are hand-tinted and will not show the familiar dots of process-printed colors. The Icart signature is crisp and definite on the etchings; on the reproductions it often looks gray and lifeless. There are other clues—pressmarks, for example, on the margins of the etchings, the famous "Windmill" seal, the character of the copyright inscription—but as the young man who offered us prints for $2.50 each pointed out, a carefully cut mat can hide a lot of otherwise valuable indications of reproduction or authenticity.

Ignorance

The dealer who suggests that he does not really know too much about this antique or that probably knows quite a lot about human nature and well understands the art of salesmanship. He may also realize that should something he sold prove to be somewhat less precious than his customer had hoped, he cannot be accused of misrepresentation, having previously established his personal incompetence. This is one instance in which ignorance can, indeed, be bliss, and quite profitable. For the seller, that is.

Indian Jewelry of the Southwestern United States

The peripatetic auctions of "Genuine Southwest Indian Jewelry" are a new phenomenon of the collecting scene. For years the traveling auction was the special province of Oriental rugs. Then "Fine Art and Signed Graphics" came along to fill the waiting walls of all those fully carpeted homes. The market for Indian jewelry will not be so easily exhausted. Even the most restless suburbanite eventually runs out of floors to cover and walls to fill, but opportunities for personal adornment are virtually unlimited—a ring for Sis, a necklace for Mom, a belt for Dad, a bracelet for Sonny ("Of course it's manly—didn't those Indian braves wear bracelets as bowstring guards?"), and then the buying can resume with another ring for Sis, and a belt for Mom, and a necklace for Dad (because Charlie, down the block, wore one to the club last Saturday), and on and on and on until the conspicuously consumptive family looks as if it is headed for a Hopi festival, even if it is only bound for the supermarket. Such extravagant acquisition is justified on the dual grounds of chic ethnic identification and sound financial investment. Unfortunately, it often fails on both counts.

Buying anything because it is the current rage often leads to the acquisition of inferior or imitation pieces, which certainly do not represent sensible investments. Many of the pieces offered at exceptional "bargain" prices—and an embarrassing number of those offered at high prices—are neither handcrafted nor Indian-made. They sometimes are set with inferior stones, or with small fragments or thin slices of stone, or with imitation stones. Some less expensive varieties of genuine turquoise are extremely porous and easily absorb dirt and grease, and will turn from a lovely sky blue to an undesirable shade of green. Exposure to extreme heat and sunlight also can alter the turquoise color. All of which makes it extremely difficult for the inexperienced dealer or collector to realize genuine bargains in Indian jewelry. Moreover, the dealer who acquires a small stock of Indian jewelry at auction often finds it impossible to sell in successful competition with other auctions and special retail promotions.

Those interested in Indian jewelry because of its ethnic associations would do much better to explore traditional Indian crafts such as pottery, baskets, and rugs. Even if new, these usually are executed in age-old shapes and designs. Much of the jewelry now on the market is a hodgepodge of Mexican and Spanish and American Indian motifs, little influenced by tribal traditions but owing plenty to the restrictions imposed by large-scale production. The only pieces worth far more than the intrinsic value of their silver and stones are examples that combine superb design and execution in choice materials. Those will have enduring appeal and value long after the current craze has been forgotten.

See Turquoise

Inexpensive

There usually is an excellent reason why an apparently good antique is underpriced. If you think about it long enough, or look hard enough, the reason probably will become quite clear. Too bad if this happens after you have made what seemed to be a remarkable buy.

Inspection

I wish I could list all the antiques I have bought that I later discovered to be damaged, incomplete, or otherwise imperfect. But the record would be too lengthy and too discouraging. (And I am careful about examining things, too.)

See Inexpensive

Ivory Miniatures

No matter how dirty it looks, don't try to clean a painting on ivory by washing it. If you do, you are almost certain to wind up with a naked wafer of ivory *sans* miniature.

You can safely wash a painting on porcelain. Even if the paint has not been fired, it probably won't dissolve, as would most paintings done on ivory.

About as bold as you can afford to get with an ivory miniature is to give it a tender dusting with a sable-soft brush. And be careful how you hold the fingernail-thin ivory, because some of the old ones will crack at a breath. If you are feeling brave enough to unframe a painting on ivory, you can help improve its appearance by washing both sides of the covering glass. Be sure it is perfectly dry, though, before you replace the picture.

And don't for a moment think that all those miniatures of French court ladies hail from the eighteenth century. Most of them are Victorian, and many of them are much, much more recent. A lot of elegant dresser sets—hand mirrors, hairbrushes, trinket boxes, powder jars, and other such items—were produced in enamel-decorated bronze that was set with impressive miniatures of noble ladies painted on ivory or bone. They only *look* as if they belonged at the Winter Palace or the Petit Trianon. That most of them are marked "Made in Germany," or "Austria," or "France," helps establish their twentieth-century origins. These pieces are decorative, and sometimes command high prices, but not because of their antique value.

Some dealers make a great fuss about the signatures on ivory miniatures, and some customers are unnecessarily impressed by them. Unless a miniature happens to be signed by a known artist of some reputation, the chances are excellent that the carefully inscribed "Henri"s and "Toni"s and "Pierre"s are the work of otherwise anonymous factory decorators whose principal claim to fame is an ability to copy famous portraits in an expeditious and often quite attractive manner.

A lot of so-called "miniatures on ivory" actually are not painted on ivory at all but are printed on plastic and dressed up with some hand-applied touches. The best way to identify these imitations, of course, is to unframe the miniature so that you can see the material firsthand. Since this is not always possible, you can draw some conclusions from the following:

The surface of a true painting on ivory usually looks rather dry.

The colors are clear and true and have a bright, lively quality.

The painting is distinct and has uniformly precise detailing.

Like wood, ivory shrinks with the grain. With time, many miniatures become slightly warped as a result. Curling edges, a slightly concave center, or an improper fit within the frame are typical of older ivory miniatures.

The printed- and painted-on-plastic imitations usually look softly blurred. They frequently have a hazy, bluish cast instead of the characteristic clarity mentioned earlier. Whether bright or somber, the colors seem to be printed on the reverse of the wafer rather than painted on its surface. This gives the picture a somewhat "veiled" look—misty instead of crisp. Details such as eyebrows, lips, an occasional flower or necklace are glaringly prominent in contrast to the rest of the "painting."

A lot of these processed "miniatures" are presented in fancy frames for the decorator's market. They certainly don't belong in the antiques trade.

J

Jefferson Lamps

Better by far than the generally more widely known and much more available Bradley and Hubbard lamps. Better design. Better execution. And—to those who know their business—better value. Look for the Jefferson signature in the metal collar around the top of the shades. You might not find it anywhere else.

Junk Shops

It is easy to overpay for the occasional antiques found while browsing in junk shops. The setting makes them seem more precious and exciting than they would appear if they were cleaned up and displayed amid many equally fine or better things. And no matter how high the price might be, if you have to blow away cobwebs, or unseat a couple of cats, or gingerly step around a dish of dog food left in the center of what passes for an aisle, it will *seem* like a bargain, largely because you expect the owner of such a shop not to know as much as you do. Should you manage to get a peek behind the open boxes of soda crackers, the mugs of neglected coffee, the tools, glue pots, torn envelopes, and other papers that litter the proprietor's desk, you probably would be surprised to see the most recent antiques price guides conveniently tucked away for ready reference.

Many years ago I paid $12 for a pair of export-ware platters that I found in a junk shop, so I keep blowing away cobwebs and hurdling sleeping pets and their unfinished meals, and hoping, always hoping. Hope doth spring eternal—don't for a minute think that the owners of junk shops don't know that!

See Howe, Edgar Watson

L

Lalique, René

Jeweler and designer of glass. Art Nouveau motifs dominate much of Lalique's earlier jewelry. Most of Lalique's glass is designed in the Art Deco manner, and consistent with the post-World War I trend toward mechanically produced works, is molded or pressed rather than free-blown, as were most Art Nouveau glass creations.

Vagabond venders at the edge of the Paris flea market used to hold up any piece of frosted, vaguely opalescent or dirty glass: "*C'est Lalique, m'sieu!*" they would insist, offering a milk bottle, a salt shaker, a thick tumbler clipped that morning from the bar across the street. Browsers would stop and buy, but I doubt that they believed they were buying Lalique.

Should you find a piece of glass that you think might be Lalique, hold the glass to the light if you cannot see the signature. The impressed "R. Lalique" that most collectors seek is sometimes quite superficial, but light passing through the glass will usually illuminate it. Particularly on powder jars, perfume bottles, and other commercial pieces, search for obscurely placed signatures. This can be fun—like looking for the hidden "Nina"s in Hirschfeld's drawings. Decorative pieces, on the other hand, often are quite prominently marked. Sometimes in several styles in several places. I once had a yellow Lalique vase that had been made into a table lamp. It carried the following signatures: "R. Lalique" impressed in block letters on the bottom; "R. Lalique" acid-signed in script across the bottom; "R. Lalique/France" engraved in script near the base; "Lalique" in diamond point at the neck. Two other valid Lalique marks are "R. Lalique" incised in block letters, or acid-stamped in "moderne" capitals. New Lalique pieces are simply marked "Lalique" in diamond-point script; needless to say, those are not the Lalique pieces collectors are looking for. Why would they have to look for items that are generally available in department stores, gift shops, and the like?

Many advanced collectors of Lalique glass have been going mad for colored pieces. Black, brown, charcoal, amber, green, blue, and —oh, boy!—red. When they speak of colored Lalique, however, they are not talking about the colored pigments that were applied to some colorless pieces in order to accent the designs. They mean real colored glass. Incidentally, those dried colored pigments can be washed away. So for goodness' sake, and for the sake of preserving whatever is left of them, don't wash them any more than you absolutely have to, and never scrub them with brushes or abrasive cleansers.

Lalique glass often has a rather soft, waxy appearance that is quite different from the hard brilliance of the lead crystals such as those produced by Steuben. Even the colorless metal often shows a slightly smoky or faintly yellow tint. In addition to the familiar frosting used to accent many designs, and the dried colored pigments and effectively controlled opalescence found in some pieces, Lalique glass is also sometimes decorated with touches of enamel. The black enamel gives an especially dramatic contrast to Lalique's clear and frosted crystals.

Lamerie, Paul

The greatest of the great eighteenth-century British silversmiths. Even experts, who seldom seem able to agree, can apparently get together without too many reservations and quibbles on this point. His French name comes from his Huguenot family, and while it has become increasingly common to refer to him as Paul de Lamerie, it seems unlikely that Lamerie himself employed the aristocratic preposition. On the other hand, he did register maker's marks showing his initials crowned above and having a fleur-de-lis below, so perhaps he was not beyond adopting the "de." With or without it, his name is so important that it adds enormous value to any piece of silver—and not only in England but in just about any market in the world. Because of this, Paul Lamerie's marks are sometimes forged or lifted from one piece to enhance a more significant one. We must be not only suspicious but incredulous if offered a bargain in silver by Paul Lamerie. If it isn't an outright forgery, it might easily be a piece marked by one of several other silversmiths whose punches closely resemble those registered by Paul Lamerie.

Some genuine Paul Lamerie pieces are decorated with engravings by William Hogarth, no less. How's that for class! Kind of like having a piece of Tiffany glass mounted in a setting by Fabergé.

Lamps, Electric

You don't have to be an antiques expert to know that any porcelain, pottery, wood, glass, or metal article that obviously was designed for use as the base of an electric lamp dates not from the seventeenth century, or from the eighteenth, or from any but the final years of the nineteenth—and probably was created sometime in the twentieth.

This is not to say that plenty of fine antiques have not been converted into lamp bases. When electricity first came into general use for indoor illumination, there weren't any precedents to suggest what an electrically lighted lamp should look like. Gas lamps were the most obvious candidates for conversion, with oil lamps and fixtures not far behind. Eventually just about anything of suitable size and strength got tapped for service—statues, Oriental porcelains, a fortune in fine Victorian art glass, ancient pottery, contemporary ceramics. If you could run a pipe through it or snake a wire around it and mount a couple of electrical sockets above, beside, upon, beneath, or even within it, you had yourself a lamp. At the same time, designers were creating forms especially for lamp bases. Regardless of style or material, these invariably had an opening at the base that was at least large enough to accept an electric cord, and an opening at the top that was small enough to contain a socket mounting. All those antique items that were turned into lamp bases had to be opened up or closed in to provide these features. So if you notice an original cord escapement or a top that would not need a metal vase cap to cover it, you can be reasonably confident that you are looking at a twentieth-century creation.

See Capo di Monte

Lillie, Beatrice

Years ago the great Beatrice Lillie starred in a musical review in which she appeared in one number with the ladies of the ensemble, who, like the star, were dressed as geishas. The chorus girls were uniformly beautiful. Beatrice Lillie was certainly no slouch, but she was, well, Beatrice Lillie. There was nothing in her costume or conduct to draw attention to the star, and yet within seconds every eye in the audience was riveted upon her. The ladies of the chorus with the blandly beautiful faces were quickly forgotten as the audience fell under the spell of a suddenly widening, wickedly impish grin.

I think of Beatrice Lillie when I see a little googly-eyed doll grinning out at me from some collector's cabinet. All the regal beauties stand around doing nothing but looking pretty, which can quickly become quite uninteresting. But that googly-eyed imp seems to know a special secret, and I, curious to share it, am captivated. I think the enduring appeal of these whimsical and cunning-looking dolls is that they evoke a response more complex than "Oh, how lovely!" To acquire an A.M. googly-eyed doll I would gladly pay double or triple the price of an A.M. beauty, for the same reason that a whole stageful of gorgeous showgirls would not have kept me from demanding my money back if Beatrice Lillie had not appeared with them.

See Marseille, Armand

Limited-Edition Collectibles

Some of those "limited" editions are not as strictly limited as they should be. In some cases infinity would appear to be the only limit set by the manufacturer—which means that the sky will probably never be the limit as far as values go. The more emphasis a distributor places upon display cases, souvenir folders, and the like, the less quality usually offered by the product itself. If you are buying some of the limited-edition collectibles because you happen to like them, great. You probably could acquire finer items for less money if you forgot all about this year's Easter and next year's Mother's Day and last year's Christmas plates and concentrated on real antiques. But where's the harm if limited-edition plates happen to be your bag?

The harm is in expecting all of those plates—especially the more recent issues—to enjoy enormous price rises. Many of them, in fact *most* of them, will not. One fairly consistent exception: the first issue in a new series. Otherwise the collector interested in financial appreciation is inviting disappointment if he invests in many of these well-publicized collectibles.

Those who insist on buying limited-edition collectibles for investment should at least find out to what number the edition will be limited. If that information is not readily available, it is reasonable to expect that the collectible in question will be. "Limited" also sometimes rather misleadingly refers to a limited time of production rather than to a controlled number of examples. In such cases there usually is quite enough of whatever it is to satisfy the market quite nicely.

See Supply and Demand

Loetz Glass

Turn-of-the-century art glass produced by Johannes Loetz Witwe at Klostermühle, Austria.

It might surprise some to find that Herr Loetz's first name was not Unsigned, since a great deal of iridescent glass, including a lot of good-looking Czechoslovakian pieces and some quite recent German and English articles, has been marketed as "unsigned Loetz."

I evidently am not alone in my weariness with "unsigned Loetz," since the current trend appears to be to have all such Loetz-type pieces signed. One should suspect all such signatures. Especially those that are particularly large and well placed for prominence. At this point I am so dizzy from looking at faked Loetz signatures that the only markings I would unreservedly trust are those that were cameo-carved into an example of Loetz's cameo glass, which, incidentally, is one of the rarer types of Loetz glass. Not long ago I came across a pair of vases marked "Lutz [sic]/Austria"—which is, I think, going a bit too far. The Lutz whose glass is sought by collectors came from France, worked in America, and as far as I know, never signed his work; if he had, he would certainly not have marked it "Lutz/Austria." Faking signatures is bad enough, but faking fake signatures is ridiculous. Even more ridiculous is paying a premium price for a worthless piece of glass carrying a worthless signature. Maybe if we would all stop doing that, we could get back to buying real antiques, with or without real signatures.

Look, Look—Oh, Look!

If you see it everywhere, how can it be old, or rare?

Visiting importers, wholesalers, gift and curio shops can be an important part of antiquing. Once I found a really attractive brass music stand in an antiques shop. I don't remember why I didn't purchase it, but I didn't—which is strange, because at $30 it seemed like a very good buy. A week or two later I saw the same stand displayed in a friend's store. "You can have it for $20," I was told, which also seemed strange, because I assumed my friend had acquired the stand that I had been offered at $30. I asked my friend if he was selling the stand at a loss. "Not at all," he said, ushering me into his storeroom, where I saw four identical stands. "I only pay $20 for them. If I could take larger quantities, I could get them for $14." I have since seen the same stand tagged $60 at an antiques show, and sold for $45 at an auction. I've also found the importer who jobs them at $14.

Shopping around is one of the best ways to avoid getting stuck with a reproduction or a "looks-like." If you see identical or similar items displayed in several antiques shops, you ought to consider just how authentic they could be. Of course it might only be coincidence. Or it might be that some new reproductions have recently come onto the market.

Louis XIV of France

His revocation of the Edict of Nantes, which had guaranteed religious freedom to the Huguenots, scattered refugee craftsmen and artisans all over the world. As a result of the families' flights from persecution, Paul Lamerie became England's greatest silversmith and Carl Fabergé became Russia's most celebrated jeweler. I am sure that if Louis XIV could have foreseen even these two distinguished eventualities, he would have thought twice before revoking the Edict of Nantes.

M

Maker's Marks on American Silver

At once simpler and more difficult to trace than the marks on British silver. Silversmiths in Colonial America followed the British style of marking their works with their initials. About the time of the American Revolution, the custom of marking silver with the maker's full last name, usually in solid capital letters, was almost universal. It is possible to trace names and initials with the help of a good complete table of American silversmiths' marks, but it is so easy to confuse silversmiths—even with the aid of the full last name—that most of us are almost better off judging the age of a piece of American silver by its style. Early-nineteenth-century American silver is a little easier to attribute, because in addition to their last names, some makers added to their marks the names of the towns in which they worked.

In 1847 (not for nothing do the Rogers Brothers use that date on their wares) silver-plated articles were first successfully manufactured. Shortly after this date American silversmiths began marking their solid silver articles "Sterling," in order to distinguish them from the silver-plated pieces then coming onto the market. American silver marked "Sterling," therefore should not be considered to be earlier than the second half of the nineteenth century, no matter what interesting names or initials it carries.

See EPNS

Marble Polish

Goddard of London makes the kind I like best. But I seldom use it for polishing marble. For one thing, I don't have that much marble lying around waiting to be polished. For another, one good polishing a year with Goddard's wax usually keeps it shining quite nicely with a little help from an occasional dusting. But this polish is absolutely unbeatable for giving a deep, gleaming finish and a nicely protective surface to cloisonné and other enamels. Sparingly applied and lightly buffed, it is excellent on bronzes. On "bronzed" lamp bases. On metal drawer pulls, finials, picture frames. You can use it—or simply the cloth with which you just applied it to some other article (always dispose of waxy cloths in a proper way immediately after use and avoid combustible surprises)—to gleam up the decorated portions of a vernis Martin cabinet or one of those intricately carved teakwood stands. And if you would like your green- or brown-patinated Tiffany desk pieces to look the way they probably did when they left the Tiffany Studios, a bit of marble polish can do the trick.

Occasionally someone tries to refurbish a piece of white metal by painting it with what I probably will go to my grave calling "dime-store gold." Instead of giving a rich effect, this usually makes the item look about as fine as the paper crown worn by Old King Cole in a kindergarten pantomime. If you happen upon such an article, you can redeem it to some extent with a light application of marble polish and a little enthusiastic buffing. You won't think that you've suddenly found an unsigned work by Fabergé, but you will have given the finish a few highlights to take a bit of the curse off that awful guggy gold.

Marseille, Armand

Porcelain manufacturer who, with his son, also Armand Marseille, produced bisque heads for dolls from the 1890s through the 1930s. The name seems so thoroughly French that I have to keep reminding myself that Armand Marseille dolls were made in Germany. I have the same problem in reverse about Casimir Bru, which sounds German to me, although I know that the Bru is currently the most desired of French dolls. Things being as they are, I don't have too many occasions to worry about Bru dolls one way or another. Things being as they are, the Armand Marseille dolls keep showing up, which gives me no excuse for not keeping their nationality straight. Especially since most are plainly marked "Germany." Authorities suggest that Armand Marseille emigrated to Germany from Russia, and probably changed his name *en route*. Perhaps. But I would not be at all surprised if this were another of those encounters with a descendant of a refugee French family that took its talents and its trades elsewhere in the wake of the revocation of the Edict of Nantes. Possibly the Marseille family, like the Fabergé family, fled from France to Russia, from where, many generations later, Armand Marseille subsequently moved to Germany.

Armand Marseille dolls are probably the most readily available of the older bisque-head dolls, which is probably why a pretty A.M. is the first doll acquired by most new collectors. Availability has kept Armand Marseille "doll dolls"—as a friend of mine terms all pretty girl dolls—at the low end of the ever-expanding spectrum of doll prices. Armand Marseille character and baby dolls bring considerably better prices, and will continue to appreciate while their pretty-pretty sisters continue to bring up the rear. So anyone buying an Armand Marseille doll to start a collection or as an initial investment in dolls would do well to try to find one with something besides beauty in its favor. Buying one that is ugly, or non-

Caucasian, or googly-eyed, or buying a character baby, or any of the more unusual dolls would be much more interesting and a better investment while searching for the costly and quite elusive Bru.

Mary Gregory Decorated Glass

Yes, Virginia, there was a Mary Gregory. Evidently. In the second half of the nineteenth century, to be imprecise, she presumably worked as a decorator at the Sandwich glass factory. Her artfully enameled vignettes of properly Victorian children became so well known that her name became associated with all such decorated pieces, even if Ms. Gregory did not actually work on them and whether or not they originated at the factory where she was employed.

Poor Mary would have been a busy lady, indeed, to have decorated all the glass that bears her name. She also would have had to live a good century longer, since a lot of "Mary Gregory" glass continues to be made.

Although there was nothing at all innovative in decorating glass objects with enamels, I have a personal—and quite unprovable—theory that Mary Gregory decorations were intended to serve as inexpensive versions of two costly British products: the exquisite pâte-sur-pâte porcelains made at Minton's, and the finely carved cameo glass then emanating from Webb, Northwood, and others. England's queen gave her name to an age, making it synonymous with the taste of the time, which British arts and industries dominated. Much American enterprise was devoted to providing available domestic equivalents for Victorian homes on this side of the Atlantic.

White enamels are the most characteristic decoration for Mary Gregory glass, but some genuine pieces also include colors. Most reproduction pieces are rather thinly painted in a chalky dead white and are not sufficiently captivating to have earned any sort of immortality for their creators. On older pieces the figures tend to be smaller and better detailed than the rather hastily executed boys and girls on the newer examples.

As if to return the compliment implied in Mary Gregory's having taken inspiration from British works, much old and practically all recent Mary Gregory–type glass is of European origin.

Maven

An expert. Beware the antiques maven! I am a passionate admirer of expertise, but the wisest people whom I have met along the antiques trail are the first to admit that they do not know everything about everything. It would be nice to think that someone might, but, unfortunately, none of us does. Except, of course, the antiques maven. The maven is an expert on all things from all periods. From antique delft to Art Deco. From Mettlach to Mickey Mouse. From Hepplewhite to Heisey. You name it, the maven knows all about it—and if you can't give it a name, the maven will be glad to supply that too. Along the way, the maven spreads much misinformation, often based upon incomplete or inaccurate research, and sometimes based upon no research at all. Most unfortunate is the maven's eagerness to appraise unseen antiques on the basis of a brief verbal description. To me that is even more annoying than the maven's frequent bulletins concerning the latest in a continuous streak of incredible finds.

Medicine Lady

A reclining nude Oriental female carved from ivory, jade, quartz, wood, plastic . . . Used by Chinese women to show their doctors where it hurt. All those new ones make me sick.

Meissen Porcelains

As Staffordshire is to England, and as Limoges is to France, so Meissen is to Germany—the district where the porcelain works proliferated because the good clay was there. And even as terms such as "Staffordshire" and "Limoges" are used to designate ceramics produced at any of the factories in the subject area, so is "Meissen" quite correctly applied to the productions of several factories. Those decorative porcelains that are called "Dresden" should really be termed "Meissen," since Meissen is where most of them originated. Perhaps the English-speaking world first called Meissen wares "Dresden" because the porcelains were sent down the Elbe River to the inland port at Dresden, from where they were shipped abroad. Or possibly Dresden got into the Meissen act in an effort to bestow some instant prestige on the products of Europe's first important porcelain factories, since Dresden was widely regarded as an eighteenth-century center for the arts. However the misnomer originated, it is another example of the sort of nominal confusion that hangs on with a tenacity seldom equaled by factual information.

The famous blue crossed-swords mark associated with Meissen porcelains is neither the earliest nor the only Meissen mark, merely the best known. Similar markings have been and continue to be used by so many factories that the marks can tend to be more confusing than clarifying. Moreover, some makers repeated earlier marks or used minor variations of them, all of which have been borrowed by imitators throughout the last century. This makes it unwise for the inexperienced to place great confidence in the Meissen marks, and suggests that emphasis be placed instead on the character of the porcelains.

Beginning collectors should be especially suspicious of bargains in tablewares in the well-known blue-and-white Meissen onion pattern and the ubiquitous Meissen monkey-musician figures. These have been done to death in factories far removed from Germany's Meissen porcelain district.

Metal

Besides brass, copper, bronze, and all the other obvious things, "metal" is also what you call the glass in a glass article. This is considered a very erudite thing to do. So why not?

Mettlach

The company that became the well-known Villeroy and Boch firm of Mettlach, Germany, in 1842 can be said to have originated in 1767 at Septfontaines, Belgium, except that Belgium was not going to become Belgium until twenty-two years later. Throughout the long history of the Boch ceramics company—later Villeroy and Boch—an incredible variety of wares in a surprising number of styles was produced, but both the firm name and the location of its principal factory have become synonymous with the widely collected stoneware steins, which, bearing the castle mark of the Mettlach factory, are universally known as Mettlach steins.

Collectors who will go to the ends of the earth—and into receivership if need be—in order to obtain a choice Mettlach stein are not nearly as enthusiastic about the vases and other decorative and useful ceramics produced by Villeroy and Boch. One exception: the more important Mettlach plaques. Occasionally the liner, or underplate, from a Mettlach punch bowl or tureen is offered for sale as a plaque. Probably because these often carry the castle mark, they are sometimes sold at inflated prices. This is especially hard to understand, since the Mettlach plaques have vertical decoration, with a definite right way up and down, while the underplates are decorated in circular borders. And is it too obvious to point out that the plain centers on the underplates would pretty much contradict their designation as plaques?

In addition to the castle mark and the widely recognized Mercury marks, there are some Villeroy and Boch signatures that are less familiar. One is an applied clay rectangle within a scrolled frame. At first glance the number within the rectangle is its most obvious feature, but a close look will reveal the lightly incised "VB" at the center of the bottom border. A more elaborate mark, also applied, consists of a crowned shield supported by a pair of birds. Upon the shield the "VB" monogram is embossed. A staff extends beneath the monogram to a small "M" set just within the shield point. A flowing ribbon supports the birds and passes through twin disks centered underneath the shield. Pieces so marked can often be acquired for a fraction of the price that would be asked if they were identified as Mettlach.

Millefiori Glass

Correctly pronounced Me-lay-fee-oh-ree, *mille fiori* means "thousand flowers," and is the name of glasswares having decorations composed of crosscut sections of colorful glass canes, which constitute the nominal "thousand flowers." Perhaps the most familiar examples of millefiore glass are the nineteenth-century paperweights in which the cane sections are encased within a dome of clear glass. However, the process of making glass rods of various colors into bundles to be drawn into long thin canes of patterned glass was known to the ancients, who used slices of such cane much as they continue to be used today. While abstract designs are by far the most common, millefiori canes have been made that yield extremely intricate sections, sometimes containing tiny animals, grotesques, miniature portraits, or naturalistic floral motifs.

Since millefiori techniques have been used throughout the last 3,000 years, it is too bad that most of the examples on the market today were made only recently. Including just about all of those lamps, toothpick holders, vases, miniature shoes, and rose bowls. Unless your interest is exclusively in decorative effect, without reference to antique value, please be terribly suspicious of any articles of this widely popular glass. And bear in mind that new millefiori pieces are quite inexpensive if bought directly from an importer or wholesaler, which makes it pointless to pay significantly more when acquiring them from an antiques dealer or autioneer.

The colorful millefiori segments should have clarity and an appearance of depth. In some of the new pieces these cane sections look like chalky surface decorations. Unless you are certain that a piece of millefiori glass is old, resign yourself to its probable newness. An occasional happy surprise is always more agreeable than a series of disappointments.

Mint

Paradoxically, the most desired quality in old things is that they survive in a like-new condition that many dealers and collectors call "mint."

When you are tempted to buy a defective piece because it is priced significantly lower than it would be if it were in mint condition, it might help to bear in mind that "mint" is what we call a place where money is coined, and also refers to the accumulation of a great fortune. Most of the dealers and collectors who have made a mint at the antiques trade are uncompromising about acquiring only articles in mint condition.

Mother-of-Pearl Satin Glass

Characterized by a silky surface of colored glass cased over a relief-molded inner layer, to achieve a pattern of apparently contrasting textures and varying depths, this extremely popular decorative glassware was produced in the 1880s in England and America. It should not be confused with ordinary satin-finished glass, since that term is correctly applied to any glass that has been treated with acid to effect a frosty-smooth surface. Mother-of-pearl satin glass is satin finished, but it isn't the satinized finish that makes it mother-of-pearl. It is the effect created by the relief-molded inner pattern, which might produce coin spots, raindrops, diamonds, zippers, spirals, scallops, or chevrons, gleaming through the satinized exterior. As if this rich effect was not sufficiently tempting to the embellishment-happy Victorian taste, some pieces were treated to elaborate decorations with enamels, applied glass ornaments, and coralene beading, and occasionally were called into service as the basis for cameo-carved pieces.

A few years ago the reproductions of Victorian satin glass had a devastating effect on the market for antique pieces. This was particularly hard to understand in view of the fact that it is not too difficult to distinguish between the old and new pieces. The old satin glasses are much lighter in weight than the reproductions, and have a satiny, lustrous sheen rather than the dead, frosted surface that is typical of the later pieces. The pattern designs that give the old glass an appearance of quilted silk are generally smaller and more finely detailed than those found on the copies. The white lining in old pieces is glisteningly white. In the new pieces it is dull, grayish, and chalky. And although the layers of glass in the antique pieces are blown much thinner than those in the reproductions—most of which are quite thick and clumsy-looking—the finished article has an illusion of depth that the new satin-glass-type articles do not possess.

Happily, many who first acquired new satin glass under the impression that they were buying old at bargain prices have learned which pieces belong in the gift shops and which are the true antiques, and are increasingly inclined to pay more for those examples in which they can place confidence. This has had a healthy restorative effect on the values of antique satin glass, which have just about recovered from their reproduction-inspired slump. Those who were smart enough to acquire and hold authentic pieces while the market was lagging somewhat behind other antiques categories can begin taking more than esthetic pleasure from their treasures. Those who would like to acquire some good antique satin glass had better begin buying any fine examples that they can find in excellent condition—pronto. The new respectability of Victorian furnishings should help support rising prices for choice Victorian satin glass.

Satin-glass pieces with coralene decoration bring premium prices. This has encouraged some distributors to gild the lily with recently applied beaded enhancements. Anyone willing to pay more for these added attractions should be sure that they are as old as the glass that wears them. Even genuine coralene decorations can be rubbed off, but beads that fall free at a touch certainly can't have been hanging around for 80 or 90 years just waiting for you to flick them away. Old coralene beading was quite finely done and busily detailed. However lacy the pattern might be, beaded units generally look slightly rounded and rather thick. Most of the new beading is skimpily applied, in wandering strands like tree branches or coral. Suspect coralene treatments that are not fussy and busy and generously applied.

Museum

An antiques shop is not a museum, and vice versa.

I wish that the proprietors of antiques shops and the directors of museums would remember this. If they did, fewer antiques dealers would keep items marked "not for sale" or "sold" tantalizingly on permanent display, and fewer museums would complain of needing additional exhibition space while continuing to convert every available vestibule into still another "boutique."

To make matters worse, many of the shops in the museums specialize in selling well-made reproductions of antiques. So, still more unhappily, do some antiques shops. At least the museum shops describe and price these merchandise offerings as reproductions. In that, at least, I wish the antiques dealers would copy them. I do approve of museum bookshops, especially as a convenient source of the museum's sometimes difficult-to-obtain publications.

N

Name (as in "What's in a . . . ?")

French gold boxes of the Eighteenth Century have been submitted to me stamped with the forged mark of Fabergé, and one could not but be amused by the fact that in order to enhance the value of Eighteenth Century productions it had been thought necessary to stamp them with the mark of a Nineteenth Century craftsman (Henry Charles Bainbridge, Peter Carl Fabergé)

Or a great name is worth a century or so any old time. So much for the presumed value that antiquers place upon age.

See Age

Negotiation

Let Henry Kissinger once try to persuade a passionate collector to part with a prized possession and he probably would gratefully return to the pressures of international diplomacy.

Almost the only way to pry loose a treasure from someone who does not want to sell it is to offer something more desirable in its place. Competition among collectors can be fierce, and for all the talk about friendly rivalries within a particular field, the bitter feuds that rage between certain collectors would make the Hatfields and McCoys look like Damon and Pythias. I know one collector who will not sell an item without first insisting that the buyer promise not to resell it to a particular competitor. I know another who will only sell one doll on condition that the buyer offer her first refusal on two. I know a young coin collector who agreed to sell a $2,000 music box for $400—but only if the $400 were paid in pre-1964 silver coins of date, denomination, and condition satisfactory for inclusion in his collection!

There is no hard-and-fast way to negotiate in the antiques trade. Just remember that if something cannot be had for money, it might be possible to acquire it, if not for love, then in exchange for that which is loved.

Nien hao

"Six-character mark under the base," the mail-order advertisement said, trying to nail down the appeal of an Oriental vase. I often talk back to ads, and my reaction to that one was, "Which six-character mark?" For centuries the Chinese have used these marks on porcelains. And the Japanese have used marks that look misleadingly similar. And to make matters worse, the Chinese had a cute way of signing later pieces with the marks of earlier reigns, in tribute to the fine work typical of that time.

There is nothing particularly complicated about the four-or six-character *nien hao*. With a good reference book and a few minutes' study, anyone can learn to read it. What it says is simply that the piece ostensibly was made during the reign of a particular emperor. If you commit a few more minutes to study, you can check out the dates of that emperor's reign, which will at least tell you when the mark indicates the article to have been made.

In the six-character signature the first character—it's in the upper right, remember, because the marks are written to be read top to bottom in vertical columns, starting at the right—is a *t* or *tau*, and is, in fact, pronounced "tä," meaning "great." The second character is the dynastic name, and on most of the pieces to be found on the market in the United States this probably will be Ching (Manchu). The third and fourth characters name the emperor. Those are the marks you will most often have to check out. With a little practice you will be able to recognize the marks of K'ang Hsi and Ch'ien Lung. The two final characters are constant, as are the first two, and mean simply "made then." So what you have is a neat little narrative that tells you the piece was made during the reign of the emperor whoever of the great whichever dynasty. And instead of worrying about each of six complex characters, your research is reduced to checking out only two.

What you get in the four-character mark is simply the emperor's name (first and second characters) and the old familiar "made then." Simple?

Sometimes you get no characters at all, only two concentric circles, such as you often find framing the *nien hao*. The traditional explanation is that the reign marks were eliminated out of respect for the emperor, for fear that if the piece were broken the damage would insult his dignity. Probably the truth about the empty circles, as well as many of the carefully written marks, is something less charming and more indicative of the thoroughness of the Oriental craftsman.

Years ago a famous actor discovered that he could economically expand his wardrobe by sending his old London-tailored clothes to be copied in Hong Kong. In fact, the Chinese reproductions were so painstakingly accurate that each of the four versions of a favorite sports jacket was received with a tiny cigarette burn scorching the lapel precisely like one on the original. Some of those empty circles and some of the seemingly genuine reign marks undoubtedly should be categorized with the meticulously accurate cigarette burns—as proof that no detail was neglected when the order of the day was: "Copy this!"

Don't confuse the carefully written six- or four-character *nien hao* with some of the mazelike seal marks found on some Oriental porcelains. Some of the seal marks are reign marks, but others are as confusing as the traditional *nien hao* are simple. Leave the seal inscriptions to the experts, and bear in mind that a lot of brand-new porcelains are showing up with similarly styled squiggles. They look like miniaturized solid-state circuits or a floor plan of the Labyrinth, and though there be those who disagree, some of them prove almost nothing.

Nippon Porcelain

Some antiques dealers who used to look down their noses at Nippon porcelain are now delighted to feature it. Until recently the only Japanese ceramics displayed on their distinguished premises were antique Imari and Satsuma. Now "blown out" (relief-molded) Nippon and tapestry-finish Nippon and other choice examples of this popular collectible porcelain are bringing significant prices—sometimes better prices than could be realized for the antique Imari and Satsuma. Is this new-found admiration for wares that were formerly scorned an additional indication that the geography of the world of antiques is constantly changing? If that is true, then those of us who wish to survive in that world must constantly adapt to it, mustn't we?

Norton, Charles Eliot

> *Our complex and exciting civilization has, indeed, developed, especially in America, a sensitiveness of nervous organization which often wears the semblance of the artistic temperament, and shows itself in manual*

> *dexterity and refined technical skill. And this tends to make mere workmanship, mere excellence of execution, the common test of merit in a work of the fine arts.* (The Forum, 1889)

It still does, Professor Norton. In the applied arts too. We've even taken to rejoicing in works that lack that distinction. The great exception: Tiffany.

See Tiffany, Louis Comfort

Nostalgia

My dictionary defines "nostalgia" as a longing to return to one's home, or a longing for something remote in time or place. I was taught to combat this feeling, which was variously known as "homesickness," "melancholia," or "the blues." One can appreciate the past without actively wishing to recapture it.

Now that nostalgia is no longer an emotion but a category for collecting, I often am stopped short at finding relics of the 1940s and 1950s creeping into the field. Since films and television programs seem committed to exploiting that era, which comes blessed with economies of setting, properties, and wardrobe—it being infinitely less expensive to simulate an "average" American living room of the period than to take a stab at the splendors of Versailles—audiences undoubtedly will continue to be sold nostalgia. And will increasingly collect and cherish things with the increasingly familiar look or sound of the forties and fifties. This means that a lot of Salvation Army furniture is going to move into the antiques shops, even as pieces from the twenties and thirties did at the start of the Art Deco boom, and that many scratched and warped "original recordings" are going to escalate in price. It isn't camp any more, or even good bad taste. It's nostalgia, and increasingly profitable.

Nouveau Riche

In current use, this description should be relieved of its insulting implications. It used to be said that the *nouveaux riches* had a passion for antiques because, having no family heirlooms, they were anxious to acquire some. Bully for them for that! Feeling as they did, they practically inaugurated the American antiques business. Where would any of us be without them? Because, let's face it, we didn't have any antiques trade until around 1900, which was just about the time that we managed to acquire some of our own *nouveaux riches*.

Most of today's *nouveaux riches* are the taste makers of our time, and are slavishly followed rather than ostentatiously following. Many of them are young and have made their fortunes in music, as opposed to the newly wealthy of previous generations who made theirs in mining, munitions, and manufacturing.

See Streisand, Barbra

O

"*Off with the Old, on with the New*"

Good advice generally, but think twice before having monograms, inscriptions, coats of arms, and other such identifying marks removed from antique silver in order to have some more personal embellishment applied, lest you eliminate something that adds great associative value or provenance to the piece. So what if it doesn't happen to be your family crest! Find out whose it was before you have it rubbed out. Most old silver that is worth having is worth leaving "as was." If you must give someone a personalized wedding gift, stick to such safe categories as stationery, household linens, or *new* silver. Or send that old piece along with a note explaining the mysterious initials or heraldic designs. This will add to the appeal of your gift, and you will have no pangs of conscience about reducing its potential value. I'm not sure what Ms. Emily Post would think of this, but any antiquer would applaud such good manners and common sense.

Ohr, George E.

Late-nineteenth-century American ceramicist. His distinctive art pottery is beginning to be appreciated by sophisticated collectors, but it still is not widely recognized by many dealers, who sometimes let it slip through their fingers for a fraction of its worth. Most Ohr pottery pieces are small in scale, rather thinly potted, surprisingly lightweight, and finely finished. The unusual shapes, often pinched and twisted into piecrust edges and oddly convoluted forms, and the distinctive glazes, suggestive of minerals, metals, and ores (no pun intended) are clues to recognition. Some pieces are simply marked "Biloxi," for Biloxi, Mississippi, where Ohr worked. Others are signed with the artist's name or initials. Either way, there are still finds to be made in George Ohr pottery. The piece that is picked up for a few dollars at a flea market can be worth a hundred or so to a knowledgeable dealer. And values are probably going to continue to rise.

Old

A three-letter word that simply means "not new."

But it is more magical than "abracadabra" for raising the prices of antiques. Of course age is one of the qualities that interests buyers of antiques. Still, I find it difficult to accept the eager response that an auctioneer or dealer can stimulate by simply declaring, "This is *old*!" I always want to ask, "How old? Two weeks? Or two years? Two decades? Or two centuries?"

I think that the thing that most upsets me is to be told that an article from the 1920s or 1930s is old. I remember growing up with so many of those things that they seem not at all old to me. I have to stop and remind myself that some of them do go back half a century. Have I become old along with them? Probably. Which may explain my objection to having such things termed "antique," unless we employ the word in a broad sense meaning simply "not recent"—or just plain "old."

Paint Remover

If someone thoughtless marks a price with one of those felt-tip pens, and ordinary methods won't remove it, try applying a tiny bit of paint remover and see if it doesn't come clean.

Paraffin

When the eyes of your old dolls are stuck, or open and close with difficulty, try touching the waxed (colored) lids lightly with paraffin, and see if it doesn't make movement a good deal easier.

Parke-Bernet

If you are truly in the know, then you are aware that the final syllable in the name of this famous auction house is correctly pronounced "net" and not "nay." Those who enjoy garnishing their antiques anecdotes with references to Parke-Bernet invariably betray themselves by mispronouncing the name. I am especially turned off by those who tell me, "I had this piece appraised by Parke-BerNAY"—a declaration usually intended to nail down some outrageous price. This was especially popular just after Parke-Bernet staged a well-publicized appraisal marathon. I always want to ask why, in the face of such a splendid estimate, the piece was not accepted for sale.

Parrish, Maxfield

American artist and illustrator whose long career included works in both the Art Nouveau and Art Deco styles that are, nevertheless, entirely distinctive, and not only because of the characteristic "Maxfield Parrish blues" either.

A few years ago we would pass up Maxfield Parrish prints at $5 or $10. Now that they sell for ten times that, I naturally regret those missed opportunities. But who would ever have thought it! Most of the paintings were done for commercial purposes and appeared all over the place in reproductions, on candy boxes, calendars, advertisements, magazine covers, jigsaw puzzles, theater programs. We just acquired a 1922 program for the Harris Theatre in New York, where John Barrymore was appearing in *Hamlet;* we bought it because the cover was done by Maxfield Parrish.

Some of the old Maxfield Parrish prints can still be purchased inexpensively. Usually these are the less familiar, unsigned, or obscurely signed works. But if you decide to sell them, you will have to find a very knowledgeable collector or be prepared to cite some recognized authority to support your contention that they are, indeed, Maxfield Parrish prints. Most of the recent reproductions now on the market are of the best known works, which means that if you find a print of one of the less popular pictures—"The Dream Garden," for example, which Parrish painted to serve as the basis for a glass mosaic by Tiffany—you can be fairly confident of its age.

Parts

If you do a lot of browsing for antiques, you will eventually come across any number of elements from incomplete objects. If the parts themselves are complete and in good condition and inexpensively priced, buy them. Pack them away in a special carton or cabinet. Fill a closet—or a room, if your collection of parts grows to require it. Whatever you do, resist the temptation to sell any of them. Should you yield to that quite pressing temptation, you are almost certain to find the perfect component that would have put your now-missing part to good use, at any time from a few days to a few weeks after you sacrificed it.

Should you fail to buy one of these apparently useless but ultimately essential parts, I can practically guarantee that you will very shortly thereafter encounter the other essential part or parts that would have made it valuable to you. Usually it will do you no good to go racing back in search of that neglected opportunity. Someone else will probably have acquired it.

Don't buy broken parts. And don't compromise when trying to effect combinations. But above all, don't let anyone shame you into parting with any part of your collection of parts. I promise you the last laugh if you don't.

Patera(ae)

It took me a day and a half to find out that this refers to a saucer-shaped carving that was popular on furniture of the late eighteenth century. If you see something described as being decorated with carved paterae, you'll know what to look for without having to waste a lot of time looking it up. Or was I alone in not having known this? Some auction galleries with pretentious pretensions delight in using unfamiliar terms in their catalog descriptions.

See Putto

Peachbloom Porcelain

Probably only the Chinese could have come up with such a poetic and descriptive name for the melting rose-to-pale-green glaze that sometimes is also known as peachblow. Since the American glass called peachblow was intended to copy peachbloom porcelain—which was very much in vogue at the time, largely because of the spectacular sale of the famous "Morgan" peachbloom vase—it is less confusing to use "peachbloom" for the porcelain, "peachblow" for the glass.

Peachblow Glass

There are four principal types of this popular Victorian art glass, and once you learn to tell them apart, they are not at all confusing.

New England peachblow is a single-layer glass that shades from a true rose red—the color of an American Beauty rose—to pure white.

Mt. Washington peachblow is a single-layer glass that shades from dusty pink to soft bluish white.

Wheeling peachblow is a cased glass having an opaque white lining within an outer layer of transparent glass that shades from a rich burgundy red to a beautiful warm yellow.

The fourth type of peachblow, which turns up a lot more often than the first three, is imitation peachblow, meaning brand-new or reproduction peachblow.

There are several ways to identify the new glass. The first indication that a piece of peachblow glass might not be as fine as you wish it were is the price. Genuine peachblow pieces are expensive, and while it is very nice to think that you are about to acquire a $500 item for a forgettable $35, the chances are good that what you are about to acquire is a $20 reproduction for $35. Of course we all dream of having it work out differently, but it doesn't—not very often. The second indication of imitation is the shape of the item. Most new peachblow pieces are rather clumsily made and are much larger and heavier than the fine antiques they purport to copy. The colors in the new pieces are not very pure. Frequently on the muddy side, they never approach the beauty of the genuine articles. And instead of blending gradually from one shade to another, as they do in authentic pieces, colors in some of the reproductions either change abruptly or appear streaky and marbleized, which should be a dead giveaway. Such streaks of color are virtually impossible in a piece of real peachblow for the excellent reason that the two-color effect was originally achieved by reheating a portion of the glass. Where the most concentrated heat was applied, the most intense color developed. From that point—usually the mouth of a vase, the lip of a pitcher, the rim of a bowl—the heat-induced second color gradually subsides until, at the base of the piece, the original color of the glass is revealed. With that in mind, it becomes pretty hard to accept pieces in which the two shades blend in a swirling, marbled effect. The illustrations of peachblow pieces in many antiques books are not especially helpful for telling reproductions from authentic items. In fact, since many of the new peachblow pieces have details similar to those on genuine examples, they can compare impressively, and confusingly, with certain photographs. What they can't compare favorably with is the real McCoy. If you don't know what that looks like, go and see some *bona fide* pieces before you start investing in peachblow glass. Once you see how good the best looks, only the most desperate urge to self-deception would prompt you to acquire any of the abundant imitations.

A word about painted peachblow. Pieces of opaque white glass sometimes are found with a collar of rosy paint. If the slightly different surface of the colored portion doesn't identify it as paint, then remember that the color in genuine peachblow is developed in the glass itself. This means that even in its most delicate shadings it possesses a glowing intensity that paint cannot equal. It also means that the interior of a genuine piece shows the same degree of color to the same depth as the exterior.

Pewter

It is so easy and inexpensive to counterfeit some antique pewter pieces that if you do not know your pewter, you had better be darned sure that you know the dealer from whom you are buying it. If he's an auctioneer, find out what (if any) guarantees of authenticity he will provide before you wind up with a lot of late "early" pewter.

Philadelphia

In antique Chippendale furniture it means "the greatest"!

Phytomorphic

It means of plantlike form.

See Art Nouveau; Gallé, Émile; Tiffany, Louis Comfort

Picker

A picker is a runner with a pedigree. Usually he buys for one or a few dealers who consider themselves at least theoretically entitled to first call upon his services and first refusal of his treasures. Sometimes, in order to secure their claims, they will pay a token retainer, or they may advance money for the purchase of merchandise on which they want a definite option. Important dealers have pickers scattered around the world like spies, and for much the same purpose. They cover the major sales and the auctions and flea markets, and once a year they fly in for a session of eyeballing and jawboning. But my favorite pickers are the three athletes, each towering a full head above the crowd, who work for a deceptively frail-looking silver-haired lady, who unleashes them upon an unsuspecting flea market, and maintains walkie-talkie contact with them while they sweep the place clean of the wicker furniture that is her specialty.

Picture Frames

Buy frames when you find them in good condition and inexpensively priced. Don't worry about having no immediate use for them. Save them. In no time at all a purpose will present itself, and you will be glad that you have a suitable frame on hand to press into service.

A frame that holds a convex bubble glass makes an attractive container for an antique fan and costs much less than a decent fan case. I like the oval brass frames with scrolled wings at either end and little rococo ornaments at the top and bottom. Many of them are designed and fitted to be hung either horizontally or vertically. Used horizontally, they are just right for framing a decorative fan.

Regular frames come in handy for holding bits of embroidery, quilt samples, pieces of patchwork, lace, crocheted doilies, valentines, theater programs, postcards, bookmarks, autographs, stamps, coins, Indian arrowheads, cards of buttons, political campaign materials, emblems, badges, cigar bands, matchbook covers, bottle caps, license plates, magazine covers, cartoons, calendars, and, of course, pictures. So while you're combing the flea markets for a little piece of Lowestoft, don't forget to keep your eyes open for usable frames. All those terribly important trifles that you have been hoarding in boxes and drawers will keep cleaner and neater if you frame them. And then you can hang them on the wall and enjoy looking at them until some more pressing use claims them. Do an especially attractive job and you can even sell them. Profitably.

Pinchbeck, Christopher

English clockmaker who developed a gold-toned alloy of copper and zinc consisting of approximately 85–90 percent copper and 15–10 percent zinc, which he introduced in 1732 as a substitute for real gold in clocks and watches. The alloy continues to be known as pinchbeck metal, but that name is really just a fancy way of saying brass. The brass that is known as Dutch metal is a similar alloy which sometimes has a slightly lower copper content. It also resembles gold; but "Dutch metal" doesn't sound anywhere near as quaint and antique as "pinchbeck," does it? And doesn't either term sound infinitely finer than "brass"?

Pink Luster

Luster decorations were popular for tablewares in the first half of the nineteenth century, when they provided an inexpensive version of the ornate and costly gilt-trimmed products of Europe's important ceramics factories. In some instances the luster applications are limited to borders or stripings on articles having transfer-printed designs. On other pieces the entire decoration is painted in the slightly metallic, thinly iridescent pink.

It is generally easy to tell the old pink lusterwares from the recent reproductions, even though the decorative patterns are much the same. Antique pieces are extremely lightweight. The white backgrounds on which the pink luster designs are painted are frequently slightly off-white, often with a faint yellow or gray tone. Tea-color stains, crazing, and hairline cracks are frequently found.

The pink luster reproductions are much thicker than the antique pieces. The paste is chalky white—rather like plaster. The decorations tend to be larger and less detailed than those of the originals. And the pink color is lighter and much less lustrous. As a final confirmation of recency, many of the new pieces are marked, which, to the best of my knowledge, none of the old ones were.

Pink Slag Glass

There is some mystery about the origin of this varicolored, molded, pink-to-white-shaded glass that was used for various tablewares around the turn of the century. Because genuine examples are scarce and have become almost ruinously expensive, various attempts have been made to reproduce it. Tumblers apparently are among the most commonly reproduced items and turn up from time to time at antiques shows and auctions, where they are presented as "pink slag."

You have to see a genuine example of this glass to know true pink slag glass from its imitations. Once you have seen it, you will never again confuse the two. Photographs and illustrations in books on antiques are no help at all in this case. Go and see the real thing before investing more than a few dollars in a reproduction.

Never mind that the pattern and shape and dimensions are proper; old molds have been used for a lot of later pieces. Just remember that real pink slag is glossy, gorgeous, and godawfully scarce. Be particularly suspicious of pieces priced at $100 or so. That is much too little for the real thing and much too much to pay for a reproduction. You stand a better chance of acquiring a genuine piece for $20 or $30 from someone who fails to recognize its true worth. At any price, the odds on being offered a reproduction are infinitely greater. So find a collector or a dealer or a museum with a genuine piece of old pink slag to show you. One look is all that you will need.

Planter's Peanuts

The jar having a large peanut at each mitered corner is one that has been reproduced. Not for a moment do I doubt that others in this popular collecting category have been (are being) copied. Signs of wear or minor damages could be indications of originality —if, that is, you want a Planter's Peanut jar having signs of wear or minor damages. Labeled jars and other Planter's Peanuts items having an address can sometimes be dated by checking the numbers in the postal zip code.

See Zip Code

Plastic Foam

The ballast for unbreakable packing of breakables.
See Disposable Diapers

Plate

We continue to call the dish upon which dinner is served a "plate" whether the plate is of ceramic or metal or plastic or paper. This use of the word actually stems from the time when silver was the material preferred for making plates, and it has much more to do with the fact that plates were made of thinly worked metal (as in armor plate, latch plate) than with the purpose they served. British antiques dealers especially tend to call silver "plate," even those articles that are not plates. And they are speaking of sterling silver, too, not of silver plate. In the United States when we say "plate" in reference to silver, we usually mean silver-plated ware, which the British, bless 'em, also call "silver plate." Sheffield plate is a kind of silver plate that is never referred to as silver plate, but is consistently identified as Sheffield plate. Sterling silver produced at Sheffield, England, can also quite correctly be called Sheffield plate, but is usually referred to as Sheffield silver, by the British, although Americans have a sloppy habit of using this term for Sheffield plate!

The familiar plate rails and the grooved shelves found in many antique dressers and cabinets were first intended for display of the family silver, which often represented the household's wealth. When porcelain plates replaced plate plates, they went into the plate racks, even though that did not provide ideal storage. But the early porcelain plates were terribly expensive and as worthy of prominent display as silver. Eventually the plate rack became a dish rack, and the dresser became a cupboard, and the silver got stored in a plate safe.

See Sheffield Plate

Plexiglas

In its favor: unbreakable; lightweight; inexpensive to install, even if it must be shaped to conform to difficult curves.

Against it: scratches easily; lacks the brilliant clarity of glass; greatly diminishes the salability of the curio cabinet or china cabinet in which it has been used as a replacement for glass panels.

So consider the pros and cons of having Plexiglas installed in pieces that require glass replacements. And check the panels in any cabinet that you are purchasing to find out if they are glass or Plexiglas. If you can't tell the difference by sight, give each panel a tiny tap and listen to the result. You'll know right enough right away. And don't assume that because one panel is glass, the rest will be. Check each and be sure.

Pompadour, Jeanne Antoinette Poisson Le Normant d'Etioles, Marquise de

Madame de Pompadour to you and me. My encyclopedia—the source of her full and proper name—discreetly says that she maintained her influence over King Louis XV of France "by her wit and capabilities," which certainly must have been formidable. Madame de Pompadour played an important role in gaining acceptance for Sèvres porcelains, which she greatly favored, and is said to have made extravagant purchases at the Sèvres' annual exhibitions in order to encourage others to follow suit. From time to time she reportedly displayed her capabilities to the king at a fabulous winter garden which she kept in a full bloom of Sèvres porcelain flowers. When Louis XV had his gold and silver plates melted down to replenish the treasury, Sèvres porcelains replaced them.

The much-admired pink background found on many Sèvres porcelains of the mid-eighteenth century was an evident favorite of Madame de Pompadour and is properly called rose Pompadour, except by those who persist in calling it rose Du Barry, in honor of another lady whose capabilities Louis XV appreciated. To be historically accurate, it was Pompadour's rose and important on the Sèvres palette long before Du Barry caught the old king's eye. Since Louis XV did not take up with Madame Du Barry until four years after Madame de Pompadour's death, it seems unlikely that he shared our unfortunate tendency to confuse the ladies. The British seem especially committed to calling the color rose Du Barry, which, in view of Madame de Pompadour's pioneering efforts on behalf of Sèvres porcelains, doesn't seem at all sporting.

The true rose Pompadour is a glowing, absolutely delicious pink and was evidently difficult to achieve. On inferior pieces it shades into yellow. Most attempts to duplicate it on later pieces and reproductions produce a pink with a somewhat blue cast that isn't Pompadour's rose at all. Since those pieces were made long after the true rose Pompadour, perhaps they deserve to be known as rose Du Barry.

Porcelain Marks

Because so much of it is marked, antique porcelains are easier to identify correctly than antique glass. But it isn't as simple as it might seem. Consider the fact that there are more than thirty European porcelain marks using one version or another of the famous crossed swords associated with Meissen porcelains. And that British porcelain marks include at least eighteen different anchors, not to mention crossed swords, arrows, and a couple of crossed pitchforks or tridents. Confusion is heaped on disorder when you find the familiar interlaced "L"s of Sèvres turning up on porcelains produced on both sides of the Channel, and also in other places. Plus which, eighteenth-century European porcelains sometimes were given Chinese markings, because Oriental porcelains were more highly regarded than the recently introduced local variety. Add to that the fact that American porcelains produced in the first half of the nineteenth century often were not marked at all, in consideration of the public's preference for the European varieties. To top everything, remember that the Japanese and other artful copyists have freely adopted and adapted the marks of nearly every well-known factory.

In view of all of which, it makes very little sense to act bullish in the china shop and go madly about turning everything upside down to look at the marks. Look at the porcelain first, and if that seems right, let the marks confirm your impression.

Price Guides

One problem with price guides to antiques is that those of a general nature tend to price some categories low, while those publications that specialize frequently assign unrealistically high values to their specialties. For example, in one general price guide a German bisque Happifats doll is listed at $20, while a guide restricted to doll prices gives $135 as the value for the same doll. Beyond contradicting each other, some guides give little more than a passing nod to the realities of the marketplace. What, for example, is the true value of a Steuben glass gazelle—the $300 quoted in one price guide, the $120 listed in another, or the $195 asked by a reputable antiques dealer? Like tequila, most antiques price guides go down best with a pinch of salt. Or with two or three other price guides in tow to confirm or contradict your findings.

I usually use three widely distributed general price guides and, whenever possible, compare their quotations with those given for a similar article in one of the specialized publications. In most cases this gives me a high figure and a low figure to set against prices advertised in periodicals such as *The Antique Trader Weekly* and *Hobbies*, or to reflect against regional preferences and trends too recent to be noted in books prepared six months or a year earlier.

In addition, price rises in such hot categories as dolls or Tiffany lamps have been so dramatic that nothing slower than a teletype could be expected to keep pace with them.

The prices quoted in some antiques books are so nonspecific that they become meaningless. One publication brackets prices as: moderate—$25 to $100; expensive—$100 to $500; very expensive—$500 and up. To make matters worse, a range is given for many items. This results in values for many pieces being expressed as "moderate to expensive." Since this, by the compiler's definition, spans a low of $25 and a high of $500, it wouldn't seem to be very helpful to the new collector or dealer who is anxious to determine a fair price for the antiques he wants to buy or sell.

It is unfortunate that the price guides, which usually include some prefatory note to the effect that the prices given are for genuine pieces in fine condition, sometimes are used to achieve an inflated price for repaired or otherwise defective items. Beginning antiquers seem to be especially susceptible to the argument that if a perfect example is worth $500, then a repaired piece must be a steal at $150. In some rare instances it might be. Most often, however, it will prove to be only an overpriced mistake, which, if it appreciates at all, never keeps pace with its perfect counterpart. In five or ten years the value of the item in proper condition might double, triple, quadruple, who-knows-what, while the defective piece still goes begging at $150. Anyone sufficiently interested in antiques values to bother consulting a price guide ought to be sufficiently interested to read all the fine print and to bear in mind such qualifications.

Price Tickets

With the seller's permission, it is wise to carefully peel away the adhesive price tickets on almost any article that you are considering. Or is it only coincidental that these stickers occasionally conceal blemishes?

Same caution applies to the numbered tags on auction lots.

If you can't manage that, at least pay careful attention to the placement of the tag and to the surrounding area.

And don't forget to replace the ticket after your examination is completed. Fair, after all, is fair.

If this procedure seems not only troublesome but symptomatic of paranoia, so be it; it is a far, far better thing to be called finicky than foolish.

See Mint

Profit

A relative matter in the antiques trade. Those who feel comfortable only dealing in merchandise carrying a fixed markup will be happier in a more precisely structured business. They probably could never justify spending $900 for something that they might, at best, hope to sell for $1,000. Many antiquers would jump at the chance, and congratulate themselves on having made $1,000. Never mind that percentagewise the profit was absurd. It *feels* better to think of the transaction in other terms. Which is why antiques dealers who avail themselves of the services of an accountant frequently do profitable things that send those rational-minded souls straight up the wall.

See Double or Nothing

Props

There is much to recommend carrying a dummy package when you go shopping for antiques. For one thing, it marks you as a buyer, which causes sellers to take your interest seriously. For another, if you want to do a little basic bargaining, you can suggest that you have previously spent a great deal on whatever it is that is supposed to be in your package, which means that a small price concession might be in order to swing a subsequent sale. Some dealers will resent the implication that you were willing to spend a large sum of money with a competitor but require an extra price break from them. You can counter this by mentioning that although you spent more than you intended to, the dealer gave you such a fantastic buy that you couldn't resist it. This is almost unfailingly effective.

You can sometimes acquire desired items by carrying an unwrapped or incompletely wrapped example when you go shopping. A doll, for instance (be sure the head shows), or a piece of art glass, or an incompletely wrapped Coca-Cola tray, or whatever happens to be your specialty. This is particularly good when shopping the larger flea markets. Some dealer who never dreamed that anyone would be willing to pay good money for "one of those" is sure to suggest that he has something similar, and you can take it from there—or from him, and sometimes for a song, if you play your cards right.

Putto (Putti)

Since it only means "cherub," I really don't see why the far more familiar term shouldn't be used. Unless, of course, one has a need to put on airs. Incidentally, Cupid is a cherub with a bow and arrow—to those of us not given to calling him a putto.

Q

Quezal Glass

From 1901 through 1925 this Brooklyn glassworks produced ornamental articles and lampshades in iridescent glass that strongly resembles some of Tiffany's lustered wares. The resemblance is not accidental. Martin Bach, who founded the Quezal Air Glass Company, originally had worked for Tiffany, as had his associate Thomas Johnson. Many Quezal pieces are beautifully executed, but possibly because their inspiration was derived from the works of others rather than dictated by personal vision or esthetic concept, they invariably lack the freshness and excitement, the sensuous richness of the Tiffany pieces with which they were intended to compete. One notable exception: the Quezal morning glory or jack-in-the-pulpit vases, which not only rival but sometimes outshine the Tiffany items of similar form.

There is a bright iridescent gold made only by Quezal. It isn't the silky gold of Tiffany or the satiny gold of Steuben, but the rich, thick gold of a fresh egg yolk. Unfortunately this outstanding color was usually used for rather uninteresting shapes—plain bowls, club-form vases. A similar gold is sometimes found in more interesting and decorated pieces made by the Durand Art Glass Company of Vineland, New Jersey. Perhaps because Martin Bach's son went to work there after the Quezal factory closed.

The Quezal firm served in other ways as a link between the Tiffany Glass and Decorating Company and other producers of Tiffany-type glass. After Thomas Johnson left Quezal he worked for the Union Glass Company, for which he produced Kew Blas iridescent glass; except for the difference in name, this is easily mistaken for Quezal glass. Conrad Vahlsing, son-in-law of the elder Martin Bach, operated the Lustre Art Glass Company, which produced many electric-light shades designed and executed in the Quezal manner.

In view of all of which, it is easy to understand why Quezal, Durand, Kew Blas, Lustre Art, and other art glass of the period is frequently mistaken for Tiffany glass. Especially since a little "L.C.T." can expedite salability and add anything from a few to a few hundred dollars to the value of an otherwise unmarked Tiffany-type piece.

Probably because Bach wished to gain recognition for his company, Quezal pieces are frequently marked. And many of the Lustre Art shades have the name traced in silver in the manner of Quezal, as does some signed Durand glass. These markings were generally done with an aluminum pencil applied over engraved signatures. With time, wear, and washings, the aluminum fillings disappeared, leaving a faintly etched marking that is best seen by holding the glass to the light. Some careless souls who believe that every piece of Tiffany-type glass should be signed by Tiffany are not as thorough as they ought to be about eliminating these marks. This can result in some strangely double-signed hybrids.

R

Redware Ceramics

The early red clay pottery that antiques dealers and collectors seek is much thicker and far heavier than the inexpensive Mexican and Spanish wares that are often mistaken for it. It is also smoother and better finished than the new pieces, which sometimes feel rather granular, pimpled, or sandy.

Repaired

Even if the work is invisible without black light, a magnifying glass, or a two-hour examination, you deserve to know that an antique you are considering has been repaired. A legitimate dealer will always point out any repairs that he is aware of. Of course he cannot call your attention to those that he has not detected. Which makes the real test of his legitimacy whether or not he will permit you to return an item should you later discover some restoration that had slipped by unnoticed.

Even a well-executed minor repair can cut an antique's value in half. Never mind the fragments and reconstructed rarities on view in museum collections.

See Mint

Repairs: Do-it-Yourself

Unless you are particularly skilled and happen to own a well equipped workshop, do not lightly assume that you can "do it yourself."

Every time that I manage this bit of self-hypnosis, I find that I do not own the necessary clamps, miter boxes, whatever—and most important the combined ability and patience that would enable me to use them effectively. The tool-rental services can close certain gaps in the equipment division, but they do not provide a very economical solution for those of us who plan to putter around on a particular repair over several weekends or dabble all winter at a tedious job. Plus which, most of us expect to be instantly expert with unfamiliar tools and techniques. And rental-service equipment sometimes is leased in little better than operable condition. Frustration and unfinished projects frequently follow.

All of my repair and restoration suggestions are based on ordinary household items. If anything more complex than the contents of the kitchen cupboard is required, I humbly pass the task on to a competent professional.

Good for you if you happen to be a master carpenter, a wizard of the workbench, an ace welder, and the fastest stripper since Georgia Sothern hung up her G-string. Be tolerant of those of us who are all thumbs and Band-Aids. You'll never know how deeply we respect your prodigious abilities.

Repairs: Dolls

Anything can be fixed.

Yes, anything.

And damned near undetectably, too.

What isn't fixed can be replaced, most dolls being things of parts.

This is done at a place called a doll hospital—which shows you how a lot of collectors and restorers feel about dolls. Never mind that it is a perfectly utilitarian workshop full of glue and paint and stray arms and legs and amputated hands and eyes . . . eyes of all sizes . . . trays and boxes and drawers filled with staring, unmounted eyes. It still is a rather charming conceit.

Repairs: Metal

When I have an antique that needs soldering or welding or brazing, I take it to a young man whose full-time job is repairing automobile radiators. He says that the crazy things I bring in amuse him and provide a welcome break from the monotony of his regular work. He charges less than a specialist in antiques repairs would to set the broken arm of a bronze dancing girl, and he does the work better and faster than any of the professional restorers whose services I formerly used. If you can find a similarly accommodating person at a nearby radiator-repair shop, your initial project might surprise him, but plenty of sincere appreciation and an occasional gratuity could win you a valuable ally.

Repairs: Porcelain

"The only thing that I cannot fix," said a friend who specializes in porcelain repairs, "is a plate that is broken right down the center."

"That isn't hard at all," I said. "I can do that with epoxy."

"But if you do that," my friend asked, "then it does show, doesn't it?"

"Well, yes, I guess—sort of," I said.

"Then it isn't properly repaired," my friend said.

And she was right.

"Invisible china repairs," the restorer's business card stated; it should have added, "except on pure white undecorated porcelain."

Repairs: Silver

The best thing most of us can do to restore antique silver is to polish it and keep it clean. And it is just as well not to overdo the polishing bit either. Incredible as it might seem, a tiny amount of silver is removed with every cleaning. Eventually hallmarks are worn down, decorations become blurred, and every polishing session increases the possibility of inadvertently scratching or accidentally dropping and denting this delicate metal.

Most experts agree that it is easier to successfully restore a large dent than a small one. This might help explain why the charge for straightening out that tiny wrinkle in the foot of the sugar bowl could equal the cost of correcting a dent as big as your fist in the side of a wine cooler.

No matter what the repair—and bear in mind that it usually is advisable to have nothing done that is not absolutely essential to your use or enjoyment of the article—retain a detailed invoice or memorandum from the expert who worked on any reasonably important piece. Having such information handy can save a good deal of time and confusion if you should want to have the piece appraised or if you decide to sell it. There are those who panic at the first sight of contemporary solder. You can soothe them by whipping out a bill of particulars setting forth what was done and when and by whom.

Revere, Paul, II

America's celebrity silversmith. Born in Boston in 1735, Paul Revere II, whom Longfellow celebrated in his poem about the midnight ride, was the son of a silversmith and learned the family trade in his father's workshop. In addition to making the silver most earnestly desired by patriotically and historically inspired American collectors, Paul Revere II did a lot of other interesting things including printing, engraving, political cartooning, revolutionary propagandizing, and dentistry. He also designed and printed the first Continental bonds, ran a bell foundry, and made a neat profit from shipping ice down to the West Indies. Nevertheless it is largely because of Henry Wadsworth Longfellow's poem about the famous ride—which Revere never actually finished, having the misfortune to be briefly captured by the British—that Paul Revere II became the most famous name in American silver. It is one Amercan name that adds sufficient coin to the price of a piece of silver to make forgeries worth the forger's effort.

The maker's marks used by Paul Revere the elder and Paul Revere the patriot are easily confused. The most convincing authority that I have found suggests that the senior Revere marked his works "P. Revere," also "P'REVERE," and sometimes "P R." The mark most generally accepted as belonging to Paul Revere II is "REVERE."

Since known forgeries exist, the best guarantee of the authenticity of a piece of Paul Revere II silver is a record of ownership existing from the time the silver left the Revere shop until the day it reaches your hands. If that cannot be done, and no comparable pedigree exists, it would be extremely unwise for any but the most experienced collector to pay a premium price for silver reportedly or "probably" made by Paul Revere II.

Revival

In antiques, the cue for rising prices and reproductions.

Rookwood Pottery

America's most important art pottery, founded in Cincinnati, Ohio, by Mrs. Maria Longworth Storer, whose father originally financed what must have seemed a rather dilettantish operation in order to "give employment to the idle rich." Probably because it did not have to depend on popular acceptance for commercial success, Rookwood experimented with glazes, decorative techniques, and styles, eventually developing pottery articles that were distinctive expressions of the principles of Art Nouveau.

Exceptionally decorated pieces of Rookwood pottery have already brought well over $1,000 and are racing to pass $2,000. But those are, indeed, exceptional pieces and bear little resemblance to the later, widely available Rookwood production pieces in the familiar mat monochrome finishes.

The "RP" monogram, with the "R" reversed, haloed in 14 incised "flames," which look like a sunburst of inverted commas, identifies most production Rookwood pieces, with the post-1900 year given in Roman numerals immediately beneath it. Knowing that the full mark contains 14 flames can save a lot of squinting and counting and calculating. If there are Roman numerals under the "RP" mark, the piece dates from 1900 plus whatever the Roman numerals say. If the mark carries the full 14 flames and there are no Roman numerals, the piece dates from 1900. If the "RP" monogram appears with no flames, the piece dates from 1886. In 1887 the first flame was added to this mark. Count another year for each additional flame. It is really very simple. But although a lot of people make a great fuss about it, and while it is nice to be able to accurately date any antiques, the date is a lot less significant than many other factors in determining the value of a piece of Rookwood pottery.

Most of the individually made pieces are also signed by the artist who decorated them. The presence of these signatures is the rule rather than the exception. It is very easy to recognize the monograms of the best known Rookwood decorators, and since the identity of the artist can contribute to the value of the piece, it is worth taking the trouble to verify the signature. Some artists spent a surprising number of years decorating Rookwood pottery, so it is not unheard of to find the same initials on a turn-of-the-century piece and on one in the "moderne" style of the 1920s.

Routine pieces of mat-glazed production Rookwood pottery are often overpriced and do not represent an attractive acquisition for an investment-minded dealer or collector. Undoubtedly they will appreciate as prices for important Rookwood pieces continue to rise, but the increase will be smaller and the pace slower than the skyrocketing values of rare and unusual examples would suggest. The best reason for collecting production Rookwood is that you happen to like it. If you do, it will give you much pleasure even if it does not enjoy any especially dramatic appreciation.

As distinguished from the mat monochromes, there are mat-finished pieces that are artist-decorated, often in soft, hazy pastels in scenic or floral designs. These are substantially more interesting and considerably more valuable than the production pieces. Still more desirable are the highly glazed Rookwood pieces that represent the company's earliest successful works. Those having a background of rich molasses-brown are more readily recognized, but the glossy pastels in the Iris glaze are much desired by today's collectors. Naturally, scenic and portrait decorations in the high-glaze pieces command premium prices. And Rookwood pottery with important or interesting silver overlay is considered the *crème de la crème.*

The value of any Rookwood piece is greatly diminished by excessive crazing. Some collectors will accept an outstanding example that has a well executed minor repair but would reject a perfect piece on which the glaze is badly crazed. A second deterrent to value is the incised "X," by which the decorator indicated dissatisfaction with the work—although it is said that artists Xed some articles that they wanted for themselves or for friends in order to take advantage of the greatly reduced prices at which these supposedly unsatisfactory pieces could be obtained. Many collectors will refuse an X-marked piece, or will acquire it only if the cost is nominal.

Rose Medallion Porcelain

Late-eighteenth-, early-nineteenth-, and mid-twentieth-century Chinese porcelain colorfully decorated in panels depicting pink and yellow flowers with green foliage, and sometimes with bright butterflies and bluebirds adding to the vivid yet—in the older wares—quite tasteful and pleasing effect. On many pieces the floral decorations are used to separate panels featuring Chinese people in rather charming, slightly stylized scenes. Sometimes the rose medallions are not medallions at all but running borders framing the various Mandarin vignettes. Such pieces are occasionally sorted into a separate category called Mandarin Canton, but generally speaking, whether the decoration is entirely floral, or has alternating panels of flowers and people, or features Mandarin scenes set in flowering margins, it is all known as Rose Medallion. At some auctions and in a few of the "better" shops the prices go up when early Rose Medallion pieces are presented as *famille rose* porcelains. There are some valid reasons for upholding this designation, but there are equally valid reasons for rejecting it, which makes the price advances a little hard to understand.

Whether it is known as Rose Medallion, Rose Canton, Mandarin Canton, or—if you must stretch a point in order to get fancy—*famille rose,* it has the happy quality of being immediately recognizable, which is, I believe, an important reason for its perennial popularity. I think this quality of being instantly identifiable is also responsible for the current enthusiasm for collecting Roseville pottery—to skip a century, an ocean, and half the continent of North America to cite an apparently farfetched but quite appropriate parallel. Many collectors give preference to antiques—and not so antiques—that they and their friends can correctly identify at a glance. With experience and study, one can acquire this knack in respect to articles belonging to quite challenging categories, but I do not think that the personal satisfaction in being able to sail into a gallery and unhesitatingly point out the three genuine Ming dynasty jars made on a rainy Tuesday in the third week of the summer of the second year of the reign of the Emperor Hung Wu is all that different from the pleasure a new collector derives from having a visitor say, "My, you do have a lot of Roseville [or Rose Medallion, or whatever], don't you!" Such joys are much more closely related than many of us would care to admit.

An additional appeal to collectors of Rose Medallion porcelains is the great variety of articles available with this unmistakable decoration. Rose Medallion china can be found in everything from the widely available tablewares and tea services to complete toilet sets, those containing not only the familiar basin-and-pitcher combinations, but soap dishes, slop jars, chamber pots, footbaths, water bottles, and bidets. Rose Medallion vases and mantel garniture pieces are plentiful, but there are also Rose Medallion barrel-form garden seats, umbrella jars, table screens, candle shields, standing screens inset with Rose Medallion tiles, enormous fishbowls and jardinieres. Such variety keeps collecting possibilities fresh and collectible fields unlimited. Moreover, there are the previously mentioned variations in design, as well as many different shapes (plain, fluted, swirling, scalloped, etc., etc., etc.), which makes it possible to build a highly specialized or deliciously generalized collection in accordance with individual preferences and available examples.

The earliest Rose Medallion porcelains are fairly heavy and rather thickly formed. Undersides of pieces usually are unglazed and show the slightly toasted surface that is characteristic of Oriental export ware. Enamel decorations are well painted in both opaque and translucent colors applied over the porcelain glaze. Mid-to-late-nineteenth-century pieces tend to be thinner, to have glazed undersides, and to be painted in a rather loose, less busily detailed manner. In the more recently manufactured pieces the porcelain becomes progressively thinner, the glaze becomes increasingly uniform, and the decorations are still more hurriedly painted, and in ever-paler colors. Most such pieces will be found to have been stamped or stenciled "China," in confirmation of post-1890 importation.

Reproduction Rose Medallion is probably the easiest of all copies of antiques to identify as such. The colors in the new pieces are vivid but hard, flat, and unpleasant. Much black, brick red, and deep rose are used with an absolutely incorrect green and a shiny bright gold that has no resemblance to the satiny gold used on the antique pieces. In weight the new porcelains fall somewhere between the thick eighteenth-century Rose Medallion and the fine, light, translucent china characteristic of the late-nineteenth-century pieces. The undecorated background of the new pieces is a dead white—neither the creamy, warm white of the earliest wares—which often have a slightly curdled texture—nor the cool, gray-blue white of the nineteenth-century porcelains. Since the reproductions are so readily distinguished from "real" Rose Medallion, it is inexcusable for even the newest antiquer to confuse the two.

Equally unforgivable is an antiques dealer who tells his trusting customers that a piece of Rose Medallion marked "China" is "older" than an unmarked piece—unless, of course, the unmarked piece happens to be brand-new, in which case we not only forgive but applaud him.

Roseville Pottery

A much earlier and far more important American art pottery than even some of its most passionate admirers sometimes realize. Established in Roseville, Ohio, in 1892, Roseville's early series compares favorably with the generally more highly regarded—and currently more expensive—works produced by Rookwood and Weller. Today's collectors tend to concentrate on the production pieces featuring relief-molded flowers and mat finishes, but the earlier pieces, which might not be so readily recognized as Roseville, would make worthy additions to the most sophisticated collection of American art pottery.

Royal Bayreuth Porcelain

The colorfully decorated novelty porcelains produced at this German factory are enormously popular with collectors, even as they were with travelers in the nineteenth and early-twentieth centuries. Many pieces were made as souvenir items and sometimes are rather awkwardly decorated with painted or decal-printed legends for American and European towns. I once had a Royal Bayreuth black bull's-head creamer gilded into a strange souvenir of Patchogue, Long Island. The inscription looked a little foreign combined with the blue Royal Bayreuth mark.

Collectors who make a big deal out of the famous blue mark must be collecting marks rather than porcelains. Some pieces of Royal Bayreuth were made only for export and are found with the company's mark in green. And despite some expert opinions to the contrary, plenty of perfectly fine Royal Bayreuth is not marked. However, it is important to remember that a lot of Royal Bayreuth items were copied by the Japanese—who have also been active on the souvenir and novelty porcelain fronts—lest all those little tomatoes and lobsters and tapestried objects be mistaken for unmarked Royal Bayreuth. The Japanese pieces are somewhat heavier than the Bayreuth originals and are less well made. Flat, unglazed bottoms showing a definite mold mark are not characteristic of Royal Bayreuth, although they are frequently found on "Bayreuth-type" pieces from other German and Japanese factories. Decorative details on most Bayreuth pieces are printed, but areas of solid color are often manually done. The painted color on most Japanese pieces looks thick and has a dull finish, in contrast to the rather lively surface typical of true Royal Bayreuth.

The popular tapestry-finish pieces of Royal Bayreuth are sometimes badly soiled, because dirt does tend to linger in those fine-textured mat-finished surfaces. Try submerging such pieces in chlorine laundry bleach and see if they don't come clean. If you don't like the way they look after rinsing in clear water, give them another bleach bath. Don't fear that the decorations will also be bleached. On the contrary, once that veil of dirt is lifted they will look prettier, if only because you can finally see them.

Royal Doulton Ceramics

One of the most diversified and commercially successful English manufacturers of pottery and porcelain, the Doulton company can be said to have originated in 1815 when John Doulton invested in a pottery concern then operating in London's Lambeth district. Doulton's son, Henry, quite literally grew up in the family business and made significant contributions to its continued expansion and success, including, it is reported, the introduction of the first steam-powered potter's wheel, an innovation that pushed the Doulton factories well ahead of the production capabilities of competing firms. The Doulton did not become "Royal" until 1901, when receipt of the Royal Warrant made the designation official.

A number of Doulton's varied productions are currently enjoying great popularity with collectors—Gibson Girl plates, the Dickens series, artist-signed pieces, especially those by Hannah Barlow. The character Toby jugs in all sizes and the charming Doulton figurines seem to be particularly popular. The jugs with the letter "A" next to the Royal Doulton mark are those that most collectors want. Without the "A" the jugs are newer, or new. Only the figurines that have been discontinued from production are appreciating. The only way that I know to determine which these are is to obtain a recent Royal Doulton catalog and see if the item is still available. It also helps to keep an eye on shops and dealers displaying a full line of current Royal Doulton figures.

Royal Doulton tablewares in the Art Deco style currently are extremely desirable and fetch fancy prices from sophisticated collectors.

Royal Flemish Glass

A line of decorated Victorian art glass produced by the Mt. Washington Glass Company. The illustrations in the antiques books can show you the shapes and the decorative motifs of Royal Flemish glass. What most pictures fail to indicate correctly is that the glass actually is frosty gray and translucent, painted with mineral stains and enamels in translucent and opaque colors—brown, orange, blue, burgundy, yellow, gold—usually in a kind of stained-glass effect, with lines of raised gold enamel separating the colored sections. Signed pieces are marked "RF" in red-brown.

Some color pictures suggest that Royal Flemish glass is decorated in vivid, brilliant shades. It usually isn't. The decorative effects are often rather somber. The colors are muted instead of bright, dark but not heavy.

In 1894 a Royal Flemish biscuit jar cost $8. If you can find one today it would be a steal at $800, and could run well over $1,000.

Royal Vienna Porcelain

Usually of ornate design, colorfully decorated and often richly gilded, the true Royal Vienna porcelains bear little resemblance to the showy but poorly executed and frequently transfer-printed pieces sold under the name. The royal years of the Vienna porcelain manufactory ended in 1864, about twenty-five years before many of the porcelains bearing the well-known "beehive" mark were made. Still, the mark itself seems sufficient to earn the designation "Royal Vienna" for an awful lot of undeserving articles. For that matter, the "beehive" mark is itself a misnomer. It never was a beehive. First used in 1744 when the Empress Maria Theresa purchased the Vienna porcelain factory, the mark represented the "bound shield" of the royal arms. It continued in use in various colors and with some variation in form throughout the period of the factory's state ownership. And it is in continuing use today on porcelains sufficiently inferior to have sent the Empress Maria Theresa straight to the booby hatch.

The Royal Vienna portrait plates that fetch such handsome prices ought to be hand-painted and absolutely gorgeous. No one should shell out several hundred dollars for a portrait plate with a transfer-printed portrait, no matter how many beehives its underside boasts. Be particularly suspicious of pieces marked "hand-painted," or "hand-decorated," or prominently signed with an artist's name. The good ones never had to declare their quality except to let the work speak for itself.

R.S. Prussia Porcelain

Manufactured in Germany in the final decades of the nineteenth century and the early years of the twentieth, the porcelain is delightful in itself. Paper-thin and feather-light. And the shapes usually are very charming. Fluted and scalloped and footed—ornate marriages of Victorian, Art Nouveau, and Edwardian styles. The decorations are something else again. Most of the decoration is both esthetically and technically unworthy of the quality of the porcelain, and it often seems oddly inappropriate to the delicate and well formed shapes to which it is applied. References are made to hand-painted R.S. Prussia pieces, but not much of this ware was decorated by hand. Hand-colored areas—borders, backgrounds—are sometimes found on transfer-decorated pieces. Possibly some blanks were sold for use by amateur china painters, but transfer decorations are characteristic of R.S. Prussia porcelains. Which means that 99 times out of 100, when someone offers a piece of "hand-painted R.S. Prussia," it either isn't really hand-painted or it isn't really R.S. Prussia. Unusual pieces or those with animal, portrait, or scenic decorations are worth acquiring at premium prices. Floral decorations are often attractive, but they also are generally available and usually do not command top-dollar prices except in the most outstanding and rare articles.

A few years ago a line of new R.S. Prussia–type wares was marketed, and some pieces are probably still to be found in shops and at flea markets. You can identify these imitations in two ways: the reproductions are heavier than the originals, and the word "Prussia" is misspelled ("Prusia") in the copy of the usual red-star mark.

At about the same time it was possible to purchase decal sheets of the R.S. Prussia (correctly spelled) red-star marks. With the decals came instructions for affixing them to unsigned R.S. Prussia pieces—or to almost anything else that might strike your fancy. That being so, there seems little reason to place great emphasis on the marks when the genuinenesss of most R.S. Prussia pieces can speak for itself. But since many collectors do, the rest of us are more or less obliged to follow suit.

Running (1)

When an auctioneer raises your bid by calling bids he does not have, he is running you.

Running (2)

Buying here, selling there. Runners know which dealers are interested in what merchandise and about how much they would be willing to pay for it. A runner who has a sufficiently varied clientele and a sharp eye for a good buy can move a lot of antiques, because he can afford to sell them at lower prices than he would have to charge if he maintained a shop or a warehouse. Everyone has his own method of operation, but most runners maintain an inventory that ranges from small to nonexistent. As soon as an item is sold, the proceeds of the sale are reinvested in another object, and then that piece is sold and the return is spent on something else, and on and on and on. A little smart running can go a long, long way. A wise runner never wears out his welcome with overpriced or substandard merchandise.

S

Salesmanship

The dealer who says, "If you're not certain about it, I would prefer that you not take it" is usually the one who takes my money.

Samson of Paris

He sounds as if he should be either a circus strong man or an expensive hairdresser, but we know him as the master nineteenth-century copyist of antique ceramics. He reproduced everything from delft to Sèvres, including the imitations of Oriental export ware for which he is, perhaps, best known in the United States. It was said that delft copies were his specialty and that they were virtually indistinguishable from the originals—except that Samson was kind enough to mark his work, as his successors continue to do. Even if they were not marked, Samson's export-ware pieces are easier to identify. The paste is thinner and the glaze is finer and seldom achieves the slightly pitted texture associated with the eighteenth-century Chinese porcelains. Samson's painted decorations are somewhat more precisely painted in colors that are a bit brighter and clearer. Samson's "export ware" is now being collected, knowingly as well as unintentionally, and is not without value. When the copies were first made they sold at prices about equal to those of the antique originals. Prices for both have since increased, but the antique pieces have enjoyed the greater appreciation. Today a pair of Samson export ware–type urns might bring about one-tenth the price of an authentic Oriental pair.

Sandwich (as in the Boston & Sandwich Glass Company)

If all the articles said to have been made by this important company actually had originated there, production would have had to continue on a round-the-clock basis for far more than the sixty-odd years the factory was in operation.

A lot of reliable identification has been based on glass fragments found at the factory site, but for the most part "Sandwich" has become a kind of *salade russe* designation into which gets tossed almost any nineteenth-century glass that cannot be otherwise attributed. Together with a good many twentieth-century reproductions of Sandwich pieces.

You can tell most of the reproductions by giving the glass a little tap and listening to it ring. Or not ring. The Sandwich metal is a fine lead glass that emits a clear bell tone. Some of the early Sandwich candlesticks have been widely reproduced, but since many of these were originally made of two or more elements joined by wafers of glass, it is easy to distinguish them from later imitations by following the mold lines up the sides of the piece. On the genuine pieces there will be no mold marks on the wafer connections, and the seams on the other elements will not run consecutively. On the reproductions the mold marks will be consistently unbroken.

I wish that someone would start a revolution and begin calling all nineteenth-century pieces that cannot be authenticated by shape or pattern "Sandwich-type glass." Otherwise I am afraid that visions of those furnaces operating full blast all the way from 1825 to eternity will continue to fire my imagination.

Schliemann, Heinrich

A wealthy retired businessman whose fascination with the works of Homer led him to embark on a series (1871–82) of archaelogical expeditions to the Near East. Reports on his findings at the sites of Troy, Mycenae, and other ancient cities captivated the public and inspired an international interest in decorative objects of ancient forms or featuring Near Eastern motifs. In ceramics, glass, and metalwares, both American and European late-Victorian and Art Nouveau creations show signs of the far-flung fallout from Heinrich Schliemann's diggings.

Scratch Test

Scratching a metal article to try to determine if it is solid bronze or brass or only some base metal that has been given a bronze or brass finish is unreliable, unfair, and hard to undertake without attracting unwanted attention.

Unreliable because the often quite superficial scratches frequently fail to cut through a heavy surface plating.

Unfair because even the most discreet exploration leaves the object marked in a way no potential buyer can ignore.

As for attracting attention, it goes without saying that whipping out a knife or file or screwdriver and digging into the underside (hopefully into the underside!) of a statue or lamp base or whatever is not likely to go unnoticed. And anything that emphasizes your interest in the article is apt to adversely influence its price.

There is a much surer and more subtle way to test a metal object. It is as nearly foolproof as any such instant analysis can be. It doesn't involve leaving telltale marks on an item. And it can, with some practice, be carried out almost without detection. All you need is a magnet, a bit of metal, and three easy-to-remember facts:

1. Bronze and brass do not hold a magnet and emit a ringing sound when tapped with metal. Even a solid-cast statue mounted on stone will be somewhat resonant.

2. Iron rings when tapped but holds a magnet.

3. White metal does not hold a magnet but responds with a dead "thunk" when tapped.

So after making sure you are not holding the article in some way that might muffle the sound, give it a little tap. If the response is flat and dull, you will know you are dealing with one of the various alloys commonly lumped together under the designation "white metal."

If you detect some resonance—anywhere from a brisk "ping" to a brilliant bell tone—take step two and apply the magnet. If the magnet sticks, you have found iron. If it doesn't, well . . . Isn't that a lot easier than digging into the underneath of something you might ultimately not even want to buy, or might subsequently wish you hadn't bought?

Occasional pieces are found with cast-iron bases or with an iron plate set into the bottom for weight and balance. Keeping this in mind will help explain why one element of an object might hold a magnet while other parts do not.

Security Blanket for Grown-Up Collectors

Some objects of great beauty possess a comforting, almost mystical serenity that makes it unthinkable to raise one's voice, to argue, to feel anger or despair in their presence. Certain fine, usually very simple Oriental articles have this tranquilizing effect on me, and help me to understand how a particular painting or an exceptional piece of furniture or porcelain might similarly soothe someone else. (Most glass and jewels are too exciting, although there is much to be said in favor of things carved from semiprecious stones.) There is a definite benefit to be derived from owning at least one such object. Display it in some safe but strategic place where you will often see it. With time it will seem to command less attention, but do not worry, for if you have chosen wisely you will continue to benefit from its presence. Eventually you will no longer realize that tensions ease slightly whenever you consider your treasure, but never mind that, because tensions will go right on easing even when you are unaware of the process or ignore its inspiration. This is a socially and personally acceptable substitute for the security blanket that you would feel quite guilty about not having outgrown, or deprived of if it had been prematurely relinquished. Devout travelers must have sustained similar comfort from wayside shrines set up along difficult roads, whether the shrine contained a serene Madonna or an all-wise Buddha.

Selling

Every collector eventually reaches a point at which he would like to dispose of something—or some things. Hopefully at a profit. If not, then at least without financial loss. This can be done in several ways, the best choice being based upon individual temperament and the nature of the items to be sold.

Before starting to sell be sure that you thoroughly understand your responsibility for reporting any local and state sales taxes that you might be required to collect. Tax laws vary, but a general rule is that the ultimate consumer must pay the sales tax. In many instances taxes have been paid several times over on antiques that have been through several changes of ownership. Usually this does not greatly impress a taxing authority, which will probably insist that you are selling something to someone for his personal use and are therefore obliged to collect and report any appropriate tax on that transaction. It doesn't matter if you paid a similar tax when you acquired the item. Out-of-state sales and dealers buying for resale are the only customary exceptions, and certain states do not allow these exemptions. Even if you intend to sell only one or two items, it is a good idea to inquire about the tax law as it applies to you. In some localities such limited activity would be classed as a casual sale and would not require you to register for a tax number or report periodically, as most venders must.

There are benefits in holding a resale certificate from your state sales-tax bureau. To some antiques wholesalers, for instance, a flash of your registration card immediately takes you out of the garage-sale category and makes you a business person worth dealing with on a professional level. And if you go out to buy antiques specifically for resale, you can avoid paying the sales tax on items on which you subsequently will be collecting taxes—unless you happen to be an out-of-state dealer shopping in Massachusetts or some other state that refuses to acknowledge any but its own registrations.

A telephone call or a letter to the local office of your state's sales-tax authority will bring all the necessary information plus a tax table that will spare you even the most fundamental arithmetic and a form that will put you officially in business. If you are planning to go out of business after a transaction or two, tell the tax people, and they might send you a reporting form that you can execute when your sales activity is completed, so that you won't have to clutter up your records or their files with a lot of unnecessary forms.

Whatever you do, don't think that you will cleverly avoid collecting and remitting sales taxes on the things that you sell. It is very simple to go about this business in the right way, but some tax authorities have an unpleasant habit of estimating the tax that should have been collected by those who neglect to register in advance. At shows and flea markets and sometimes in response to advertisements for tag sales or garage sales, a field auditor will size up the display and present the vender with a bill for what he estimates the tax would be, and the seller is responsible for it—even if he doesn't make a sale. It is a lot easier to avail yourself of a resale number and report the taxes that you collect after you collect them.

If you decide to dispose of your things at auction or by consigning them to a retail antiques shop, the auctioneer or the retailer will collect and report the tax and you won't have to bother with that detail.

SELLING AT AUCTION

If you have one really sensational item that you want to dispose of or if you would like to clear out a great many things of no great importance, and you would like not to be troubled with the tedium of keeping records and collecting money and advertising and corresponding with mail-order customers, and you feel that you are probably not the world's greatest salesman, and you do not wish to open your home to the casual browser or the merely curious or the downright suspicious, and you do not want to wait until a regular dealer can dispose of your things on consignment, and you would like your selling activities to remain anonymous, consider the advantages and disadvantages of selling at auction.

For many who consign antiques for sale at auction a principal advantage is that certain items will bring significantly better prices at auction than through any other kind of sale. There also is considerable comfort in the fact that consignments will be sold at a definite time and that—with the rarest exceptions—the sale will be irrevocable and payment will be received within a specified interval. The auctioneer and his staff will do all the work, leaving the consignor free to sit back and enjoy the spectacle.

For his services the auctioneer will deduct from the gross proceeds of the sale a commission ranging from as little as 10 percent to as much as 50 percent, depending upon his custom, your willingness to agree to a higher or lower fee, and the auctioneer's eagerness to handle your consignments. If you have something particularly choice, which the auctioneer feels will greatly enhance a sale, he might even agree to sell it for you at much less than his usual commission or for a token charge to cover catalog and other advertising expenses. On the other hand, if you wish to dispose of a great many items of little or no consequence, none of which can be expected to realize more than a few dollars, the auctioneer might insist that he will handle the sale only if you agree to a 50–50 sharing of the proceeds. Commissions of 20–25 percent are fairly standard with most metropolitan galleries, although the auctioneer, being a businessman—often a particularly shrewd one—will try to take the best possible advantage from the deal. He also might routinely or especially charge you for insurance, special handling, unusual catalog descriptions or illustrations, or special mention of your things in his advertisements or brochures. Such charges usually are minimal and perfectly proper. The important thing is to know in advance that the auctioneer will be deducting the cost of these and any other items from your share of the proceeds of your sale. If that is the case, you might want to consider whether or not to incur the extra expense of photographing certain lots for catalog illustration or giving them some other special emphasis.

Even if you maintain adequate insurance to protect yourself from loss as a result of theft, breakage, fire, and other eventualities, you might want to take advantage of the inexpensive coverage available under the auctioneer's policy. For one thing, your insurance might or might not cover items that were removed from your private premises and displayed in a public place. And if it does, and circumstances oblige you to file a claim under this provision, you might find future premiums enormously increased or your coverage canceled.

Once you have agreed upon the auctioneer's commission and the additional charges, you need only establish a mutually satisfactory price below which the auctioneer agrees not to sell your things. Some auctioneers will balk at any mention of a reserve price. Others will go along with almost any reasonable reserve that a consignor sets. It is best to be realistic. Bear in mind that neither you nor the auctioneer will profit from lots that remain unsold as a result of outrageous reserve prices. Rely on the auctioneer. If you don't feel that you can trust his judgment in this respect, you should not be doing business with him under any circumstances. At the same time, don't be too easily discouraged by negativism on his part. I once placed a $300 reserve on a consignment that the auctioneer doubted would realize more than $50. I insisted that I could not allow the lot to be sold on any other terms, since the $240 proceeds of the sale would just cover my investment in the item. "Well," the auctioneer said finally, "we've done a bit of business in the past, so I'll run the piece through for you with a $300 buy-back on it, and if it doesn't make it—as I don't think it will—we won't charge you anything for bidding it in." Fortunately the right combination of buyers showed up in a briskly competitive mood, and the lot that the auctioneer would have written off at $50 easily made $400, giving me a small profit and the auctioneer a commission that made handling the lot more than just a gesture of friendly accommodation.

If you are going to establish a reserve on your consignment, you will need to know in advance what penalty you will pay if the lot fails to reach that figure. Some auctioneers will handle reserved consignments without charge. Others will not accept a lot that carries a reserve price. For the most part, fees ranging from 5 percent to 20 percent of the buy-back bid are arranged at the time a consignment is accepted. Instead of a percentage, some galleries apply a standard fee—$20 an item in many cases—to every lot bid back by a consignor.

Whatever you do, don't think that you can cleverly protect yourself by establishing absurd reserves on your things or by attending the sale and blithely bidding up your consignments. The auctioneer who would encourage you in such tactics probably figures that he can derive his profit from the buy-back penalties he collects from you. You, on the other hand, are only defeating yourself—assuming, of course, that your reason for having consigned things for auction was to have them sold. If you really are interested in selling, find an auctioneer you can trust, be sure that you understand his conditions and that he agrees to yours, and then leave the rest to him.

You can sometimes help the auctioneer achieve a better price for your things by giving him any meaningful information that might enhance their value. Don't try to puff everything up into something it isn't, but don't be shy about pointing out signatures, labels, hallmarks, and other confirmations of authenticity that might be overlooked in the rush of assembling and cataloging a sale. Be equally honest about pointing out anything that might detract from the value of an item. Leave it up to the auctioneer to decide whether or not he will make use of that information, but avoid postsale complications by having the condition of your consignment clearly understood when the auctioneer accepts it.

Ordinarily you will be given a receipt for your things. If the auctioneer doesn't volunteer one, ask for it. Your receipt should show the date the consignment was accepted and identify each item by a brief description, so that there is little possibility of error in the event of subsequent dispute. Some auctioneers write their catalog copy directly from these consignment sheets, which means that it is a good idea to add to the receipt any special notation that you want included in the catalog. Be sure that any reserve prices that you have established are also correctly indicated, and if there is to be any special waiver of commission or reduced commission rate, those conditions should also be spelled out. It is not always sufficient to assume that you have an understanding with the auctioneer. Probably you have. And probably that understanding will be honored by the auctioneer and his accounting staff and any other concerned parties. But suppose the auctioneer forgets to mention some concessions that he made to you? Or suppose that he becomes ill, or sells his business, or consigns the sale to another gallery? Auctioneers are human, too, you know. And since your receipt constitutes a kind of contract setting forth the terms of your agreement, it ought to incorporate any special features of that agreement.

You also will want to know approximately when the auctioneer plans to sell your things and how long after the sale you can expect to receive your share of the proceeds. Some galleries are consistently good about sending advance notices to their consignors. Others will leave it up to you to inquire. If you deal directly with the auctioneer, he usually can tell you when he will schedule your things.

Many auctioneers will offer to buy your things outright instead of selling them for you on a commission basis. Depending upon the auctioneer's offer, this might or might not be a favorable agreement. Don't mistakenly assume that if an auctioneer tries to buy something he will be willing to pay only a fraction of its worth. Certainly he is going to try to make the best possible deal, but that doesn't mean that he will offer only $20 for a $1,000 item. Not unless he is more than a little confident that he can get away with it. More often he might offer as much as $700 or $800 on a lot that he thinks he can sell at $1,000. The economics of the auction business are quite different from those of the retail antiques trade. The auctioneer who moves several hundred items in the course of a sale is frequently willing to accept a small profit on many lots, concentrating on the aggregate proceeds of the auction to determine success or failure. And in every sale there are apt to be a few lots that take off into unanticipated realms, thus more than compensating for an occasional miscalculation. Especially if you cannot enjoy the slight element of chance that adds so much to the excitement of an auction sale, you might want to favorably consider an auctioneer's proposal for outright purchase of your things.

If you like to gamble, however, and you are working with an auctioneer who is well known for achieving healthy prices, you might like to cast your lot with him and have him sell your consignments on a half-over-cost basis. Depending upon what you paid for the item and what the auctioneer realizes for it, this arrangement can be financially advantageous to you, or it can favor the auctioneer. In most instances the higher the price goes, the more the auctioneer makes—at your expense. Remember, though, that if he is selling your consignments under this arrangement, the auctioneer will probably strive just a bit harder to achieve the best possible price. That can be to your advantage too.

Here is the yield on a half-over-cost arrangement for an item that cost the consignor $320, compared with that on a regular 20 percent selling commission.

Selling Price	*Consignor's return at cost plus 50% of the profit*	*Consignor's return after deducting 20% commission*
$400	$360	$320
$450	$385	$360
$475	$397.50	$380
$500	$410	$400

(Until this price, the half-over-cost sharing has given a small and gradually diminishing benefit to the consignor. Notice the change as the selling price rises.)

Selling Price	*Consignor's return at cost plus 50% of the profit*	*Consignor's return after deducting 20% commission*
$550	$435	$440
$600	$460	$480
$650	$485	$520
$700	$510	$560

(The auctioneer's advantage in sharing the profit instead of taking a standard commission becomes apparent. If the lot sells high enough, the difference becomes more impressive.)

$1,000	$660	$800

You will receive the maximum return on your auction consignments if you let the auctioneer share the profit on lots that you expect will sell at only a few bids over cost, while reserving those treasures that you picked up for a song and expect to sell at a handsome return to be sold on a straight commission basis.

Depending on the auctioneer and the manner in which he keeps his accounts, you will receive your share of the proceeds at any time from a few minutes to a few weeks after the sale. If an auctioneer says that six weeks is his usual time for settling a sale, and you have waited seven, you might want to make a polite inquiry about the delay. Most auctioneers have an absolutely uncanny knack for keeping consignments straight and payments properly directed, but since a sale can involve hundreds of transactions, an occasional error is understandable. Not surprisingly, the larger the auctioneer's staff, the greater the opportunity for mistakes. I once waited two months to receive the proceeds of a sale handled by one of New York's busiest galleries. When I finally questioned the delay, one of the bookkeepers said, "Oh, we closed that sale out long ago." After a good deal of searching, most of it predicated upon my furnishing the correct lot numbers and selling prices, the errors were located, and the payments, which I was told had been posted to a suspense account for unidentified consignors, were released. "Suspense" was an appropriate word, all right. If I hadn't bothered to inquire, I probably would still be watching the mailbox and soothing my impatience with excuses about how busy—but dependable—that celebrated auction house must be.

SELLING VIA THE NEWSPAPERS

Whether or not it pays to advertise your antiques depends on what you have to sell and what condition it is in. If you can accurately identify it, and especially if you can give a specific reference for it, or if it belongs to one of the currently hot collecting categories, and if it is all original and perfect, the answer probably should be yes. There is little point in paying for a newspaper ad in which you cannot be more particular than "Lovely old pink-and-white dishes" or "Beautiful old porcelain centerpiece." Most antiques are lovely and beautiful—at least to the person who bought them—and all of them certainly ought to be old, so if those are the most appropriate descriptives you can come up with, you will do much better to consider selling your things in some other manner.

An advertisement, whether for direct sale from your home or via mail order, should not only create a desire for the item but also should convey a ruthlessly honest impression of it. Which means that with the exception of rarities that are acceptable even in less than mint condition—which you probably would not resort to advertising in the first place—the items that you advertise ought to be perfect. If they aren't, you are going to have to spell out the flaws, and in the brief context of an ad these will gain undue emphasis. There are ways to sell "as is" antiques: give them to an auction, where condition sometimes has little effect on price, or take them to a flea market and be satisfied to turn them over at cost. But don't expect to move them successfully through advertising, because the mere mention of a defect or repair is sufficient to discourage most prospective buyers. And if you don't mention it, whether the buyer orders the item through the mail or makes a special trip to examine it, disappointment will magnify a flaw into something much more prohibitive than it might be.

The fastest and least expensive place to advertise probably is the classified columns of your local newspaper. Don't assume that no one but you ever reads them. You probably would be surprised at the responses your ad might draw. And not entirely from nearby antiques dealers either. The number of auctioneers and prominent antiques dealers who have pickers combing the countryside in their behalf is one of the great incalculables of the business. It must be enormous. Plus which, you never know how many antiquers will be passing through your area on their way to or from a show or flea market. One of the first things the sharp ones do is scan the merchandise offerings in the local daily. In fact, if you know that a major show or a large flea market is going to be held in your vicinity, schedule your advertisement to run at that time. You might as well take advantage of the crowds attracted by the main event. Some of the curious are certain to be looking for an auction or a garage sale to broaden their shopping experience, and if your advertisement suggests it, they'll get in touch with you too. Collectors' publications reach subscribers all over the world. *The Antique Trader Weekly* carries the largest number of advertisements for name collectibles. The pages of periodicals such as *Hobbies* are filled with offerings of fine antiques.

If you don't want to be bothered by strangers ringing your doorbell at their convenience rather than yours, don't include your address in your ad. List a telephone number, not forgetting your area code, or rent a post-office box and let potential customers contact you by mail. Either way, you eliminate a lot of curious and casual browsers. Since more people will place a telephone call in answer to an ad than will bother to write a letter, use of the post-office box will tend to reduce the number of responses that you receive. On the other hand, with the exception of some correspondence-happy types who will write about almost anything, the replies that you receive through the mail probably will come from more serious buyers. If you do include a telephone number, be sure to give a name—a first name will do—just so people who are interested can ask for someone definite instead of going through a whole spiel and then finding out that they only have been talking to the baby-sitter. Don't depend on your plan to sit by the telephone day and night the instant your ad breaks. Sooner or later Junior or Uncle Joe is going to answer for you, and you will wish you had taken advantage of this simple hint. Besides, a telephone number or a post-office-box number is terribly impersonal. Simply adding "Marie" to your listing can make all the difference in the world. People can relate to "Marie," which is something that they find quite difficult to do when faced with "P. O. Bx 509." Antiques is a strangely personal kind of business, so personalize your ad at least that much. So help me, it helps.

Using a post-office box as your address for all correspondence connected with the sale of antiques also offers some protection against robbery. If it is at all practical, you might consider renting a box at a post office in a nearby town rather than at the station serving your residence. There's no need to become paranoid about the problem of theft, but there's nothing wrong with using a little foresight. Friends who for many years have been selling antiques by mail continue to use their home address in their advertisements. They also have installed elaborate and expensive alarm systems, and have taken to storing their better things in a vault. "If we were starting out today," they admit, "we'd choose the anonymity of a postal box, but we've published our address for so long, there's nothing to be accomplished by withdrawing it now." Even if you think that your first ad is likely to be your last, you might want to bear in mind that fine antiques have become highly negotiable, and that thanks to the miracles of modern transportation, the bronze that was lifted in Massachusetts can be sold in Oklahoma before the owner returns from an all-day auction and calls the police. Since the cost of a post-office box is negligible, you might as well do whatever you can to insure that your advertisements attract customers, not thieves.

In addition to a precise description and an honest appraisal of condition, should you include the price in your ad? I think so. Especially if you are running a classified ad rather than going into one of the specialized publications. Someone who feels that your price is too high is not going to buy the item anyway, so you might as well not be bothered by his inquiry. If your price is at all reasonable, you probably will receive more responses than you can keep track of. Consider carefully before advertising anything at a shockingly low price. A lot of potential buyers will assume that there is something wrong with the piece, or that it is a reproduction, or is undesirable for some other reason. If you are determined to dispose of something at less than half its current market value, better withhold the price and let your respondents be happily surprised. Descriptives such as "greatly reduced," "priced below cost," "sacrifice," and other such terms will help convey your message without seeming to downgrade your merchandise.

Some dealers prefer to eliminate the prices of choice items advertised in various trade publications and simply to say "expensive," or "for the advanced collector," which means the same thing. I wish that these advertisers would have the nerve to go ahead and put down $20,000, or whatever amount they consider "expensive" to be. I don't think anyone any longer expects the prices of fine antiques acquired from a knowledgeable dealer to be "cheap," so what's the value of "expensive," except to add an extra touch of snob appeal? Good pieces do not need that sort of enhancement, while no inferior piece ever was redeemed by it. As increasing numbers of buyers acquire antiques for investment, dealers probably will become less coy about quoting prices. You don't find evasions like "expensive" and "for the advanced investor" in the stock market listings, do you?

By all means, refer whenever possible to illustrations of identical or comparable items in currently available publications, but make sure that the reference applies and that you are not making allowances that would favor your things. Especially if you advertise in one of the antiques publications, you will be expected to stand behind your merchandise; but even if you only spring for a six-dollar space in the local daily, please be accurate in your presentation.

There's nothing wrong with warming up an otherwise precise description with an occasional adjective such as "luscious," or "magnificent," or "great," or "a knockout," as long as it truly applies. Just remember that the facts are what most buyers want to know. Get them down first, then if you have room for a subjective comment to jazz up your copy, you can be as clever as you choose. Again, personalization can help. Especially if you plan an extended series of advertisements. Even a phrase as hackneyed as "Private collector offers . . ." can help. If you want to get really chatty—and some dealers are enormously successful with this approach—you might even go for an opening like "Help! My attic's caving in!"

Don't advertise that you are moving unless you actually are moving. The readers who follow antiques advertisements have a knack for recognizing repeaters and quickly learn to ignore those who "sale" under false colors. If you run a year-round basement or garage sale and you want to promote it with an occasional ad, don't try to make it sound like a once-in-a-lifetime event. Even a dealer or collector who has never before visited you will immediately recognize the situation for what it is and feel a little cheated—unless, of course, he happens to make the buy of the century, in which case you will certainly see him again, and often.

Selling by mail entails certain problems in collection and delivery. Some dealers insist that payment be made by money order or certified check. Others withhold shipment until a customer's check has cleared. If merchandise is shipped on approval and happens not to be accepted, the whole process of payment and shipment has to be repeated in reverse. This is time-consuming and frequently costly. It can also cause the seller to lose sales. He may have held an item off the market while waiting for a customer's check to clear, and then the article may be refused and returned because it doesn't satisfy the customer. If the seller has kept a waiting list of potential buyers and reapproaches them to offer the item a month or more after an initial expression of interest, he may find that they have purchased something else in the interim or that their enthusiasm is greatly diminished by the fact that someone else has, for whatever reason, rejected the piece. Never mind that they might originally have bought the item and been delighted with it. Should you find yourself in this position, the best explanation to give for the canceled sale is that the initial customer's funds proved to be insufficient. This might not entirely rekindle the buyer's interest, but at least it will not turn him off as even an ill-founded rejection would. Otherwise there is not much that a seller can do to retrieve such a situation except to keep the piece off the market for a while and advertise it later when it can get off to a clean start.

If you or someone who helps you does not enjoy wrapping things and packing them for shipment, then you might as well forget all about selling by mail, because it never will be anything but an aggravation to you. Double boxing is the best guarantee against breakage, and once you have acquired suitable cartons, it really doesn't take much more effort than single boxing. But don't just stick a packed box inside a larger box, letting it rattle around like crazy, and then pride yourself on your excellent double boxing. The whole point is to make sure that the inner box doesn't shift no matter how vigorously the package is handled. And if you don't think that your package will be vigorously handled, watch some of those "Fragile—Handle with Care" cartons getting pitched around at the post office. Plastic foam or crumpled newspaper makes a good lining for your outer carton. Allow a few inches of insulation on all sides of the main event, not forgetting the top, and pack the carton tight enough so that nothing, but nothing, moves. Even if your package does not require it, tie it around with a good sturdy cord. It will give the deliverer and your customer something to hold onto, making dropping and possible breaking just that much more unlikely.

When including individually wrapped small components such as covers, finials, washers, and the like, it is a good idea to enclose them in some bright-colored plastic or tissue so that they attract immediate attention and aren't lost in the shuffle and tossed aside with the ballast.

If you ship something on approval, be sure to ask your customer to save all original wrappings so that if he should want to return the merchandise to you, it can be properly packed for safe shipment. You'd be surprised at how many people think that a wisp of tissue paper and a shoe box are sufficient as long as the package is stamped "Insured."

When I first read some of the antiques publications, it took me a foolishly long time to figure out that "S.A.S.E." in an ad meant that the seller requested respondents to include a self-addressed, stamped envelope for reply. If you become very active in selling antiques by mail, you probably will want to make the same request. Postage can run into money. It stands to reason, doesn't it, that someone who goes along with your S.A.S.E. request receives the courtesy of an answer?

SELLING AT ANTIQUES SHOWS

In *How I Feed My Friends*, the author, Max White, writes: "There are two kinds of movies, westerns and society pictures, and, if you think about it long enough, you see that this is so." If you think about it long enough, you see that a similar distinction can be made between antiques shows. There are those that are fast-paced and full of action, with herds of customers stampeding through and sales made at breakneck speed. And then there are the "society" shows, at which the exhibitors and the customers seem to devote as much time to enjoying their tea or coffee or cocktails as they do to buying and selling antiques. Sometimes a show that ought to be a genuine Western unintentionally becomes a society show, and occasionally, though very seldom, a typical society show turns into a Western. Most indoor antiques shows large enough to accommodate 100 or more exhibitors are *supposed* to be Westerns. Those having fewer than 50 dealers *usually* are society shows.

In selecting a show in which he wishes to participate, a new exhibitor must first decide whether he will be more comfortable and more successful in a Western or in a society situation. In every region there are enough shows of each type to provide ample experimentation. But experiments can be costly, frustrating, and an extravagant waste of time and merchandise. The best way to choose a show in which you wish to participate is first to attend that show as a customer, and then, if it seems attractive, sign up for a future edition. This gives you a chance to evaluate the physical setup of the show—the size and general arrangement of the booths, the lighting, entrances, exits, and ventilation, the food and sanitary facilities for exhibitors and public—the pace of the show, the kinds of customers it attracts, the sort of merchandise displayed and sold—or unsold—as well as the caliber of the currently participating dealers.

Years ago, on the recommendation of friends, Betty and I booked a space at one of the large weekly antiques flea markets.

Only after the die was cast did we realize that we knew nothing about the event in which we were about to participate. Luckily, as it turned out, we were unable to secure space for the first weekend in the series, and were booked into the second instead. On opening day we went to the market as customers and got a firsthand look at what would be an entirely new selling experience for us. We had been accustomed to society shows, but that market that season was a definite Western. We hardly had walked past the entrance before our plans for the following week started to change. We realized that the mob that jammed the aisles would make it impossible for us to closely supervise the kind of display we usually set up at smaller shows. Immediately we decided to cut our booth in half and to concentrate on a single area instead of having customers coming at us from all sides. Then we purchased a pair of inexpensive small shoulder-strap pocketbooks, so that each of us could take cash and make change without having to work from a central cash box. This also eliminated the possibility that an ill-concealed or unconcealed and tempting money box might be stolen. We also divided our supplies of wrapping paper and paper bags so that each of us had an adequate cache at his station. Then we agreed to arrive early enough to be fully unpacked and set up before the first admission was sold. Finding that the nearest food was a block away, and expecting no relief in the market's frantic pace, we realized that it would be more convenient to pack our lunch than to have to take turns going for food, which would have left one of us alone at our booth.

Such advance consideration is ideal. Unfortunately it is not always possible. You might, for instance, want to consider exhibiting at a new show or at an established show that time and travel conditions have prevented you from previewing. If you know a dealer who has previously participated in the show, you can learn a good deal by questioning him, as long as you understand that certain factors that present no problem to one exhibitor can be real roadblocks to another. For example, a dealer who sells only jewelry might not think twice about having to carry a couple of flat closed cases up two flights of narrow stairs to an exhibition area, although a dealer who sells furniture could find that a considerable hardship.

If nothing else, the furniture dealer might want to arrange for some extra muscle at setup time, and even, perhaps, throughout the show, in case his customers also needed help.

Before signing a contract for any show at a location with which we are not familiar I always ask the manager these questions:

Is it possible to drive onto the exhibition floor? If it is, is it possible to unload directly from the car at the booth, or must merchandise be moved from an unloading area? This last involves double handling of everything and might advise against exhibiting large, heavy, or awkward-to-manage items. It also can mean that if the management does not provide hand trucks or dollies, the wise exhibitor will arrange to supply his own. In certain situations union regulations require that only authorized personnel deliver and remove merchandise, which means that you would have to trust the crew to handle your things without loss or breakage and that you might have to pay anything from a nominal tip to a standard fee, depending on the arrangements that the show manager has made.

If displays are being set up on more than one level, is the main room upstairs or down? Whichever it is, that is the floor on which to obtain space. Don't for a moment believe that all things are equal. They never are. And don't let any promoter persuade you that all booths receive equal attention. Most shoppers probably do cover the entire show, but invariably the displays in the main room get better attention. Customers might give secondary floors or subordinate rooms a single look, but they frequently will circulate throughout the main room, which means that the displays there receive multiple exposure, if only subliminally. Space in a corridor, even if it is at the principal entrance, might not be as choice as some managers suggest. Corridors are for getting from one place to another, and that is what most patrons will use them for. Sure, it's a high-traffic location, but if the traffic just keeps rushing past, you might be happier were your booth situated at one end of the hallway or the other. Remember, too, that if the show is busy and corridors are crowded, people will have trouble reaching your booth. Not a few of them will get discouraged and will keep moving. If there is a stage or balcony or other display space set apart from the main exhibition area, think twice about renting a booth there. Only if you are going to have a spectacular display that is sure to attract attention, or if your merchandise is so specialized that it will appeal primarily to a select group of collectors, are you apt to be truly successful in such a spot. There is one advantage in setting up on a mezzanine or stage, especially if you are the only exhibitor so situated—usually you will have a little more elbow room and can set up with greater freedom than you would have in a regular booth. A more favorable situation, however, is a corner location, which might allow you to stretch a little without invading your neighbor's territory. At some shows corner booths cost a bit more than others. At some corners they are worth the difference.

Is food to be sold at the show? There are advantages and disadvantages to being situated near the refreshment stand, dining room, tea shoppe, or whatever. It is true that many people pass the booth immediately adjacent to the restaurant. Not only once, but twice, or many times more. This can be very comforting, especially at a society show, where the pace is leisurely. At a busier show it can mean that you will spend a lot of time picking up sticky paper napkins and paper cups and other debris and brushing crumbs off the edges of your tables. The booths nearest the food can also become focal points for small gatherings that prolong their tea-table conversations. Unfortunately not many of the members of these groups stop talking long enough to buy your antiques. When they finally disperse, nine times out of ten they stride briskly off to shop two or three tables away. This is reflexive and should not be taken personally. Think about it when selecting your space. You might also want to remember that the booth next to the food probably won't be too far from the kitchen. Which means that in certain situations there will be constant reminders of cooking together with other manifestations of food service—noise, steam, and sometimes the inescapable vibrations of dishwashers and other equipment, not to mention the excitement of an occasional contretemps among the workers. Do not lightly assume that such things would not disturb you. For a few minutes they might not. After a few hours they can become maddening. Endured for several days, they can send some of us straight up the wall.

Will the show be open consistently during the hours of exhibition, or will there be a lunch or dinner recess? If the show closes for an hour or two, consider what you will do with yourself during that interval. Is there enough time for you to have a meal, do a little shopping, some sightseeing, your laundry? Or will you simply be stuck with some time to kill and nothing better to do than write a letter to your Great-Aunt Minnie? If that's the case, better be sure that you provide yourself with stationery. Will you have to close your booth—dust covers, lights out, and locks on? Are security provisions adequate? Is there a place nearby where you can grab a nap or a shower? And if there isn't, maybe you would like to consider the convenience of a handy motel. Many society shows schedule dinner breaks on the theory that attendance would be drastically reduced during the customary dinner hour, so that the number of admissions that might be sacrificed would be minimal. True, no doubt, but also indicative that the manager's first concern is selling admissions rather than having the exhibitors sell antiques. If there is to be a recess of any sort, by all means find out if complimentary re-entry will be accorded customers whose shopping is interrupted by the break. If not, try to arrange to get some passes for discriminating distribution to customers who were seriously interested in something but couldn't quite make up their minds before the whistle blew.

What will be the general admission charge? A fundamental question that I never thought of asking until Betty and I signed into a show that was a couple of states and an equal number of days from home. A four-day show that was promoted as the biggest thing to hit the area since the last hurricane. For four days and four nights we sat and stared at each other and at our fellow dealers. I don't think there were more than 300 admissions sold throughout the show. Why? It was a good show, with many fine exhibitors displaying an excellent range of antiques. The location was terrific. The week before the antiques show a crowd estimated at 40,000 had attended a garden show at the same arena. There was one enormous difference, and that made the difference between the success of the garden show and the failure of the antiques show. Admission to the garden show was $1. A ticket to the antiques show cost $3. Fortunately, most of those who attended the show were serious buyers, so the venture was not an utter disaster for the exhibitors, but the $3 charge ultimately cost the management many thousands in lost admissions and ruined what should have been a highly successful show. If I had known in advance that the admission was going to be so steep, I would have had second thoughts about registering for that show. There are only a few major antiques shows that can succeed on a high-admission policy. Usually, unless the show is a specialized exhibition—guns, depression glass, dolls, bottles—an admission charge that exceeds the local norm had better promise (and deliver) something extraordinary to offset the public's resistance to the price. Ask, too, if there will be an additional charge for parking at the show, and if there are any other extras. And what about free admission or reduced prices for children? Small children tend to be a nuisance at antiques shows, but their attendance frequently is what makes possible attendance by the mothers of small children. At the famous $3 fiasco, children were charged full fare. The only discount tickets available gave the lucky bearer a big twenty-five-cent advantage. Patrons told us repeatedly that their friends had been discouraged from attending the show because the admission was too steep. An additional fee for parking and the need to hire a baby sitter or bring the kiddies at $3 a head made the show prohibitively expensive.

Are electrical outlets available, and will there be an additional charge for electricity? Even if your merchandise does not require electricity for proper display, you might want to consider having a couple of spotlights to brighten your booth, especially if you happen to be next to a brilliantly lighted display. On the other hand, if that feature is going to add another $50 to your booth cost, it might be advisable to do without it. Ask yourself how much additional business you can expect to do to offset the expense. Unless there is a good chance of increasing your gross receipts by at least three times the additional charge, you might not find it worthwhile. If you are selling lamps, or feature an illuminated display case, you are going to need electricity and undoubtedly will sign up for it regardless of the cost. Or maybe you would like to consider leaving your lamps and your lighted showcase at home that time around. Whatever you do, don't assume that there will be an electrical outlet handy for your use. There might be an outlet, but it might not be terribly handy. We once exhibited in a show at which the manager assured me that every booth included an electrical outlet. Great! What he did not mention was that the outlet was in a box connected to a crossbeam twelve feet above the floor. I always carry a heavy-duty extension cord and a tangle of subordinates in my antiques show take-along, so I managed to overcome that little technicality. Some of my fellow exhibitors were less well prepared and had to do without their complimentary but unreachable electricity.

Does the management supply tables? Table covers? Pegboard? Drapes or other background? Chairs? How many? Are these items included in the cost of the booth, or will there be additional charges? Do you have a choice of table sizes? Maybe you would rather use fewer or smaller tables so that you will have space for displaying some furniture or a counter of jewelry? I think it is ridiculous to have to pay extra for chairs, but some show managers insist that they are not charging for the chairs, only renting them as a convenience for their exhibitors. I suppose it is like the meals that you are served on a flight—you pay for them, even though you may not realize that you are paying for them, because the charge is hidden in the cost of the flight. The additional $5 for a rented folding chair can be concealed in the booth rental, and most of us wouldn't blink an eye. Slap it on as a surcharge and we'll darned well bring our own folding picnic chairs, we will! Be sure that if the management is not supplying chairs, you provide some for yourself, even if you have to go out and rent them. The "rent-all" places are excellent sources for equipment that you might want for one-show or occasional antiques-show use. If you are going to do quite a few shows, you certainly will want to own your chairs, tables, and other necessaries, but if you are thinking that you might want to do only one or two shows to get your feet experimentally wet without loading up on a lot of equipment, consider renting what you need the first time or two around.

Is the building air-conditioned/heated (choice of one depending on place and time)? Don't laugh. I once booked a show in the heart of the Southland in the middle of a heat wave. "It's air-conditioned, of course?" Betty asked optimistically. I shrugged. "Well," I said, "sure"—although I was not at all sure. "I guess it would have to be. They would never schedule a show at this time of year unless the place were fully . . ." But even as I spoke I knew that I was absolutely wrong, that they not only would but could, and, in fact, had. People came and complained and swore and sweated, and, thankfully, they also purchased antiques, but they didn't stay as long as they might have if the hall had been one degree below unendurable, and by closing time the exhibitors were only heartbeats away from heat prostration. Winter weather can be equally treacherous from the dealer's point of view, although much less uncomfortable for the public. To a customer dressed for outside and spending a few hours at the show, an inadequately heated hall can be preferable to an overheated, stuffy place that browsers can't wait to get out of. Dealers, however, grow progressively colder, especially those with booths near entrances and exits. It isn't so bad to be set up near a door in the summer. In fact, it might be an advantage if air conditioning is nonexistent or inefficient. So ask about heating and air conditioning. Especially if you are thinking of signing up for one of the increasingly popular shows being booked into state fairgrounds buildings or similar facilities that originally might not have been designed for year-round use. And don't reach for reassurance in grandiose names. You can't imagine how primitive something called "Center for Contemporary Living" can turn out to be.

What is the earliest move-in time? What is the latest move-out time? If you have only two or three hours for establishing your display, you certainly will want to eliminate any complex features requiring painstaking adjustment or installation. Ditto for shows that close at 10:00 P.M., at which the management says, "Everybody out and on his way by midnight." Whatever you do, don't optimistically calculate that you will sell so much that packing and loading will be a snap. Because Betty and I love to buy, it is not unusual for us to leave a show with a larger load than we arrived with. At times I am reminded not to overpack the van in case we are lucky enough to do some healthy buying. If you also happen to be an enthusiastic shopper, you might want to observe the same precaution. At most major shows, setup time includes a day or two before the opening, with a similar after-closing allowance for moving out. One advantage of moving in as early as possible is that it will be much easier to set up your display without having to worry about interfering with your neighbors' already established booths. Also, you will be more relaxed than those who are rushing to get squared away at the last moment, which means that you will be far less likely to break or lose things. Not being pressed for time will give you a chance to have first look at other exhibits in the show, enabling you to do a little buying if you're so inclined or pick up tips that might help improve your display. One disadvantage in completing your display early is that security measures are not always as effective as they should be before a show opens. Some managers provide adequate overnight protection once the show is under way, but tend to be a little conservative with the advance guard. In such cases you might want to consider moving into the show in two stages. Set up your tables, shelves, backing, cabinets, lights the first day, then, if it is at all practical, move in your merchandise—especially the most valuable or most breakable items—on the second. And it would not be unheard of to show up with your Tiffany lampshades on your arm just before the ribbon is cut.

There is one question that you should ask yourself before signing up for any show: Do I have sufficient salable merchandise to equal twenty times my expenses for the show, and, if so, can I adequately display it at my booth, and can I efficiently transport it to and from the show? Don't think that last consideration is silly. I once watched a neighboring dealer try to dispose of a large antique trunk during the closing minutes of a show. Throughout the evening she had repeatedly reduced the price of the trunk, and as the end drew near and the trunk remained unsold, she actually began pacing back and forth and mumbling ominously. When I could no longer stand it, I asked what she was so upset about. "My brother brought this monster down for us," she explained, "in the back of his truck. But he's gone off on a hunting trip, and I don't know what to do about getting it out of here. I was so certain I'd move this darned thing, it never dawned on me I'd have to face taking it home!" Don't let that happen to you. If you have merchandise that has required special handling for delivery to a show, be sure to have equivalent help on tap to aid in its removal. There are dealers who have an uncanny ability to predict what will sell at which show, but none of them is always on target.

If the retail value of your merchandise is only about ten times your booth rent, you probably ought to consider exhibiting on a smaller scale. Perhaps you can find someone to share part of the space and part of the cost of your booth. If you don't know a dealer whom you would like to approach with this suggestion, ask the manager of the show to recommend a partner for you. Some co-ordinators are extremely good about this and feel that by including more dealers they add to the variety and balance of the show, making it more interesting for the public. Other managers frown on having dealers share space, just as certain landlords frown on unauthorized sublets. Choose carefully in casting about for some-one to share with. Betty and I once shared a booth with a young couple, their many friends, their parents and in-laws, their dog, and enough cold meats and mustard to stock a small delicatessen. There was such activity at our booth that not many customers bothered to interrupt the hullabaloo to express interest in antiques. Conviviality was high that day, but business was decidedly down, and when the dog choked on an ill-advised morsel and spat up on our needle-point-covered stool, Betty and I looked at each other and silently vowed, "Nevermore." We have subsequently shared spaces. Many times. With friendly dealers and with unfriendly dealers. Generally speaking, the friendliest dealers to share with are those whose merchandise is radically different from yours. If they sell jewelry and you don't, you probably will get along just dandy. If you sell bric-a-brac and they deal only in furniture, you shouldn't have any problem—unless, of course, one of you shows up with a dog, a legion of noisy friends, a full complement of in-laws, and about fifty pounds of salami.

The one essential in the antiques trade is merchandise. If your prices are realistic and you have the right things, you can display them on the bare floor and people still will buy them. Certain show promoters might frown on this, but there are situations in which the plain-pipe-rack approach is decidedly possible and productive—as long as you have the merchandise.

Since you probably will not want to do such a primitive display, you will need something to put your things on. If the manager does not supply tables, or does not supply all the tables that you need, you will have to arrange to have some of your own. The party rent-all services can help. At some shows tables, chairs, pegboard, showcases and display cabinets, spotlight, carpeting, ashtrays—everything—can be rented on the premises for the run of the show. At other shows the exhibitors must make arrangements with an outside agency for rental of such equipment. The rent-all services sometimes will conveniently deliver your things directly to your booth at the show. If they balk at delivering your small order, check some of your fellow exhibitors to see if they would not like to combine their requirements with yours. And don't forget to ask about table coverings while you are with the rent-all people. Not everyone has cloths that will do justice to those six- or eight-foot tables. Double-check to be sure that the rented banquet cloths have been flameproofed.

If you are going to buy tables, you probably will go for those folding six-foot aluminum ones. There are many such on the market, but they are basically of two types: A—those with leg supports that open and close with a folding angle the way old-fashioned card tables open and close; and B—those with leg supports that consist of sliding metal tongues that self-lock into position. Tables of the B type are generally stronger and more expensive than the simpler, lighter-weight A tables. They would seem to be the better choice for antiques exhibitors—or so I thought until I had a chance to road-test examples of each. Truth to tell, type B can be a bloody nuisance. These tables are tricky to open, since they must be placed face down, flat on the floor—and that means *flat,* or those metal tongues just won't groove as they're supposed to. They can be equally tricky to close. As a result of which not a few dealers have been known to drive home from shows with unclosed tables awkwardly lashed to the roofs of their cars. If a tiny bit of gravel happens to get stuck in the works, it can jam the whole mechanism. Even the most innocent application of force can lead to bent legs and a crooked table. Plus which, they lock with a tricky little pushbutton business that, when not functioning just right, could set Job to tearing his hair. Not with your simple A table. Yes, you have to be sure that those old-fashioned clamps are secure, and yes, the tops tend to be made from lighter-weight metal, which makes them easier to dent. But, folks, I never saw a dealer sweating through setup time over an inoperable A table, and I have yet to see an incompletely closed A riding home on the roof of a car. Metal tables having little drop-leaf extensions are not very practical for antiques shows. The extension flaps easily get disoriented (read: crooked), and they aren't really strong enough to trust with a load of valuable things. Wood-top tables are heavy to transport and difficult to handle, and sooner or later the tops get splintery, which means that sooner or later you do too.

Folding metal tables are available in widths up to 36 inches, but the widest table is not always the most practical. If the maximum width of your booth happens to be 10 feet, and you use a 36-inch table at either side, you are going to have a miserable little 4-foot space left open at the center, which won't give you or your customers much room. Moreover, two such tables set to form a right angle will yield a corner with a diagonal depth of 51 inches. Whatever is displayed there will be a long and awkward reach away. Twenty-four-inch-wide tables are more suitable to most booth sizes. Widths less than 18 inches are too small to provide adequate display space. In any width, tables 6 feet long are more adaptable and easier to handle than the 8-foot variety. Some show managements will provide one, two, or three tables for each booth. How many tables of what sizes you will need to complete your exhibit will depend on the available space, the merchandise you plan to show, and your use of pegboards, easels, display cabinets, showcases, and the like. A sturdy card table with folding legs makes a useful extra table for special displays or to fill an odd area in which a larger table could not be used. Because they collapse easily and are readily knocked over, most folding tray tables, snack tables, and other such unstable stands are unsuitable for antiques display. Some dealers use them to build a more interesting exhibit on top of regular tables, but I don't recommend them. It is great to get some elevation into your display, but whatever you use should be sturdy and dependable.

After you have acquired tables, you will need some cloths to cover them. Buy fabric wide enough to drape to the floor. This not only makes your booth look neat but also provides useful concealed space where cartons, wrappings, tools, and personal articles can be stored. If the material has not been flameproofed, have it properly treated or do it yourself with flame-retardant solution, which you probably can purchase or order from a hardware or paint store. Should your local source seem uncomprehending or uncooperative, try the nearest theatrical supply house, which probably stocks flameproofing compound for use on stage scenery and curtains. Not all show managements will insist that you use only flameproof fabrics in your display, but even if they don't, you should. The cost is forgettable and the reassurance factor is considerable.

If your merchandise includes whatnot stands, bookcases, curio cabinets, or other items of furniture that can also be used to display small objects, do not overload them with bric-a-brac and expect them to sell. Some customers get so involved with the contents that they fail to notice furniture. I remember a beautiful Victorian walnut whatnot that I was certain would sell at one of our first shows. Because we had bought it right, we were able to offer it at an unusually low price, and yet throughout the show it sat unnoticed while customers gradually picked it clean of the bric-a-brac with which I had crowded its shelves. Toward the end of the show the whatnot was left holding only a few items. "My goodness," said the dealer with the booth across the aisle, "when did we bring this pretty piece in?" I said that it had been right there since the show had opened and that I was surprised no one had bought it in view of its bargain price. "I'll take it," she said. "I think it's smashing. Only I don't understand how I stood here all through the show and didn't notice it before!" I realized then why neither she nor anyone else had, and I never again displayed more than a few token accessories on any piece I wanted to sell.

I keep a duffel bag packed with the following tools and supplies and drag it along to every show—I don't always need every item, but sooner or later they all come in handy: a ball of twine, a roll of masking tape, a roll of transparent tape, a package of straight pins, some blanket pins (in case a table cover needs a little help keeping a table covered), a few safety pins, a staple tacker and staples, a screwdriver, a healthy heavy-duty electrical extension cord, a pair of regular extension cords, a pair of multiple-outlet electrical connections, a scissors, some aspirin, some Band-Aids, an extra sales book, a package of unmarked price tickets, a couple of felt marking pens, a couple of extra ball-point pens, an assortment of pegboard hooks, a loop of picture wire, the last of a roll of paper towels (for dusting, polishing, last-minute cleanups), a small bottle of window cleaner, some big red "Sold" tags (very impressive —use them proudly), replacement light bulbs, a magnifying glass, a tape measure, a magnet, a hammer, assorted nails, and two large plastic garbage-disposal bags. Be assured that if you forget some of these items, you will be able to borrow most of them from a neighboring exhibitor or from the show manager or the building custodian. If you do that, you will not only acquire use of the things you need but also the instant reputation of "nuisance." So plan ahead. Then you can be the one from whom others borrow these small necessaries, and you will acquire the instant reputation of "fine person," which is far more flattering. When you ask a forgetful borrower to return your things, however, you will risk becoming a "petty person," which is less flattering but worth enduring, since you will again have all your tools and supplies ready for the next time out.

Don't forget that you will need wrapping paper and paper bags, and try to have some sturdy shopping bags available for your customers and for your own convenience in wrapping large purchases.

When you apply for space in a show, most managers will submit an exhibitor's contract for your signature. Be sure that you completely understand all of your obligations under any contract that you execute. Most of these agreements are fairly standard and not intended to be forbidding or tricky, nor is the average show manager inclined to be rigid about enforcing various contractual provisions, but it is essential to know that the manager enjoys that right. This was indelibly impressed on me at a four-day show in which we participated. The contract specified that all exhibits would be completed one hour prior to the show's opening and would not be dismantled before the show officially closed. Late on the third day one of the exhibitors, for whom the show had proved quite unsuccessful, decided that he would minimize his loss by moving out a day early. He hoped to recoup some of his expenses from the show by setting up at a local fair the following day. When the show manager discovered this, he dispatched two armed guards to the half-packed booth and advised the exhibitor that his merchandise was being impounded and could not legally be removed from the premises until the following night, after the show had closed. "You can leave any time you like," the manager advised the exhibitor, "but under the terms of your contract your things stay until the show is over." The exhibitor decided to stay the additional day, and for his time and pains made not one additional sale. Not many show managers would treat an unhappy exhibitor in this way, but it is worth remembering that an apparently simple contractual condition might grant them the right to.

YOUR OWN RETAIL SHOP

After you have participated in a few shows or sold successfully through the mail or at auction, you might feel prepared to take the big step into a little shop of your own. It looks tempting. And easy. None of the repetitive packing and unpacking that the antiques shows require. None of the advertising expense and detailed correspondence demanded by a lively mail-order operation. None of the fat commissions that the auctioneers have been collecting from the sale of your things. And you probably know a dozen dealers who are making a respectable living in the retail antiques trade. There would seem to be no reason why you shouldn't also.

The most important factor for successful operation of a retail antiques shop is not where the store is located or how minimal the rent might be, or how modest you will manage to keep all other expenses, or whether you will be open or closed on Mondays or Fridays, or even that you have accumulated an astonishing stock of fine and interesting antiques as an opening inventory. No. The one essential for survival in the retail antiques trade is sources from which you can continue to obtain antiques suitable for replenishing your stock. It isn't sufficient to open with a bang—not, at least, if you do not want to close with a whimper in six months or less. How many disappointing times I have seen a new shop unveil an exciting collection of antiques on opening day, and then, as the stock is picked over and the best pieces disappear in the first flush of business, go relentlessly downhill because the owner is unable to regularly replace quality items with items of equal quality. Faced with insufficient inventory, an antiques dealer can always cancel a show or withhold a few auction consignments or skip a couple of mail-order advertisements. But a retail shop cannot open and close at whim, depending upon the owner's mood and the status of the inventory, and hope to be successful. And nothing is more discouraging to those important repeat customers, whose consistent patronage will be the cornerstone of a flourishing shop's success, than seeing the same items displayed week after week without the occasional stimulation of some stunning new addition.

Before signing a lease for an antiques shop, consider how much time was spent accumulating the things that you own. How many hours inspecting and attending auctions. How many days browsing in antiques shops and at shows. How many weeks when not one notable acquisition was made. Would you still be able to buy in the same ways if you had to devote several hours a day to taking care of your shop? If not, then how do you plan to sustain the kind of inventory that launched you into the business? It is true that private individuals and antiques runners will sometimes bring things to you. This can be highly productive. I know one dealer who buys only in this way, and she gets some great things too. It is also highly unpredictable. A new shop will have to establish itself as a potentially worthwhile stop for runners and pickers, who count time as money. And many of the private individuals who turn up with things are not really prepared to sell them but only to take advantage of the traditional free appraisal that they expect to get from a dealer's expressed interest.

Wholesalers and importers of antiques can help solve the merchandise problem for a new retailer who has access to such people and confidence in them. Shops that rely heavily upon such sources, however, often wind up looking very much like many other shops that obtain antiques through the same channels. And wholesale suppliers, geared to large-volume business, cannot always provide the unusual or important items that would be most interesting to a selective retailer. Plus which, much as they might like to encourage new customers, many wholesalers will first offer choice pieces to the auctioneers who can buy regularly in great quantity or to retailers whose patronage they have enjoyed for years. Neither will they very often come through with the kind of sensational buy that can go a long way toward covering the expenses of a new shop. Markups are fairly well fixed and true finds are rare.

Antiques accepted on consignment can also help, but profits on consignment pieces are apt to be modest, while prices based upon an owner's demand and a seller's percentage are not usually conducive to a lot of lively sales activity.

All of which just about leaves the new retailer pretty much where he started out—dependent upon his wits and such sources as he has managed to establish in the past. How plentiful these are and how productive they continue to be will make the difference between success and failure for most new shops.

So look far into the future before you leap into the retail antiques business. Never mind how gorgeous and exciting your shop is going to look for its grand opening. Think how it is going to look when you sit down to pay the third month's rent. Or the fourth's. Things being as they are in the antiques trade, you might find it necessary to replace your hand-picked treasures with available collectibles. From there the road can quickly lead to "limited-edition collectibles," to giftwares, plants, flower arrangements, mineral specimens, "wall décor"—and before you realize what has happened, the antiques shop of your dreams has become a hodgepodge shoppe, and you aren't any longer in the antiques business. Not really. No matter what the sign in the window says.

Before resorting to such nonantiques sidelines, you might better consider adding an antiques-related feature to stimulate interest in and cover expenses for your store. If you, or someone you know—or someone you don't know whom you can meet through a classified ad or a mutual acquaintance—is expert at chair caning, clock repairs, porcelain mending, art restoration, picture framing, furniture refinishing and recovering, doll restringing and repairs, lamp electrification and rewiring, jewelry repairs, quilt mending, needlepoint, crewel embroidery, or any of a thousand other services that would be of value to your antiques customers, this can be a traffic-and-profit-building feature for your shop. In fact, if you could round up a group of people to cover all of these service bases, you probably could not only keep your customers and your landlord happy but you would also be able to afford a couple of extended buying trips that would help solve your antiques inventory problems. You would not even have to convert your shop into a general-repairs service. Just promote that feature with a sign in your window and an occasional plug in your advertising. The number of antiques sitting around in garages and basements waiting for a helping hand is sufficient to keep an army of skillful repairers busy as elves from here to eternity. The number of customers who will happily pay you anything from a token honorarium to a princely commission for helping them realize some use for "that old thing" should be sufficient to keep your shop running in the black while you keep busy running down more treasures.

An additional and valuable sideline that can enrich an antiques shop is a selection of books on antiques. General and specialized price guides, reference and appreciation books—all will sell if you give them a small shelf of display space. You don't have to stock every antiques-related book ever published. Take in a representative selection and offer your customers prompt special-order service for other titles. When you find three or four customers ordering the same book, you won't need some snappy publisher's representative knocking on your door to tell you that that title is one you should add to your regular stock. Book discounts vary from 20 to 50 percent off cover prices, with 40 percent fairly standard. You won't get rich selling antiques books in your store, but you will add income-producing interest to your shop without resorting to handmade potholders and penny candy. And as a special bonus, in otherwise idle moments you can read the books yourself—free!

Animal lovers of the antiques trade, bear with me. I love my pets too. But no matter how devoted you are to Rover or Tabby or (heaven forbid!) Simba, please don't give your creatures the run of your shop. Not all of your customers are going to share your affection or admiration for your furred or feathered friends. A barking dog might help discourage robbers, but it will discourage a lot of customers too. Laughing and saying, "Don't be afraid, they're not going to bite you" does no good at all. At the very best it makes a frightened visitor feel foolish, which adds embarrassment to fear. Hardly an attitude contributive to comfortable, relaxed browsing. On the other hand, those customers who are absolutely nuts about animals will be so enthralled with your companions that they will neglect the merchandise. If your pets cannot or will not be confined to quarters, please make other arrangements for their care and entertainment during those hours that you devote to the antiques business.

Even while you are busily engaged in operating a retail shop you can profitably diversify your business by exhibiting in an occasional antiques show, by running a mail-order ad every once in a while, and by feeding appropriate consignments to auctioneers. People interested in antiques who have never crossed the threshold of your store will be introduced to you and your merchandise via your advertisements and at antiques shows. Which is a good reason for not marking up your shop prices in order to offset the booth rent at a show or the expenses of mail-order advertising. Smart retailers often exhibit at antiques shows held in their neighborhood in order to meet new customers. If you are going to offer things at auction, either restrict your consignments to antiques that have never been displayed in your store or give them to an auctioneer whose sales are held well away from your location. Otherwise someone is certain to remember having seen this or that at your place and will feel either that he can pay less for your things by waiting to buy them at auction or that there is no profit in bidding for them at auction since they undoubtedly would be protected by healthy reserves. Even though both assumptions might be incorrect, you will probably lose your customer as a potential retail buyer *and* as a contender for your auction consignments. For the same reason it is extremely unwise to tell anyone in or out of the trade that certain auction lots were consigned by you. Let ownership be a matter of confidence between you and the auctioneer. It isn't anyone else's business. I don't know from where most buyers think all those auction lots come, but both dealers (who ought to know better) and private buyers (who are otherwise quite sensible) seem to cherish the image of antiques falling from some misty nowhere down onto the auction block. All the romance goes out of the situation if you destroy their illusions by pointing out that they might have acquired the same item at half the price had they bought it directly from your store.

Many retailers maintain a file of customers' wants. This is a very good thing to do, and such a list comes in handy when you happen to acquire something for which you have had a specific request. It should not, however, encourage you to invest in things that you would not ordinarily buy at prices other than those you would routinely pay. Some collectors are apt to come on pretty strong when they describe the wonderful things they want and the fantastic prices they would be willing to pay for them. They can talk quite differently when confronted with the object of their dreams, especially if it carries a price that is straight out of yours. No matter that you described the piece accurately. Showed true-color photographs. Made long-distance telephone calls. Sent registered letters. Paid shipping charges. Sustained travel expenses. Not to mention having paid through the nose to buy the item. If it turns out to be "just not quite" what your customer had in mind, you are both going to be disappointed. Your customer's disappointment, however, not resting on any significant financial investment, is apt to be more easily borne.

Sheffield Plate

From 1743 until the advent of electroplating, approximately a century later, the principal alternative to making wares of solid silver involved a process whereby a layer of copper was sandwiched between two sheets of silver, the three layers being fused together before the result was worked into the desired article. Since the edges of the finished piece would have shown a stripe of copper metal running through the silver borders, it became customary to work the silver sheet slightly larger than the copper so that there would be a projecting silver flap to fold over and conceal the copper stripe. On pieces having irregular borders that would have made the flap concealment impractical, a band of silver wire would be soldered to the exposed edge.

This process, which is the true process for manufacture of old Sheffield plate, was developed by Thomas Boulsover at Sheffield, England, but it was utilized by at least 125 other makers of Sheffield plate both at Sheffield and at Birmingham. In 1784, makers were legally required to register marks for Sheffield plate, which makes articles from that date forward fairly easy to authenticate.

Although the layer of silver applied in a piece of genuine Sheffield plate is much heavier than the thin film of silver that results from electroplating, just about any piece of genuine Sheffield plate will show some signs of bleeding—pinkish areas where the silver has worn thin enough to expose the copper. This is part of the appeal that Sheffield plate holds for some devoted collectors, who deplore the brazen practice of having such pieces newly replated. So if you happen to acquire such a piece and the bleeding bothers you, do yourself and them a favor and leave it alone. Especially if you would someday like to sell it.

Shirley Temple Collectibles

Those who decry the current enthusiasm for collecting dolls, dishes, and other memorabilia featuring "The World's Darling" of the 1930s, when she was, indeed, the darling of the world, ought to accept it as part of a tradition of utilizing popular folk and literary characters for decorations. Think of all the famous characters from the works of Charles Dickens who have been represented on everything from ornamental china to coffee tins. Or the countless statues and ornaments featuring heroes and heroines from Shakespeare's plays. Or characters from *Uncle Tom's Cabin*. Isn't Shirley Temple in composition as perfectly representative of the popular taste of an era as is Little Eva in Staffordshire pottery? If John Rogers had been around, I'm sure there would have been a Rogers' group of "The Good Ship Lollipop." Now, wouldn't that have been something!

Signatures

If the artists responsible for the fine objects sought by today's antiques collectors had suspected our enthusiasm for having everything signed, they undoubtedly would have been more conscientious about marking their work.

Many of us, unfortunately, are so insecure where authenticity is concerned that we are inclined to give a spuriously signed reproduction or a properly signed but defective piece preference over an unmarked but perfect original. I'll never forget the auction at which a signed Wavecrest box that had been wretchedly overpainted sold for twice as much as a perfect but unmarked Smith Brothers biscuit jar, which was presented as unsigned Wavecrest. Bidding was lively and high on the first piece. I sailed off with the second for a fraction of its worth! But, then, I am more interested in antiques and in their condition than I am in signatures.

Occasionally a reproduction is marked as such, but in some obscure way that can be highly misleading. Some new Bye-Lo Baby doll heads, for example, carry the maker's name, but placed well below a facsimile of the signature found on the originals. In fact, once this head is installed on a body, the mark that would identify it as a copy is just about, if not entirely, concealed.

Be suspicious of terribly obvious signatures on most antiques. They were the exceptions, not the rule.

Suspect paper labels too. Particularly on articles that show some signs of wear and which in the course of use would have been subjected to frequent washings. Certainly some labels did survive, but there are a lot of counterfeit labels abroad in the antiques market. And plenty of genuine labels that have been removed from authentic but damaged pieces and affixed to objects that might or might not deserve them. Perhaps the blame for such practices should be equally divided between the opportunistic merchants who undertake them and the buyers who are willing to pay premium prices for the reassurances provided by some often questionable authentication.

Silence

The hush that pervades certain museum galleries is not prompted by boredom or considerate courtesy toward fellow browsers, but is a natural response to being in the presence of wonder. Those who break this silence to exclaim that words fail them or that they cannot articulate the powerful feelings generated by the experience are actually groping for ways to reduce the moment to something manageable, familiar, not overwhelming. It is unfortunate that guided tours, tape-recorded lectures, electronic explanations, and occasional museum mavens find it necessary to invade this void with an unbroken flow of hints on what to look for in order to more fully appreciate that which the silent observer might have been breathlessly appreciating very nicely on his own, thank you. The dreadful recorded "living" dramatizations intended to revive the past are even more deadly. To make matters worse, and perhaps to try to enliven what they suspect to be a basically boring place that no one in his right mind would visit if it wasn't jazzed up with some special events, some museums toss an occasional cocktail party or fashion show amid the treasures. Surely there are better places to go to drink and to meet people and to see the latest styles. But where are we to go in search of wonder? Museums that wouldn't know what to do without all those awful "auditory aids," or without the income derived from their rentals, should consider replacing the lectures with music appropriate to the exhibits they now—often unintelligibly and usually too rapidly—drone on and on and on about. Music that wouldn't disturb the rapt silence but would only complement it. There is definitely something to be said in favor of looking at late-eighteenth-century French furnishings and art to the accompaniment of a little something by Mozart or Gluck. Vocal selections should be performed in foreign languages—preferably lost languages—or in nonsense syllables, so that no familiar words or phrases would intrude upon the silent awe that fills our minds and hearts.

See Silk Flowers

Silk Flowers

The last time I went to look at some of the porcelains at the Metropolitan Museum of Art in New York City, certain vases and bowls displayed in the room settings held gorgeous arrangements of colorful silk flowers. These bouquets were very pretty, but they frequently asserted themselves to the point of hiding their containers. I'm all for seeing antiques displayed in a functional manner, but I also like them to be displayed so that they can be seen. Which means not by artfully reduced illumination and not peeping out from beneath a big bunch of gauze poppies and organdy roses. Such self-defeating touches remind me of the grotesque recipes that were a specialty of the late Tizzie Lish, a radio comic whose hideously complicated instructions usually ended with such simple advice as "Throw everything out the window and open a can of salmon!" There are situations for which Tizzie Lish certainly had the best possible solution.

Snobbery

A sin of the small-time antiques dealer. Most of the really important antiques dealers whom I have met are not at all snobbish. Even if they wanted to be, their enthusiasm wouldn't let them. Tyros sometimes feel obliged to put on airs, but don't let them put you off. It's only because they're young. Give them time. They'll learn.

Arrogance sometimes is a refuge of dealers and auctioneers with questionable merchandise or business practices. If that is the case, you have an additional good reason for not buying from them.

Snuff Bottles, Oriental

If you don't believe that a majority of those Chinese snuff bottles on the market today are brand spanking new, take a look at the little dippers and see if they show any signs of use.

These bottles used to be sold in what I came to call the "auctioneer's assortment," which consisted of two figural bottles (often an old man on an elephant and an old woman on an elephant), two of "Peking" glass, which certainly never saw the city limits of that old town, two in imitation carved ivory, two with beads of presumed turquoise and coral, two in imitation cinnabar lacquer, two in Rose Medallion–type porcelain, and two in amber or jade or rose quartz or whatever the color code of the day might be. By trickling one or two into each auction a clever auctioneer could realize significant profits on these little numbers. Those who just put them all out at once as a "collection of antique snuff bottles" sometimes fared less well. I often wonder how those who paid something close to antiques prices feel about their treasures now that similar snuff bottles are showing up in the Oriental specialty stores and gift shops and department stores and even at the flea markets. It certainly would make me sad to think that for a few more dollars I could have bought a real antique snuff bottle . . . or inro . . . or netsuke . . . or . . .

Spider

A crisscross crack—as distinguished from a line, which is a single-line crack—in glass or porcelain. A spider often results from stress and can be caused by temperature shock in the firing or annealing. It can even happen to pieces in the dishpan or displayed on a windowsill.

A very superficial spider is common in the glazed underside of a piece of decorated porcelain, and probably occurs during the additional firing used to set the decoration. Most often these cracks go no deeper than the surface glaze, in which case the porcelain should not be considered to be damaged. An otherwise perfect piece with an enormous spider in the glaze will still ring like a bell if you tap it. But a lot of people will insist that a crack is a crack, so, as a rule, it is prudent to avoid porcelains with a spider, even though you know it represents only a minor defect rather than a serious damage. If you know that the spider is only glaze deep, and you would like it not to be on the underside at all, you can eliminate it by having the glaze ground off in the offending area. You will be left with a rough patch of unglazed porcelain, and the whole business might be more trouble or expense than the results would justify, but it is one possible solution. Some crafty types conceal porcelain spiders by overpainting, but that is, to me, an obvious and often unattractive stratagem. I think the best thing to do if you own a piece with one of these superficial spiders is to ignore it. If it begins asserting itself by looking dirty or discolored, a brief bath in chlorine laundry bleach will clean it into near invisibility. And don't let anyone bully you into thinking that the piece is broken if it only has a spider in the glaze.

Spiders in glass articles are something else again. Most often found in multilayered glasses, they are caused by the unequal expansion of different metals. Often difficult to detect unless the crack is exposed to light passing through the article, such a spider significantly lessens the appeal and value of what might otherwise be a desirable piece of glass. The best thing to do about spiders in glass is to avoid acquiring pieces that have them. The best way to do this is to carefully examine the article in good light and to further check it with light passing through it. Use a flashlight if there is no other light suitable for this.

See Tongue Depressor

Stein, Gertrude

In *The Autobiography of Alice B. Toklas* Gertrude Stein wrote:

> *Gertrude Stein says that if you are way ahead with your head you naturally are old fashioned and regular in your daily life. And Picasso adds, do you suppose Michael Angelo would have been grateful for a gift of a piece of renaissance furniture, no he wanted a greek coin.**

So considered, the appeal of some of today's collectibles becomes a lot easier to understand.

* Gertrude Stein, *The Autobiography of Alice B. Toklas* (New York: Random House, 1933).

Stevens and Williams

The name of this famous English glassmaking company is rapidly becoming the new catchall for unidentified examples of Victorian art glass. "Probably Stevens and Williams" is getting to be such a common descriptive phrase for pieces that cannot be otherwise authenticated that it is almost meaningless. I have for years been allergic to the term "unsigned Loetz" as a designation for anything from unmarked Tiffany glass to iridescent Czechoslovakian pieces or Imperial's stretched "jewels." The latest thing, obviously, is to forget about "unsigned Loetz" and concentrate on "probably Stevens and Williams." The Stevens and Williams company did sign some glass with an acid-stamped fleur-de-lis that looks very much like the signature used on Steuben glass. I wish that those who offer unauthenticated Stevens and Williams pieces would be considerate and use the word "type" after the name instead of the word "probably" before it.

Stiegel, Henry William

In 1765, after having operated another glassworks for two years, Henry William Stiegel opened his first plant at Manheim, Pennsylvania, and soon built it into the most productive glass house in the North American colonies. Stiegel's personal history has all the elements of a typical rags-to-riches-to-rags saga. He was twenty-one when he arrived in Pennsylvania from Germany. He first worked at and subsequently purchased his father-in-law's ironworks, where he developed a ten-plate stove that stood free of the wall and served for cooking as well as heating. The ironworks eventually became the site of Stiegel's first glass factory. Stiegel helped lay out and found the town of Manheim, where, in addition to his glassworks, he built a lavish home complete with private chapel from which he sometimes preached. To man his rapidly expanding enterprises Stiegel brought many glassmakers from Europe, and eventually employed well over 100 workers at one Manheim plant. In order to finance his overextended business Stiegel finally sold his fine estate, and after the money ran out and the glassworks failed, he spent the final decade of his life in relative obscurity working as a caretaker and as a schoolmaster. While he was still operating the ironworks, Stiegel's preference for a more luxurious life-style than that favored by his plain-living Pennsylvania neighbors earned him the nickname of "Baron." The nickname stuck—and, indeed, it has stayed with Stiegel for more than two centuries, since some authorities persist in referring to Stiegel as "Baron," and even occasionally add an aristocratic and superfluous "von."

Stiegel's own carefully maintained records show that the Manheim glassworks produced some items in quantities as large as 8,000 and 9,000. These impressive statistics have been used to encourage beginning collectors in the pursuit of Stiegel glass. Don't convince yourself that every little piece of colored pattern-molded glass was produced at the Stiegel works. If you do, you are probably going to be inaccurate by at least 50 years. If there is any genuine Stiegel glass around these days, it is in museums and private collections. Go ahead and appreciate those beautiful nineteenth-century Midwestern pieces for what they are. But stop calling them Stiegel.

Other Stiegel-type articles that keep turning up on the antiques trail are vases and other containers of aquamarine bottle glass, usually bubbly and decorated with a carefully or crudely etched scene of fishermen in a boat. Calling these Stiegel can put you off by 150 to 200 years. Surely no one wants to be all that inaccurate!

Enthusiastic and optimistic collectors have been known to acquire—sometimes at considerable cost—examples of contemporary Mexican glass, which often resembles eighteenth- and nineteenth-century American pieces. Chalk it up to wishful thinking. Since there are plenty of shops around that sell this inexpensive glass for what it is, there seems little point in paying a premium price for it just because it resembles the Stiegel glass pictured in the antiques books.

Streisand, Barbra

Her enthusiasm for antiques helped to glamorize collecting in quarters that otherwise might never have dreamed of getting into the field.

See Stein, Gertrude

Supply and Demand

It's more than just a law of economics. In the antiques trade it is a fact of life. Anyone who loves old things so passionately that he loses sight of this can expect to lose his shirt along with it.

Swap Meet

In some areas a colloquialism—and a euphemism—for "flea market." I have been to hundreds of swap meets, but only once did anyone suggest an actual exchange of merchandise. What usually gets swapped at a swap meet is your money for someone else's old things.

T

Tag Sales

There are three kinds of tag sales of interest to antiquers. The first is really a glorified—or not so glorified—garage sale, which for some reason is not called a garage sale but a tag sale. The second type of tag sale is a reduced-price sale held by an antiques retailer or wholesaler in order to move inventory. The third is a household sale, usually run by a team of professionals who establish prices, advertise and supervise the sale, and take a percentage of the proceeds for their services.

Aside from the difference in name, the principal distinction between a garage sale and a garage-sale-type tag sale is that many of the tag sales are perpetual. In such cases there is apt to be a somewhat larger selection of merchandise than the average garage sale offers, with some furniture and a few higher-priced items in addition to the usual garage sale standbys. Most continuing tag sales have fairly permanent signs—wood or metal instead of the customary cardboard placard that announces the more ephemeral garage sale. At many of the perpetual tag sales, prices are not low, and seldom are they negotiable.

What usually happens at a tag sale of the second type is that the dealer places a special tag on all the merchandise that he wants to reduce. Sometimes the ticket is in two parts, either or both of which carry the price and a description or identifying number for the item. If you want to purchase the piece, you tear off the buyer's portion of the tag, pay the price and claim the item. Sometimes the owner will mark further reductions on the tags as the sale progresses, or will announce special discounts or prices applicable for limited periods. At a really good tag sale of this kind it is not unusual to find buyers swapping tags or buying them from each other—often at a significant profit.

The household tag sale is becoming increasingly big in the suburbs, and while one might yield a fine antique or two, most feature recent useful or decorative items for which the sales specialist asks —and receives—healthy prices. Quite a few dealers have established mutually beneficial understandings with tag-sale promoters who reward them with advance word of choice pieces in upcoming sales. In such cases the sale will have been quite thoroughly shopped well in advance of its opening, leaving the general public and less-favored dealers to scrap it out amid the leftovers. If you can curry such favor with one of the tag-sale operators, you too could benefit from having first refusal of the treasures in future sales. If you don't think that a chocolate cake or a dozen green orchids would do the trick, just come right out and offer a healthy finder's fee over and above the cost of the item on whatever you acquire through such recommendations.

Therapy

Many collectors and dealers begin buying and selling antiques as a form of therapy. Their doctors frequently encourage this. And why not? It gets the patients out of the house, which is usually desirable. It gives them something to look forward to, which is essential to survival for any of us. It encourages new contacts with people, most of whom are friendly and supportive, which is a lot better than dragging along with the generally limited group of relatives and friends whose antagonisms might have contributed to the need for therapy in the first place. It provides an inexhaustible field for investigation, which is more challenging than trying to solve the daily crossword puzzle. It fosters independence of thought and action, which is necessary for self-realization and personal maturity. It demands early rising and busy days, which is preferable to oversleeping, brooding, and being addicted to the late-late-late-late TV show. It transforms the ho-hum of everyday life into an endless treasure hunt complete with occasional tangible rewards to prove that all is not fantasy. It requires good health, which discourages hypochondria, melancholia, headache, and the common cold. In addition to all of which, it can also be financially profitable.

Some caution must be exercised, however, that the cure does not become a curse. Compulsive behavior of any type can be devastating.

See Greed

Thonet Brothers

Of Vienna. The bentwood people. They were not the first to make bentwood furniture—possibly not even the ancient Egyptians were the *first*—but they were the first to succeed in adapting the wood-bending processes to mass-production techniques.

Someone who invariably knows about such things once informed me that the name is correctly pronounced to rhyme with "sonnet," but if you pronounce it that way instead of rhyming the final syllable with "day," hardly anyone will know to whom you are referring—which makes this one of those unfortunate matters about which it probably is just as well to be incorrect.

See Parke-Bernet

Thrift Shops

Two kinds of stores are called thrift shops. One is operated to benefit a charity, or charities, is staffed mainly by volunteers, and is stocked largely by donations. The other is basically a secondhand store, privately operated as a profit-making enterprise. Although antiques can sometimes be found in both, it is important to distinguish between the two. If a shop's name doesn't make its status perfectly clear, go ahead and ask if the store is a charity shop or a private business. A secondhand store is still a secondhand store, you know, even if it has "thrift" in its name. Any real charity shop will be happy to identify its beneficiary. The charity-supporting shops are the real thrift shops. The others are not only uncharitable, but many of them aren't even especially thrifty.

The best charity shops for the avid antiquer are those supporting causes that appeal to elderly and wealthy donors, because that's where most of the real goodies come from. Shops that are run to benefit hospitals, settlement houses, religious activities, libraries, and museums are much more likely to receive donations from the stately homes of your community than are those contributing to some of the more contemporary causes, such as birth-control programs or the rehabilitation of ex-addicts—although the recent phenomenon known as "radical chic" caused a degree of rub-off in favor of some of the more radical causes. If you want to know where the rich and mighty of your town are contributing their treasures, and you happen not to be on a first-name basis with any of them, take a look at the furs and the formal attire in the charity shops. The better the quality—although not necessarily the condition—of the donations in these categories, the better are your chances of one day happening upon a choice piece of furniture or jewelry or bric-a-brac.

Some charity shops have a schedule according to which new donations are put on sale. Knowing it can save a determined shopper a lot of time and effort. If your particular favorite happens not to maintain such a schedule, your chances of making a really fine buy depend upon: (1) luck; (2) persistence—being on the threshold every day when the shop opens, for instance, or following some similarly dogged routine; and (3) charm—which in Basic English means persuading the manager or one of the clerks that you are such a steady and reliable patron that any treasures in which you would be interested should be tucked away in the office or under the counter until your next visit. Some successful charity-shop shoppers have even been able to wangle personal telephone calls or notes when something truly special turns up. If you can manage such treatment—usually a reward for a fairly sustained period of generous patronage—consider yourself blessed, and don't turn down too many proffered treasures in succession unless you are willing to risk demotion to the "Oh"—shrug—"hello" status the next time you stop by.

Price bargaining is a ticklish proposition in most charity shops. Some managers will give antiques dealers or favored customers a fixed or special discount every time out. Others are adamant about holding the price line unless an item remains unsold for a certain time or until the shop has one of its periodic sales. Some charity shops hold regular half-price sales on all merchandise in a particular category. Others consistently maintain a reduced-price table or display marked-down things in a special cabinet or show window. It's up to you to find out what the procedure is. Almost without exception, the price of the most expensive item in the shop will be open to a reasonable amount of negotiation, particularly if there is a significant gap between its price and those of most of the other things on display. If you are genuinely interested in the one article bearing a $500 price tag, and everything else is marked under $100, you stand an excellent chance of getting that $500 shaved a little —maybe quite a lot. Certainly it will do no harm to try. Politely. Same goes for a large piece of furniture in a crowded store or in one principally devoted to clothing and jewelry. Some managers will sacrifice hundreds of dollars just to get the darned thing out of the place fast!

Those shops with a weekly or monthly mark-down policy generally are the least willing to make special price concessions. But if you can find out that an item is soon due to be marked down, you might be able to buy it at the lower price a few days to a week before the reduction would be official. If a shop has a dating code —and most do—it usually does not take the talents of a James Bond or Mata Hari to crack it. Many shops simply mark the article with the date at which it went on sale. Some try to confuse you by using roman numerals—which is kind of silly once everyone realizes what the game is. Speaking generally, you can disregard most of the zeros and "X"s used as prefixes and suffixes to what otherwise would be a perfectly obvious date. Other markings might identify the benefiting charity or a donor's account number. Some shops color-code their price tags—white for January, blue for February, pink for March, yellow for April, and on through the spectrum of the year. You don't have to be a genius to separate February's blue bargains from April's golden arrivals, or to know that come May, all remaining pink March prices are scheduled to be halved.

One caution: especially in the charity shops consistently receiving the choicest donations, check carefully for "as is" antiques. The "as is" frequently is the reason a particular piece wound up in the donations box in the first place. Some shops automatically mark all things "as is," even when there is no apparent damage, in order to protect themselves against returns. Since many charity shops maintain a strict "all sales final" policy, be sure the articles you buy are in such condition that you would want to keep them. If you happen to pull a lulu of a mistake and greatly overpay for something defective, don't be too shy about trying for a refund. No matter what the signs say, many managers are responsive to a just and reasonable approach.

A word to the wise: never inquire about a price concession on any item until you are sure that you want to buy it. Most charity shops are managed and manned by volunteers whose reaction to numerous requests for special prices on subsequently unpurchased things can run the gamut from hysteria to rage. Save your ammunition for those occasions when you are out for big game, which is when you will want, and most often receive, generous consideration.

And don't forget to look at the books in any charity shop. Often priced and shelved without regard for potential value, old and rare books can represent the best buys on the premises.

Tiffany, Louis Comfort

His has become a magical name. Perhaps the most magical name in American antiques. People who never heard of Philadelphia porcelain manufacturer William Ellis Tucker will respond to the mention of Tiffany. Those to whom Myer Myers is only the name of one of the cops in the 87th Precinct novels instead of an important American eighteenth-century silversmith immediately recognize "Tiffany." They might tend to associate Louis Comfort Tiffany with the jewelry business that his father founded. Or with some perfectly dreadful lamps that neither Tiffany nor any of his associates would or could have had anything to do with. They might not think of Tiffany in conjunction with pottery vases or enameled boxes, but the famous scenic windows, the iridescent art glass and bronze desk sets mean Tiffany to them, and that means quality, and in today's market it also means big money.

Probably because so many Tiffany pieces bear his name or initials, there is a widespread misconception that Tiffany personally made many of the Tiffany glass items. But he did not. What he did was make it possible for others to produce these remarkable pieces by bringing together artists and workers, by supplying financial backing, discriminating taste, imagination, impeccable standards and high-class merchandising methods which he was not beyond boosting with an occasionally flamboyant bit of public relations.

The first piece of Tiffany glass that I acquired was a footed salt dish for which I paid $57.50, and which I later sold for $57. So much for the fantastic profits to be made by dealing in Tiffany glass. The second piece I bought was a beautiful iridescent gold bowl with a deep stretched rim. I paid $250 for it and was subsequently delighted to sell it for $250. At least I broke even on that one. As far as I was concerned, the Tiffany business was definitely looking up. Just to prove my point, I paid $150 for a Tiffany glass candlestick lamp with an exquisite miniature chimney that was as pretty as a lavender hyacinth. I was so enthralled with the chimney that I was willing to forgive an interior crack in the candlestick base. Not many prospective buyers felt as I did, however, and after a memorable series of disappointments, I sold the lamp at a forgettable $10 profit. I then acquired a small Zodiac-pattern inkwell from one dealer and a matching pen tray and blotter ends from another. I think that all three items (I will not count a pair of blotter ends as two pieces, although I know dealers who do) represented an investment of $125. That time I got lucky and made $35 on the deal. That was more like it! Next I bought a floor-lamp base—a good one. Only thing wrong with it was that one little rosette was missing from the adjustable shade loop. A trifle, I thought, until I tried to replace it. I paid $140 for the lamp base, and sold it for $190 after I gave up trying to find the proper rosette for it. In its way that too was a mistake, just as each of my other transactions in Tiffany had been.

Let's look at my record. I started wrong. I was anxious to have a piece of Tiffany glass—any piece of Tiffany glass. So I bought one that seemed relatively inexpensive. Actually, especially at that time, I paid more than I should have for a piece that still has not appreciated much. The salts and nut dishes and finger bowls and other gold tablewares are the most available examples of Tiffany glass and have increased in value only slightly while prices for important Tiffany pieces have soared.

Although an infinitely more exciting piece, the gold bowl was a similar mistake. It had great color and smashing iridescence. But, as I discovered, the only customer for such pieces was someone in very much the same position I had been in when I bought it—a beginning collector who wanted a showy example of Tiffany glass and didn't want to spend $500 or $600. Today the bowl might bring $350 or $400 *if* a new collector could be found who would prefer to shell out that much for a bowl instead of applying the money to the purchase of a more significant Tiffany article. Some of the pieces bringing $500 when I bought the bowl now hover around the $1,000 mark and a few have gone considerably higher.

The lesson of the candle lamp is simple: just about everyone wants Tiffany, and almost anyone will pay a fair price to obtain a good piece in good condition, but a damaged, defective, repaired, or incomplete article is usually an overpriced and unwise acquisition. With rarest exceptions, an imperfect piece of Tiffany will be a poor buy. The rationalization that if the item were perfect it would be worth many times the asking price absolutely does not apply here. Most Tiffany collectors would happily pay the higher price in order to obtain a perfect piece. With rarest exceptions, they will not be interested in a defective piece at any price. To ignore this is to ignore one of the principal attractions that Tiffany's works hold for those who appreciate, admire, and acquire them—the perfection with which Tiffany's creations were executed in the finest materials. It is true that the Tiffany Studios used to sell damaged pieces at reduced prices and that glass that otherwise might have been considered defective was often decorated with touches of engraving to disguise the elimination of the imperfection. Pointing this out will not greatly impress a collector who wants his Tiffany to be mint. He wants perfection, not bargains. If bargains were his principal interest he would be buying depression glass. Instead he is buying Tiffany. It is one status symbol that delivers the goods. Emotionally. Esthetically. And financially. That being so, he is probably not going to be terribly impressed with a cut-down piece at a cut-rate price. More than in any other category of antiques, complete original and perfect condition is essential to successful buying, collecting, and selling Tiffany articles. If the candle lamp for which I eagerly paid $150 had not been damaged I could have sold it at double or triple the price. As it turned out, I was finally well satisfied to take a token profit that I could invest in a piece in proper condition.

I made a small profit on the desk pieces, but they also were related to an error in judgment. When I bought the small Zodiac inkwell, another dealer offered me the largest Zodiac inkwell mounted on a large Zodiac tray. A handsome piece and much harder to obtain than the several items for which I gladly had spent $125. The price for the more unusual piece was the same—and I turned it down! I didn't think I should invest so much in

Tiffany desk articles. How insignificant was the $35 that I finally pulled out of the items I bought. I could have realized a healthy profit on the better piece.

With the floor-lamp base I made a different sort of mistake. I gave up too soon and for too little. I worried about a missing rosette when I should have concentrated on searching for a suitable shade. If I had not chickened out, I could have made something quite desirable out of the floor lamp. I would have had the pleasure of using it for years, and I probably could have sold it at any time for substantially more than I let it go for. Proper shades for that particular base are not impossible to obtain. This is not true of suitable shades for all Tiffany lamp bases. It is risky to buy bases for Tiffany lily lamps with the expectation of someday acquiring a set of lily shades. Easily broken, often improperly matched, these shades seldom survive in completely mint sets. When they do, they seldom find their way into the general marketplace. One dealer who has been stockpiling Tiffany lily shades for years simply will not sell them except installed on a completed lamp. Another will sell one set only after a replacement set has been acquired. In view of the lily-shade famine, it would be prudent to be certain that shades are available before investing in one of the fixtures requiring them. As one expert put it, "The easiest way to get three shades for a triple-lily base is to buy a seven-lily lamp that has four shades missing."

The spectacular price rises of Tiffany lamps have been widely reported, even in such unlikely places as whiskey advertisements and bank promotions. Less well known, perhaps, but equally impressive has been the appreciation in Tiffany enamels and Tiffany pottery. Some of the more important Tiffany candlesticks now bring prices in the thousands, and the growing popularity of collecting these examples of Tiffany's work will probably keep pushing prices higher. Tiffany's small bronze animal paperweights can still be acquired reasonably and can be expected to increase in value as prices for other Tiffany items rise. Certainly, good examples of Tiffany pottery, any of the unusual candlesticks, or the small Tiffany animals would represent a more interesting and more promising investment than would the more routine examples of Tiffany's iridescent gold glass.

The Tiffany flower-form vases are currently having an astonishing wave of popularity with an appropriate increase in price. The paperweight vases and other more complex examples of Tiffany glass have been beyond the reach of all but the most advanced collectors for several years. Because of which, those little gold salts and ordinary iridescent bowls and cracked candle lamps seem increasingly desirable at their appreciably lower prices. Those who would acquire Tiffany items for their personal pleasure or for potential profit ought to remember that the pleasure and profit in Tiffany pieces usually depend upon perfection. No matter what is paid for a choice piece of Tiffany today, bought and kept in good condition, it will look like a bargain in the future.

Tongue Depressor

If you spend a lot of time looking down into vases and pitchers and other things difficult to see into, you might find it worthwhile to acquire one of those flashlights that doctors use to look down into a patient's throat. The tongue depressor that extends from the flashlight will carry the illumination down into the vessel you are inspecting, and maybe you will be the lucky one to say "Ah!" Or maybe you will see that it has been repaired—or ought to have been.

Transportation

Some who claim to be in the antiques trade are more precisely in the transportation business—carrying the same merchandise back and forth, from shop to auctioneer, from show to show. They seldom sell anything, largely because their prices are too high or their offerings too slim. If transportation is going to be their principal business activity, they probably could do much better if they would forget all about antiques and concentrate on light trucking.

This is not to be confused with "running." Runners sell!

See Running

Tucker Porcelain

The first porcelain factory in the United States to produce chinawares of quality equal to the imports that dominated the American market was founded in 1825 by William Ellis Tucker in Philadelphia.

Beset by technical and financial difficulties, and faced with definite preference for articles of foreign manufacture, the Tuckers unsuccessfully appealed to the Federal government for aid, both in direct financing and through an increase in the duty on imported porcelain. After thirteen years and several management changes—although always including Tucker or his younger brother, Thomas, as part of the company—the factory was closed.

Because Tucker china was intended to satisfy a market devoted to Sèvres porcelain, many pieces are designed and decorated in the French manner. Less refined than Sèvres, Tucker china is often mistaken for Old Paris porcelain, while, at the same time, many French pieces have been incorrectly attributed to the Tucker factory.

There are two clues to the identification of Tucker porcelain. The first and easiest is simply that all Tucker decorations were hand-painted. No transfer decorations were used at the Tucker factory. The second clue is that when Tucker china is held to the the light, most pieces show a lovely soft green translucence. Now, not every piece of porcelain having a green translucence is genuine Tucker, and not even all genuine Tucker pieces display this characteristic. But if the shapes are right, and the decoration seems proper, and the green glow shows when light passes through the porcelain, you have three factors favorable to attribution. And don't grow discouraged if you make a few mistakes along the way to becoming a Tucker expert. Professionals do it all the time. Only recently an important antiques dealer advertised an elaborate Old Paris urn that he freely admitted had several years earlier been sold as Tucker.

Genuine Tucker pieces are currently bringing good prices—much higher than those indicated in some of the antiques price guides—and probably will enjoy a gigantic rise in conjunction with America's bicentennial celebration.

Turquoise

To the Indians of southwestern United States turquoise stones possessed many of the same esthetic, medicinal, and magical properties that the Chinese attribute to and admire in jade. In both American Indian and Chinese folklore there are references to heavenly mountains of turquoise or jade.

Individual preferences vary greatly, but the blue stones mottled by lacy black veining are among the most favored kinds of turquoise.

Type (as in "Tiffany-Type")

A catchall word that makes a convenient crutch when describing antiques that cannot be more positively attributed. I wish that some auctioneers and all self-styled experts would occasionally lean on it.

U

Use

What most of today's buyers want from their antiques. Which is why practical furniture, lamps, clocks, rugs, mirrors, pictures, and other decorative items are easier to sell at higher prices than some of the better pedigreed objects that can only sit around waiting to be polished or dusted.

V

Vacuum Cleaner

Can your vacuum cleaner be set to expel as well as inhale? If so, you can use it to blast the dust from the involved interstices in a deeply carved piece, such as an Oriental stand or an elaborate picture frame.

Once you have the dust out of the depths, you can finish the more accessible spots with a few swipes of a virginal paintbrush.

Value

Probably the most often asked question in the antiques trade is "What's it worth?" It is difficult to answer.

Some articles can be appraised on the basis of intrinsic value. The materials from which they are made have a basic market price that can be used to calculate approximate worth. We frequently hear auctioneers cry that the bid for a silver piece has not yet reached the price it would bring if sold for scrap. The intrinsic worth of objects of gold, silver, or including precious and semiprecious stones can be measured rather precisely. For that matter, so could the scrap-metal values of copper, brass, iron, and on and on and on. But estimates of worth based upon intrinsic value can be very misleading. When I was in the fourth grade I remember being shocked to learn that the various chemical components of the human body had a market value of about 99 cents—an estimate that made no allowance whatsoever for the things that folks like Einstein, Picasso, and Gypsy Rose Lee were able to do with their 99 cents' worth. That is where extrinsic value comes in.

An article can acquire extrinsic worth in so many ways that consideration of them boggles the mind. Anything from who made it to when he made it and how many of it he made and why and where it was sold—or if it wasn't sold—and who purchased it, and who else perhaps owned it, and where it was displayed—or hidden, for that matter—and most of all, who wants it and how much it is wanted at that precise moment.

Which means that the only sensible answer to "What's it worth?" is "Whatever someone is willing to pay for it." This sounds like a terrible evasion, but it is the only realistic answer, and anyone who suggests otherwise is being misleading.

It is not the seller, whether antiques dealer or auctioneer or housewife running an annual garage sale, who establishes the value of an item. It is the buyer who shells out hard cash to acquire the article who thereby establishes that at that time, in that place, that particular item is worth that much to him. Never mind what the appraisers say, or the antiques price guides. If the most that anyone is willing to pay to acquire something is $100, all of the citations from all of the experts and books in the world will not make it worth $1,000. Much comfort, however, can be taken from the fact that the market for fine antiques is today a sellers' market. It is much easier to find buyers who will pay fair prices for good things than it is to find good things to sell.

See Supply and Demand

Van Briggle Art Pottery

One of the earliest art potteries established in western United States was founded in 1901 in Colorado Springs, Colorado, by Artus Van Briggle. Van Briggle had been a decorator at the Rookwood Pottery, but moved from Cincinnati to Colorado Springs in search of a climate that might prove more favorable to his health. Unlike much of the earlier Rookwood pottery that he had worked on, Van Briggle's pottery featured molded rather than glaze decoration and a rather velvety mat finish.

I remember being taken to the Van Briggle Art Pottery when I was twelve. Visitors were ushered into a large, airy room in the middle of which a potter sat forming shapes out of clay thrown onto a spinning wheel. The wet clay was creamy beige, but the finished pieces on display in the showrooms were vivid turquoise and rich burgundy. Oddly enough, although the demonstrations of pottery being formed on the wheel were the featured element of the tour, most of the pieces that we saw appeared to have been molded rather than thrown. My uncle, Ben Berg, was then busy raising prize roses, so he purchased a Van Briggle centerpiece with a figural flower holder of a kneeling female feeding swans. I can't recall what it cost at the time, but it seemed quite expensive to us there at the tag end of the Depression and might have been $20 or more. A few years ago an antiques dealer offered me a similar Van Briggle centerpiece for $120, and I'm sure that it would cost much more today. If I could have anticipated such happy appreciation, I probably would have paid more attention to the ceramics instead of concentrating on the real butterflies trapped between sheets of plastic to provide shades for Van Briggle's pottery-based table lamps. At least I had sense enough to insist that we buy one of the lamps. My uncle still has it. The shade no longer sends me, but I have developed a genuine appreciation for the elegantly stylized turquoise pottery base. Buy good things for young people, even if you happen to buy them for the wrong reasons. Except that it is the original shade designed for that lamp, I wouldn't give ten cents for that butterfly shade today, but I'd be happy to forfeit a respectable sum for the lamp base.

Veblen, Thorstein

> *The visible imperfections of the hand-wrought goods, being honorific, are accounted marks of superiority in point of beauty, or serviceability, or both. Hence has arisen that exaltation of the defective, of which John Ruskin and William Morris were such eager spokesmen in their time.* (The Theory of the Leisure Class)

Aw, c'mon, Mr. Veblen, you can't just dismiss the whole arts-and-crafts movement that way. Not at today's prices, you can't.

Vernis Martin Furniture

Vernis is French for varnish. Martin is the family name of the brothers who patented *vernis Martin* lacquer. Correctly, the term applies to furniture with lacquer decorations done in relief in the Oriental style. Most often, however, the furniture described as *vernis Martin* is decorated with painted or printed pictures that might have been given a protective coat of varnish. Wouldn't it be proper to call all those curio cabinets and music cabinets simply *vernis,* since the Martin brothers really had nothing to do with them? Or could we simply say "decorated"? Or "decorative"? That being their main attraction. I suppose that if we are going to go on misapplying the term *vernis Martin,* it is a matter of little consequence whether or not we bother spelling it correctly. Auctioneers, I forgive you.

Vienna Bronzes

Strictly speaking, any bronze cast in Vienna is a Vienna bronze, but the term generally suggests small figures produced in unlimited numbers and having much surface detail rather than sculptural detail, usually decorated with polychrome enamels instead of the patination or doré gilding associated with more formal works. In addition to being decorative, many of these small bronzes are designed for some functional purpose—inkwells, penholders, ash receivers, stamp boxes—which tends to move them still further from the fine-art category. Finely finished they might be. Art they seldom are. But they are bronze, which seems sufficient to excite a lot of people. And since they tend to be on the small side, quite a few can be contained in one cabinet, which makes it possible for a new collector to display his Vienna bronzes with much pride in little space. Some consider this a definite advantage. It never seems to occur to them that for an equal investment in money and space a single fine bronze could be acquired and displayed. And that one good bronze could pay significant dividends—both esthetic and financial—as none of those little roosters and cats and Arabs probably ever will.

To make matters worse, someone must be issuing new Vienna bronzes. The marketplace has become alarmingly busy with them.

See Look, Look—Oh, Look!

Vuitton, Louis, Luggage

The best and most expensive ever made. Almost the only second-hand luggage with substantial resale value. In good condition it is avidly sought—even collected. Choice pieces sometimes can be inexpensively acquired at a thrift shop or flea market. A sign of the times: at auction a Vuitton valise sold for twice the price of a large fitted Vuitton steamer trunk.

See Use

W

Water Pik

Useful for washing the last traces of grime or lingering soapsuds out of intricate relief patterns or difficult-to-reach areas in porcelain, glass, wood, or just about anything else that you would like to wash clean with water. No need, however, to risk damage by employing the most intense pressure. The Water Pik will do a perfectly fine job even at a gentle setting.

Don't forget to surround your work area with some sort of shield. Spritzes like crazy. If you can't improvise a suitable shield, how about moving the entire project behind the shower enclosure?

You also can get pretty good results with an ordinary bulb baster —like the one you use for the Thanksgiving turkey.

Wavecrest

A line of decorated glass accessory pieces produced in the 1890s by the C. F. Monroe Company of Meriden, Connecticut. "Produced" is technically inaccurate, since the blanks used for Wavecrest glass were the work of other manufacturers. Strictly speaking, Wavecrest refers to the painted and enameled decorations applied by the C. F. Monroe Company rather than to the glass itself. Wavecrest was a registered trademark of the company and is correctly used only to identify articles decorated at that factory and included in their Wavecrest line. The two signatures most often found on Wavecrest ware are the elaborately designed red-banner mark, which isn't red at all but a somewhat liverish pink, with "Wavecrest" displayed on a billowing banner, and—at the opposite pole —simply "Wavecrest/Trade Mark" austerely stamped in black. The black-stamped signature frequently is found faded to near-invisibility. In addition, many Wavecrest items of unquestionable authenticity are found unmarked. Some of these pieces probably once carried an ink-stamped signature; some, we know, had paper labels; and others simply never were signed. The fancy red-banner mark seems to carry a bit of extra weight with some dealers, which is strange when one considers that items identical in all other respects are found with the simpler marking.

The C. F. Monroe Company also produced Nakara and Kelva, two similar lines of decorated glass, which frequently are confused with or are deliberately grouped together with Wavecrest. There are, in fact, some authorities who have suggested that the various designations were used rather loosely and that the differences between Wavecrest, Nakara, and Kelva pretty much exist in name only. This is not true. There are decorative characteristics typical of each series. These are basic to the identification of unmarked items.

Most Wavecrest pieces have a waxy look, especially in background areas where color has been thinly applied. The molded relief decorations on many items are left uncolored, adding scrolls and curls of pearly white that make the name "Wavecrest" seem somewhat less fanciful than it might otherwise. While scenic, figural, and geometric decorations are found, the majority of Wavecrest pieces are decorated with pastel flowers—and very pretty they are too.

The name "Nakara" suggests a pearly luster, which is odd, since that quality is more typical of Wavecrest. Darker colors and a rather mat finish are characteristic of Nakara pieces. Although some of the same pastel colors found in Wavecrest are also found on items marked "Nakara," the richer Victorian palette is far more typical of this line. The mauves, olives, browns, and grays found on Nakara pieces are often used in combinations—brown shaded to gold, moss merging with mauve. While the molded decorations on most Wavecrest items are highlighted, on Nakara these often are painted over to subtly enrich the background. Portrait and scenic decorations more extravagant than those used on Wavecrest are found on some Nakara items, but florals, again, are the most characteristic. Which is why portrait and scenic pieces fetch the best prices.

Kelva items share the darker color schemes typical of Nakara but are distinguished by a mottled background that is painted to suggest a plushlike surface. At first glance some Kelva pieces appear to have a chipped-ice texture into which dark pigments—brick red, raspberry, charcoal gray—have been rubbed. Actually the surface is smooth, the effect resulting from the intricately strippled paint. Upon this quasi-textured background rather subdued flowers are arranged. The Kelva mark is stamped in brownish red: "Kelva/ Trade Mark."

From the frequency with which pieces are found, it would seem that the C. F. Monroe Company produced a considerably varied amount of Wavecrest ware, some Nakara, and not much Kelva. This ratio also applies to the length of time that each series was in production. Unusual pieces of Wavecrest keep turning up. Nakara items seem to cover a more limited range, while production of Kelva appears to have been pretty well restricted to such typical articles as dresser boxes, fern bowls, and the like.

Because there is less of it around, a Kelva piece usually brings a somewhat better price than a comparably decorated item in Nakara, while Nakara will tend to be valued ahead of a similar piece of Wavecrest. But a Wavecrest piece of unusual size or purpose or having a rare or especially beautiful decoration can command top dollar and will continue to increase in value when most of those pretty little trinket boxes have been forgotten.

Wholesale

Some antiques dealers who call themselves wholesalers are wholesalers in name only. They charge healthy retail prices to anyone buying less than a carload of merchandise at a clip, and discourage customers unable or unwilling to cope with similarly large consignments. Dealers who want to pick and choose only two or three select items usually can buy more advantageously from a retail dealer, who will extend courtesy discounts to others in the trade. Many retailers routinely take 15 or 20 percent (sometimes more, sometimes much more!) off the ticket price of antiques purchased for resale by another dealer. Some so-called wholesale dealers act as if they are making enormous concessions by granting a 10 percent discount on sales totaling less than $500. Others simply act as if they do not want to be bothered with your patronage no matter what volume of business you might bring them. A few—darned few—blessed souls will knock themselves out being helpful, will sell one item or a thousand with equal concern and enthusiasm, and will work as closely with a new dealer who only wants a small bronze or a few examples of art glass to dress up a display at a show as they would with an auctioneer from Texas who has a certified check and a couple of empty vans waiting at the freight dock.

Whether they are friendly or deprecating, reasonable in their prices or ridiculous, wholesale dealers invariably will require some assurance that a new customer actually is in the antiques trade, or is an interior decorator, photographer, display or scenic designer, or other professional interested in acquiring things for uses other than personal possession, although what ultimately happens to the items after they have been sold is of no great consequence to most wholesalers. They usually will be quite well satisfied with some proof that the customer would have a legitimate resale or professional use for whatever he buys, and anything from a sales-tax registration number to a business card or a piece of stationery with a commercial letterhead might serve that purpose. Some wholesalers are more finicky than others about the sort of evidence they will accept, but many will be satisfied with nothing more official than a business card printed "Jane and Joe Smith/Antiques" presented at the door. Others will insist upon seeing a resale registration from the state sales-tax bureau. Since that is easily obtained (*see* Selling), there is little excuse for not being able to furnish it on request. If you do not have a tax number and you do not want to bother having a batch of business cards printed but would still like to do some wholesale browsing, you probably can gain entry to the frequently disappointing warehouses if you can borrow some cards from a friend or if you can persuade an auctioneer or decorator to give you an introductory note on his letterhead. It doesn't matter that he doesn't know the wholesaler you will be calling on or that the wholesaler never heard of him. Just a note saying "Jane and Joe Smith will appreciate your courtesy to the trade" could do the trick, since all a wholesaler usually wants is some justification for doing business with you rather than with just anyone who schlepps in off the street.

A word of warning: some so-called antiques wholesalers carry virtually nothing but brand-new items, which they import in quantity. Even if you cannot immediately tell that the merchandise is new, you will learn to recognize these displays by the number of examples available. If you are not entirely certain, ask if you could buy two, three, six, a dozen (?) of whatever it might be. If the answer is immediate and affirmative and you are really interested in acquiring only genuine antiques, you probably ought to go to some other wholesaler.

Wicker

Three kinds of wicker furniture are being sold in antiques shops: antique, old, and new.

Antique wicker can be a lot older than you might expect. In Europe, wicker has been used in furniture construction for centuries. A wicker cradle that was brought to America on the *Mayflower* is in the collection of the Pilgrim Society at Plymouth, Massachusetts. Most of the available antique wicker, however, dates from the Victorian era, and is not only beautifully fussy in design but also is well constructed. Moreover, since it survived generations without being consigned to the junk heap, usually it will be found in excellent original or well restored condition.

Old wicker furniture dates from 1900 to the late 1930s. These are the pieces that used to decorate the verandas of the summer palaces to which Americans who had made their fortunes went to live like royalty, and the great resort hotels where those who had not quite made their fortunes went to live as if they had. Wicker-style furniture made of rope and of cardboard filament belongs in this same category. Since such wicker-type pieces cost less to produce, they were made in astonishing quantities, often in complete matching sets that included a sofa, a couple of armchairs, a table or two, possibly a desk, a floor lamp, a table lamp, and one or two plant containers to furnish the "outdoor rooms" that the middle class was making of its old front porches. A lot of this wicker wound up indoors too. In the sun parlors of hospitals. In the lobbies of hotels with Newportish pretentions. And in homes where its easy informality and resort associations added a note of continuing holiday that was as appropriate to the spirit of the times as the cocktails that were created to disguise the bad taste of prohibition booze. Most of this furniture is strongly built on heavy wood frames. As part of a general break with things of the past, the curls and whirls and deliciously intricate designs that had been lavished on Victorian wicker pieces were abandoned in favor of uncluttered lines and—where wicker had once been lacy—densely woven panels. Uncomplicated designs were also infinitely less expensive to produce, which gave a large plus to modernity in the marketplace.

New wicker is being produced in Europe and in the Far East and probably in a good many factories closer to home. Most of the new wicker furniture is wretchedly constructed, and while old and antique wicker pieces have held together handsomely for 50 and

100 and 150 years and longer, not much of the new wicker will survive a second season. Yet masked by a couple of coats of white paint, it can look almost as good as its betters, and it sometimes costs as much as—or more than—they would. The best way to tell new wicker from old is to check its weight. Most wicker furniture is lightweight—that being one of its more appealing advantages. But because most of the new pieces are woven from thinner reeds and built on flimsy frames, they are as feathers when compared to the well-built pieces from the past. Not only are the reeds in new wicker spaghetti thin but they tend to be quite uniform in size, which is not true of the reeds in older pieces. New wicker will feel somewhat hairy or thready, while the reeds in old wicker tend to feel smooth. The proportions of old wicker furniture are usually quite generous, with wide armrests and deep-woven aprons. New pieces are designed on a more stingy scale, and although some factories have been buying good antique pieces to reproduce, not many of the new pieces show the variety of techniques and well-finished details that characterize the originals. A desirable piece of old or antique wicker purchased in good condition can be expected to appreciate in value. If it lasts long enough, new wicker will never be anything but secondhand furniture.

Think twice before acquiring wicker that needs repair. There are some gifted souls who will undertake this work, but many of them are all but exclusively committed to particular dealers or decorators and are downright finicky about which extra assignments they will take on. Others, with more jobs than they can possibly fulfill, can be terribly temperamental when it comes time to discuss matters of price and delivery. You will understand why this is possible if you try to do a few repairs on your own without having sources for reeds and raffia (try the crafts shops) or knowing about soaking and wrapping and other techniques that make the difference between a good job and an unfinished mess. There is one restoration trick that needs nothing but a sharp knife and a steady hand to bring it off: if a strand is broken or a curl is missing, you can frequently even out the design by cutting back the broken piece or by removing an opposing curl or curls.

Spray-on paints are a blessing to the wicker lover. If you are painting any piece for the first time, or want to turn a red- or pink-painted piece snowy white, try applying an undercoat of aluminum paint. The white paint will cover better and you won't have to worry about blushing undertones showing through.

Wine

It is not coincidental that nations such as Italy and France, which have traditions of wine production, also developed important glass industries. Ever since the ancients learned to fuse sands into glass, it has been the preferred vessel for wine. In imperial Rome glass wine cups were much prized, taking precedence even over those made from gold, for the excellent reason that when drinking wine from a glass, one could easily avoid impurities, dregs, and other unpleasantnesses that might lurk undetected in an opaque container.

Nations in which grains took precedence over grapes, not only in the fields but in the fermentation vats, had less need for transparent drinking vessels and so went happily along quaffing their beers from jugs and mugs of clay and metal. Wine was responsible for the introduction of the drinking "glass" onto the boards of Britain, and for the eventual displacement of silver cups and pewter tankards.

Those of us who like to rhapsodize and romanticize about antiques need to be reminded from time to time that there usually was some splendid practical, often quite crassly commercial reason for their development and introduction. Articles and materials that could not succeed on these counts seldom were long for their worlds, which means they almost never make it to ours. Most of those items that seem so exceptional to us because of their current rarity were, with impressive exceptions, the commonplaces of their times.

Z

Zip Code

Helpful in dating collectible items bearing a maker's address.

In mid-1943 the postal service inaugurated two-number zones in cities served by more than one branch post office. This continued until July 1963, when the five-number zip code was introduced on a nationwide basis. If you find a label or other identifying mark using the two-number system in the address, you can at least be sure that the article was made sometime before 1963 but after 1943. Use of the five-number zip code confirms fairly recent manufacture. In a field crowded with confusing reproductions, we can't afford to ignore any possible clues.

Zsolnay Ceramics

Familiar examples of this famous Hungarian pottery are in the Art Nouveau and Art Deco styles, but there are earlier pieces, properly Victorian in concept and decoration, dating back to the beginning of the company about the middle of the nineteenth century. Iridescent glazes in brilliant red, bright, light green, or gleaming dark blue are characteristic of the later pieces, which include small stylized animal figures and other purely decorative items as well as vases, flower holders, bowls, and similar articles. The superb iridescence achieved in the Zsolnay glazes leads some to confuse this pottery with works by Tiffany, or with the Weller Pottery's Sicard pieces, but even the most casual acquaintance with characteristic examples of each will quickly eliminate such possibility.

The most exciting piece of Zsolnay pottery I have seen: a simple canoe-form centerpiece in satiny iridescent green, with a bird in glossy, flaming scarlet perched at either end.

Index

B

C

D

G

H

M

N

Q

R